To my wife, Stefanie, and our two sons, Nicholas and William.
Thank you for all your support and patience.

—Michael W. Geoghegan

To Melissa, Hudson, and Tallu, for all your patience and love.
Thanks for the smooches. Well, except for Hudson, who
won't smooch me, because he's way too cool for that.
Hudson, thanks for the firm handshake.

——Dan Klass

Podcast Solutions
The Complete Guide to Podcasting

Michael W. Geoghegan
Dan Klass

friendsof

DESIGNER TO DESIGNER™
an Apress® company

Podcast Solutions:
The Complete Guide to Podcasting

Copyright © 2005 by Michael W. Geoghegan and Dan Klass

Library of Congress Cataloging-in-Publication Data

Geoghegan, Michael W. (Michael Woodland), 1968-
  Podcast solutions / Michael W. Geoghegan, Dan Klass.
      p. cm.
  Includes bibliographical references and index.
  ISBN 1-59059-554-8 (alk. paper)
  1. Webcasting. I. Klass, Dan, 1963- II. Title.
  TK5105.887.G46 2005
  006.7'876--dc22

                    2005019932

Printed and bound in the United States of America 9 8 7 6 5 4 3 2 1

Trademarked names may appear in this book. Rather than use a trademark symbol with every occurrence of a trademarked name, we use the names only in an editorial fashion and to the benefit of the trademark owner, with no intention of infringement of the trademark.

Distributed to the book trade worldwide by Springer-Verlag New York, Inc., 233 Spring Street, 6th Floor, New York, NY 10013. Phone 1-800-SPRINGER, fax 201-348-4505, e-mail orders-ny@springer-sbm.com, or visit www.springeronline.com.

For information on translations, please contact Apress directly at 2560 Ninth Street, Suite 219, Berkeley, CA 94710. Phone 510-549-5930, fax 510-549-5939, e-mail info@apress.com, or visit www.apress.com.

The information in this book is distributed on an "as is" basis, without warranty. Although every precaution has been taken in the preparation of this work, neither the author(s) nor Apress shall have any liability to any person or entity with respect to any loss or damage caused or alleged to be caused directly or indirectly by the information contained in this work.

The source code for this book is freely available to readers at www.friendsofed.com in the Downloads section.

Credits

Lead Editor Chris Mills	**Assistant Production Director** Kari Brooks-Copony
Technical Reviewer Doug Kaye	**Production Editor** Kelly Winquist
Editorial Board Steve Anglin, Dan Appleman, Ewan Buckingham, Gary Cornell, Tony Davis, Jason Gilmore, Jonathan Hassell, Chris Mills, Dominic Shakeshaft, Jim Sumser	**Compositor** Dina Quan **Proofreader** Liz Welch
Associate Publisher Grace Wong	**Indexer** Broccoli Information Management
Project Manager Denise Santoro Lincoln	**Artist** April Milne
Copy Edit Manager Nicole LeClerc	**Cover Designer** Kurt Krames
Copy Editors Nicole LeClerc, Ami Knox	**Manufacturing Manager** Tom Debolski

CONTENTS AT A GLANCE

CONTENTS

Chapter 3: Podcasting How-To 27

Chapter 4: Planning Your Podcast 33

Chapter 5: Podcasting Tools

CONTENTS

Chapter 8: Preparing Your File 131

Chapter 9: Serving It Up 147

FOREWORD

In early 1980 I was working Saturdays at an electronics store just a few miles south of Amsterdam. The store mainly sold components for hobbyists who needed capacitors, resistors, and early transistors. My salary was used for gas money to get me to the studios of Decibel Radio, Amsterdam's leading illegal pirate radio station, which broadcast from Friday afternoon to Monday morning from a canal house apartment in the city center.

At the time in the Netherlands, there were no private radio stations, and the lack of popular programs on the government-controlled station had created quite an underground movement of small groups of enthusiasts who were connecting with local audiences through pure supply and demand. None of these stations ever turned a profit—any advertising income was saved for the inevitable raid by FCC agents, who would confiscate our equipment with a wink and a nod, since they knew we'd be back on the air the very next weekend. Heck, they were fans as well.

Those days were some of the most exciting of my youth. It wasn't about money or fame, but connecting with an audience hungry at a subatomic level. In fact, the most popular part of our programming was the hourly phone-in, when we opened up the phone line to allow anyone to say hi to friends and family also listening to the show. Everyone loves holding the microphone, if only for a few moments.

Around the same time, the Commodore VIC-20 home computer was introduced, and the electronics shop I worked at was selling them. I gravitated toward this device almost immediately, intrigued with its capability to share data through audiocassettes. The sounds recorded on the tape largely inspired a fellow Saturday worker and me to set about building our own acoustic modems to share data in real time across a phone line connection. Among a few components we "borrowed" from the shop was a pair of 75-baud modems that allowed a keystroke typed on my machine to display on my friend's monitor through a phone line. From that day, I knew something powerful was starting to happen.

I kept my broadcast career synchronized with my interest in computer communications, and in 1987 when I started working at MTV, my Mac Plus connected me directly to my audience, primarily college students who had access to terminals connected to the Internet. Nothing fancy—this was all pre-web.

With the advent of the web, and as connection speeds increased, I became more excited about the possibility of broadcasting in the same unregulated fun fashion that we did at the pirate stations, except this time, the world would be our audience . . .

As you will learn in this book, which starts with a history of podcasting, my longtime wish came true. Now the power of audio communications with global distribution is within the means and budget of anyone with something—or nothing—to say. And podcasting can be a great conduit for us all. Gone are the gatekeepers of spectrum, content, and time.

Podcasting is only the tip of an iceberg slowly revealing itself. What started with weblogs is people's desire to take back our media—not into our hands to hold, but into our hearts. In the short time podcasting has been around, it has revived this element of multimedia that has been taken for granted for many years. The art is alive and kicking, with readily available tools (see the CastBlaster podcast creation tool supplied on this book's companion CD). And we are so frustrated with traditional broadcast outlets that the demand is now creating its own supply.

At the heart of this media disruption lies the power of subscription. The publish subscribe model has been perfected over the past eight years and has found its way onto our desktops and portable devices. Our media is adapting to our lives, instead of the reverse status quo.

Michael and Dan, two true podcasting pioneers, certainly know what they are talking about. As such, this book is an important part of a rapidly emerging movement. As the new spectrum expands with MP3 players emerging in every device imaginable, it serves as a launch pad for the millions of voices and hundreds of millions of ears that will participate in this collaborative "media hacking" initiative.

Adam Curry
Guildford, England
Summer 2005

ABOUT THE AUTHORS

Michael W. Geoghegan has been involved in podcasting since its earliest days. His first podcast production, "Reel Reviews – Films Worth Watching" (www.reelreviewsradio.com), was the Internet's first film review, discussion, and commentary podcast. With the success of "Reel Reviews," and building on his enthusiasm for podcasting, Michael began helping others get involved in podcasting through his production company, Willnick Productions. His second production, "Grape Radio" (http://graperadio.com), is the top-rated podcast about wine.

Michael is the first podcaster to have ever been contracted by a Fortune 100 company (The Walt Disney Company) to both host and produce a podcast. The Disneyland Podcasts (www.disneyland.com/podcast) represented a watershed event in podcasting as large, established media players began to recognize the value of this emerging communications medium.

Michael's entrepreneurial focus is now directed at podcasting. He has just launched his newest venture, PrivaCast (www.privacast.com), a first-of-its-kind enterprise-level solution for secure corporate and educational communications among organizations and their employees or constituents. In addition, Michael has participated in numerous presentations on podcasting and taught the very first "Podcasting 101" classes. He is frequently scheduled to speak about podcasting, its impact on new media, and opportunities for its utilization and monetization. Michael is also often sought out for comments on podcasting by various media outlets, and his insights have appeared on CNN as well as in the *New York Times*, *USA Today*, *Wired Magazine*, and the *San Francisco Chronicle*. He is widely regarded as a leader in producing quality podcast audio, and many of his online how-to articles on podcasting remain some of the most popular and widely linked on the web.

Michael lives in Newport Beach, California, with his wife and two young sons.

Dan Klass has been involved in the Internet and interactive entertainment fields for almost 20 years (yes, there was interactive entertainment 20 years ago!), including working on interactive video toys for Ideal and developing online "stand-up comedy" performances. Recently he was the creator/writer/producer/star of NewsPop, an animated series for a joint Internet venture between Steven Spielberg's DreamWorks SKG and Ron Howard's Imagine Entertainment.

Dan is currently devoting most of his time to podcasting. He produces and hosts two original podcasts: the weekly "Old Wave Radio: New 80s Music" (www.new80smusic.com), a retro-80s music show, and the much acclaimed twice-weekly "The Bitterest Pill" (www.thebitterestpill.com), a comedy/talk show that revolves around his musings as a stay-at-home dad on the outskirts of the entertainment industry. "The Bitterest Pill," arguably one of the most popular entertainment podcasts to date, has been featured on NBC, NPR, and Fox News, and in the *New York Times* and the *Christian Science Monitor*.

Recently, Dan established Jacket Media (www.jacketmedia.com) as the central hub of his podcast production, syndication, and sponsorship empire.

Dan lives in Los Angeles with his wife, two kids, and two Macs.

ABOUT THE TECHNICAL REVIEWER

 **Doug Kaye** is the creator and executive producer of the IT Conversations podcast network (www.itconversations.com) and a major new nonprofit network that was unnamed at the time of this book's publication. Before he began his distinguished 28-year career as a computer-software and dot-com CEO and CTO, Doug cut his audio teeth as a field and studio engineer in radio and as a sound editor and postproduction mixer in film and television. It all makes sense when you consider that he started college in the 1960s at the University of California, Berkeley, studying engineering physics, but graduated with a degree in drama, and then dropped out of New York University's Graduate School of Film and Television.

Somewhere along the way, Doug found time to write two books of his own: *Strategies for Web Hosting and Managed Services* (John Wiley & Sons, 2002) and *Loosely Coupled: The Missing Pieces of Web Services* (RDS Press, 2003).

ACKNOWLEDGMENTS

This book would not have been possible without the help of countless people whom we have been fortunate enough to meet through podcasting. Special thanks to Adam Curry; Doug Kaye (IT Conversations); Dawn and Drew ("The Dawn and Drew Show!"); Brian Ibbott ("Coverville"); Paul Figgiani (PodcastRigs.com); Dave Slusher ("The Evil Genius Chronicles"); Michael Butler ("Rock and Roll Geek Show"); Craig Patchett ("The Godcast Network"); Chris McIntyre (Podcast Alley); Leigh Older, Brian Clark, and Jay Selman ("Grape Radio"); Ray Slakinski and August Trometer (iPodderX); Jennifer Sanchez; Sam Levin; Tim and Emile Bourquin ("The Podcast Brothers"); Eric Rice (Audioblog.com); K. Todd Storch ("Business Thoughts"); Greg Cangialosi ("The Trend Junkie"); Duncan Wardle and the incredible team at Disneyland Parks and Resorts including Tim O'Day, Ken Langdon, and Joe Popp; Jason Niedle, photographer extraordinaire; the entire iPodder Lemon team; The Association of Music Podcasting; Forum E; The Podcastoutlaws; Mike Spataro; Bob Goyetche ("Mostly Tunes"); and Tim Schwieger and the entire team at Broadcast Supply Worldwide. To all you whom we've forgotten and are only reading this section to look for your names, we tried to work you in but the editor cut you out.

INTRODUCTION

Welcome to *Podcast Solutions: The Complete Guide to Podcasting*. We had a simple goal in mind while we wrote this book: to give you a straightforward overview of podcasting and share the information necessary to get you up and running with a quality podcast. Within the pages of this book, you'll find everything you need to know to get started in podcasting. We'll cover the history of podcasting, how to listen to podcasts and, most important, how to produce and distribute your own podcast.

We're not geeks, and this isn't a geek book. There's no way to detail step-by-step instructions for every piece of software that conceivably exists for podcasting, and we're not going to try to impress you with an exhaustive (and therefore exhausting) list of every website that has anything to do with podcasting (that's what Google is for). Things are moving so quickly in podcasting that it seems every day brings a new product or service announcement. If we covered them all, you'd never make it to the end of the book, and you'd never begin doing the one thing we really want to help you do: start making your own podcasts. Instead, we've used our combined experience to carefully select and detail the software, hardware, and services we feel stand out and deserve mention for helping people get started in podcasting.

While we're at it, we don't think you're a "dummy." Podcasting isn't for dummies. There's too much involved in the production and promotion of a successful podcast for it to be that easy. However, we've worked hard to provide simple explanations for processes that can be somewhat confusing at first, and we've tried to ensure that even a total beginner will be able to use and understand the information we present.

It's an exciting time in podcasting, and we're glad you've chosen our book to help guide you on your way to producing a podcast you'll be proud of. Let's get started.

ABOUT THE CD

The CD that comes with this book is jam-packed with useful programs to help you receive other people's podcasts and create the best podcasts you possibly can. It contains podcatchers, feed generators, and audio studio programs. Most of these programs are trial versions, which should be enough to give you a taste of the program. We have included links to go to for further information below, and electronic manuals on the CD where possible. There are also some *Podcast Solutions* podcasts included on the CD. These are interviews and discussion among some of the original podcasting pioneers. Check the site www.podcastsolutions.com for all the interviews we conducted.

Adobe Audition 1.5

Version information: Timed trial version
Platform: Windows 2000 and XP (Professional and Home Editions)
Website: www.adobe.com/products/audition/main.html

Adobe Audition is a professional audio recording, editing, and mixing environment. Designed for audio and video professionals in studios, broadcast facilities, and postproduction facilities, it delivers advanced audio mixing, editing, mastering, and effects processing capabilities, as well as tight integration with Adobe's video products. Using Audition, you can mix up to 128 tracks, edit individual audio files, create loops, and use more than 50 DSP effects.

Audacity 1.2.3

Version information: Full version
Platforms: Windows (98, ME, 2000, and XP); Mac OS 9 and OS X; Linux (various flavors)
Website: http://audacity.sourceforge.net

Audacity is a free, easy-to-use audio editor and recorder. You can use Audacity to

- Record live audio
- Convert tapes and records into digital recordings or CDs
- Edit Ogg Vorbis, MP3, and WAV sound files

- Cut, copy, splice, and mix sounds together
- Change the speed or pitch of a recording
- And more!

Audio Hijack Pro 2.5.1

Version information: Fully functional demo version. Noise is overlaid on recordings lasting over 10 minutes.
Platform: Mac OS X 10.2–10.4
Website: www.rogueamoeba.com/audiohijackpro

Audio Hijack Pro is an audio recording program that allows you to sample and record audio from any source your Mac can handle, from CD and DVD audio to Internet streams and downloaded MP3s. Once the audio is recorded, you can enhance it using industry-standard VST and Audio Unit audio effects.

CastBlaster 0.17 Beta

Version information: Beta version
Platform: Windows XP with Internet Explorer installed
Website: www.castblaster.com

This is a beta (prerelease) version of the CastBlaster podcast creation tool. Keep an eye on the website for updated versions and development news. Future versions are expected to allow for the ability to publish directly to the supported PodShow network.

DSP-Quattro 2.1.1

Version information: Fully functional demo version (but no saving of work is allowed)
Platform: Mac OS 8, 9, and X
Website: www.dsp-quattro.com

DSP-Quattro is a professional creative tool for audio editing, plug-in hosting, and CD mastering. It includes a host of recording and editing features to ensure that output is recorded just as you hear it and edited to perfection using editing functions and digital effects. It also supports plug-ins, both included effects and third-party plug-ins (from Akai, Roland, Yamaha, and many more). Finally, it boasts many CD-creation facilities, including fully programmable playlists and effect chains.

Feeder 1.1.2

Version information: Timed trial version
Platform: Mac OS X 10.3 and later
Website: www.reinventedsoftware.com/feeder

Feeder is an application for creating, editing, and publishing RSS feeds on Mac OS X. With Feeder, you don't need to understand RSS to create and publish feeds to the web—it is packed with features to help automate and enhance the experience from start to finish.

Feeder supports the full RSS 2.0 specification, including enclosures for podcasting. RSS has many powerful features, but not everyone needs them all. Feeder provides customizable templates to hide unnecessary fields, an autocomplete feature to save repetitive typing, and automatic updating of publication dates.

Feeder validates your feed to the RSS 2.0 specification and generates an HTML preview so you can see how your feed will look in a newsreader, check links and images, and proofread text. When your feed is ready, Feeder can publish it and upload enclosure files using FTP, SFTP, or .Mac.

iPodderX 3.0

Version information: Full custom version with preloaded feeds
Platform: Mac OS X 10.3 and later
Website: www.ipodderx.com

iPodderX is a podcatcher that is both powerful and easy to use. It allows you to subscribe to RSS and Atom news feeds to bring you fresh content regularly. It can collect not only podcasts, but also any other audio, movie, image, or document feeds you are subscribed to.

iPodder Lemon 2.1

Version information: Full custom version with preloaded feeds
Platforms: Windows 2000 and XP; Linux (various flavors); Mac version also available from the website
Website: http://ipodder.sourceforge.net/index.php

iPodder Lemon is a popular podcatcher that uses RSS feeds to bring you fresh podcasts of your choice to play anytime, anywhere.

Ozone 3.0

Version information: Trial version that is fully functional for 10 days, then mutes the output for about 1 second every 40 seconds or so
Platforms: Windows (98, 2000, ME, and XP); Mac OS X 10.2 and later
Website: www.izotope.com/products/audio/ozone

Ozone is a complete suite of mastering processors and plug-ins that provides everything you could possibly need to professionally master your audio files. Ozone is a plug-in for other programs, so you need to have a compatible host application.

Peak 4.14

Version information: Timed trial version
Platform: Mac OS X
Website: www.bias-inc.com/products/peak

Peak is an industry-standard stereo audio recording, editing, and processing application. It is the ideal audio utility for podcasters and audio professionals and enthusiasts. In addition to fast and powerful audio editing, Peak integrates a wide variety of effects and signal processing tools to create custom fades, adjust audio gain, repair digital audio spikes, add real room ambience, change pitch and duration independently, and more, all while offering additional real-time effects such as parametric EQ, compression/limiting, reverb, dozens of other special effects, and access to third-party VST and Audio Unit plug-ins, as well as additional solutions from BIAS such as the highly acclaimed SoundSoap family of audio noise reduction and restoration tools (for more information about SoundSoap and SoundSoap Pro, visit www.bias-inc.com).

Other tools include automated loop creation, unlimited and independent undo/redo for each audio document, a highly customizable work environment (colors, key commands, toolbar), and advanced batch file processing. Peak 4.1 can master content in a variety of formats, including Red Book audio CD and popular digital file formats used for delivering a podcast, such as MP3, MP4/AAC, and others.

Personal Audio Recorder 3.0

Version information: Timed trial version
Platforms: Treo 600/650; Palm Tungsten T/T2/T3/Z72; Sony Clie Palm tops
Website: www.toysoft.ca/par.html

Personal Audio Recorder (PAR) is all you need to turn your Palm into an audio recorder. PAR can record voice memos to RAM or to an external card such as SD and MMC. Recorded voice memos can easily be beamed or transferred to your desktop using a card reader or card exporter software. Voice memos can also be e-mailed using your e-mail client.

Propaganda 1.0

Version information: Fully functional trial version that inserts a demo message into completed recording every few minutes
Platform: Windows XP
Website: www.makepropaganda.com/products.html

Propaganda software is a powerful tool that you can use to create commercial-quality podcast shows with a minimum of effort. Propaganda handles music and sound effects as easily as spoken-word recordings. When you're satisfied with your production, simply click the Publish button and share it with the world. Propaganda will upload your completed podcast to your website, with full RSS, XML, and HTML support.

Sound Forge 8

Version information: Timed trial version
Platform: Windows 2000 and XP (Professional and Home Editions)
Website: www.sonymediasoftware.com/products/showproduct.asp?PID=961

Sound Forge is an audio recording and editing program. It enables you to analyze, record, and edit audio; produce music loops; digitize and clean up old recordings; model acoustic environments; create streaming media; and master replication-ready CDs.

Sound Forge Audio Studio

Version information: Timed trial version
Platforms: Windows 2000 and XP (Professional and Home Editions)
Website: www.sonymediasoftware.com/Products/ShowProduct.asp?PID=945

Sound Forge Audio Studio is very similar in functionality to Sound Forge 8, but it has fewer features and is aimed toward the hobbyist and home user markets. Podcasters will probably find this software to be more than powerful enough for their needs. If you think you're going to need a more professional environment, then you should consider using Sound Forge 8 instead.

1 PODCASTING 101

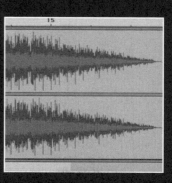

Podcasting is one of the most exciting and wonderfully disruptive technologies to emerge in recent history.

Podcasting is exciting because anybody can get involved, express themselves, exchange ideas, or pitch their products. Whatever interests people have, there is a place for them in podcasting.

Podcasting is disruptive because, like any worthwhile new technology, podcasting breaks all the rules. Can you make a podcast about retro kitchen appliances? Sure. Can it be a minute long? Of course. Can it be an hour long? If you'd like. Can it be in slang? Uh-huh.

Podcasting puts the power to communicate into the hands of *individuals*. Thousands of people are already involved, each as unique as their podcast. There is no working within "The System." In fact, there is no system. You don't need a fancy studio or an FCC license. You only need a microphone, a computer, and something to share with the rest of the world. Yes, you read that correctly: *the world*.

A stage has been erected on which the "common man" (or woman, for that matter) can stand tall and be heard: the Internet. The price of admission is some basic equipment and a desire to communicate—that's all. Podcasters, with their first podcast, can reach a more geographically diverse audience than a radio station with the most powerful AM/FM transmitter in the world. All with no transmitters, no satellites, no regulations. Listeners located in the United States, New Zealand, Japan, India, France, and many other countries are common for popular podcasts. The whole world really *is* listening. Access to such a huge potential audience was a privilege once reserved only for large corporations and governments, but podcasting has changed everything. The individual has been empowered and given an equal voice—this means you.

> **This revolution will not be televised; it will be podcast.**

There's one thing we'd better clear up right from the start: *you do not need an iPod to listen to podcasts, make podcasts, or learn about podcasts*. It's true. Thousands of people are creating and enjoying podcasts without ever having touched an iPod, or any other piece of Apple hardware or software. Yes, the word "podcasting" does borrow a little interest from the "pod" in iPod, but that's where the connection ends. No one group or company controls any aspect of podcasting, from the hardware and software used to create podcasts, to the hardware and software used to listen to podcasts. It's anybody's game.

What grew out of an experiment between a former MTV VJ and a computer programmer quickly became a form of media distribution that would grow and spread faster than perhaps any other new media development in recent history. First, it was the technical folks podcasting—the early adopters who were more interested in the fact that it actually worked than anything else. Soon, more people came to the party. Less "techie" folks embraced the opportunity and got involved. A married couple started podcasting out of a old farmhouse in Milwaukee, the bass player of a San Francisco rock band started spinning tunes and talking about his life at home between gigs, and a young father in Denver started a show made up exclusively of cover songs. By mid-2005, it seemed everybody, from radio stations to sci-fi television shows, from religious evangelicals to caustic drag queens, was getting into podcasting.

Sound like fun? Let's get started and on our way to getting you, dear reader, set up and producing your own podcast. We'll save the gory technical details for a bit later on (but not too much later). In this chapter, we'll focus on the following topics:

- The history of podcasting so far
- What exactly podcasting is and why it has become so popular
- A brief overview of how podcasting works, to help you get your bearings

A brief history of podcasting

In 1877, Thomas Edison made the first sound recording on what was to be known as the phonograph. It wasn't until 1887 that the first commercially available gramophone was made available. OK, maybe we should jump ahead a little bit . . .

We want our MP3

Former MTV VJ and interactive media developer Adam Curry had been trying to find ways to use the Internet to broadcast video and audio streams for years. Curry surmised that with the coming abundance of broadband, there must be a better way to use that pipeline to transmit content to the masses. His theory, which he coined "The Last Yard," was that since a broadband connection is "always on," people could have huge files downloading at night as they slept or in the background while they worked, and they could then be notified when the file download was complete. Instead of users feeling like they are sitting and waiting for hours for something to download, they simply click a button and voilà! The file is there.

In 2000, Curry met with respected programmer Dave Winer, who was instrumental in developing several computer and Internet applications as well as being the creator of **Really Simple Syndication** (**RSS**). RSS is the means by which news stories and weblogs (aka blogs) are syndicated throughout the web. Together, Curry and Winer theorized that there must be a way to use RSS to deliver not only headlines, but audio or video files as well. As a result of their discussions, Winer created the <enclosure> tag within his RSS specification, enabling applications to fetch files off the Internet by simply following the URL within the feed pointing to that file.

Audioblogs

Enter **audioblogs**. The first audioblog may have been posted as early as August 2001 by a Canadian blogger living in San Francisco named "Jish." (Podcasting is largely seen as an evolution of blogging, which uses a similar means to distribute text entries to readers.) Over the next two years, audioblogging started to pick up some steam as people began posting audio posts and various recordings on their sites. Many started to use Winer's <enclosure> tag. In October 2003, at the annual blogger conference known as

BloggerCon, a blogger named Harold Gilchrist headed a session on the emergence of audioblogging, including demonstrations of some applications for downloading the associated enclosures (audio files).

During the same period, Christopher Lydon, a popular radio host, was posting audio interviews with an associated RSS feed that Winer helped him set up. (An **RSS feed** is simply a page of code, in this case pointing to the MP3 file—but more on that later.) Now that there was some audio content appearing, Curry went to work. He wanted a way to get Lydon's interviews to not only automatically download to his computer, but also go a step further and sync to his iPod. Curry knew he needed an application that would check several RSS feeds, one at a time, for the <enclosure> tag and, when it found a new enclosure (MP3), download it automatically and move it onto his iPod. Unfortunately for Curry, he was not a computer programmer and he had a hard time convincing any computer programmers to write the application for him. Soon he found himself learning to program in AppleScript so that he could hack away and carve out the first version of his **iPodder**. In Curry's words, the first version of iPodder "really sucked, because I'm not a developer. Observing open source projects led me to believe that releasing my code would attract other developers who might consider fixing and/or contributing to my work."

Source code

Curry soon realized that, for programmers to have the best chance at truly testing the system, they would need a real-world testing situation. While others, including Dave Winer, Harold Gilchrist, and Christopher Lydon, had been occasionally publishing audio content using the <enclosure> tag mentioned earlier, Curry decided to help move the development process along by launching the first show produced on a consistent basis. "Daily Source Code" (whose name was carefully chosen to attract tech-heads) enabled developers to accurately test the software outside of a lab setting. With the launch of Curry's show in August 2004, what would eventually be called podcasting was born. Of course at the time, there was no agreed-upon name for syndicated audio content using RSS, so most people just called it audioblogging.

"If you build it, they will come," as the saying goes. Curry did, and they did. Soon developers and programmers from around the world were tinkering with the program, adding to it, fixing it, and testing it. Some developers even decided to create their own versions of Curry's program.

Curry's "Daily Source Code" served as the bar that anyone could reach for. Through his easy charm and years of radio experience, Curry created a show of such casual professionalism and sincere enthusiasm that he naturally became a Pied Piper of sorts for anyone who ever dreamt of getting behind a microphone. Soon he was not the only one producing a show. Before you knew it, the revolution was well under way.

The revolution has a name

Other early adopters included Dave Slusher, with his show "Evil Genius Chronicles," and Doug Kaye, who had already been producing "IT Conversations" with RSS syndication of his audio content for a little over a year. Throughout early September 2004, things really started to move, but still without an agreed-upon name. Earlier, in February 2004, Ben Hammersley wrote an article about audioblogs and online radio in which he speculated about possible names for what people were doing, "podcasting" being among those names. Yet, barely recognized, the word would disappear for roughly seven months. In the interim, some people who liked the term registered domains, including Dannie Gregoire, who had independently created the name and registered podcaster.net. Then it happened: a confluence of ideas and little bit of luck.

Dave Slusher of "Evil Genius Chronicles" wrote on September 18, 2004, "I've been noticing something downloading audioblog posts with the user agent of 'podcaster.' There is an URL in there that points to podcaster.net, but there isn't anything yet. I wonder what this is? I do like this as a term for what it is when you are creating things to distribute via the iPod platform . . . 'Podcasting!' Right on."

Shortly thereafter, the term "podcasting" gained traction and became associated with the movement that was already under way. Throughout the following months, more and more people, led by the pioneers such as Adam Curry, Dave Winer, and Dave Slusher, picked up the microphone and got involved. New shows were created and released at a breakneck pace. Directories and groups of podcasters were formed. Just a year after Gilchrist's session on audioblogs, at the BloggerCon held in November 2004 was a session led by Curry dedicated to podcasting that was attended by an overflow crowd. This was an opportunity for many of the early pioneers to sit in the same room and talk face to face. By now it was too late to turn back; the word "podcasting" had taken hold. (Michael was fortunate enough to attend that BloggerCon session and says it was one of the magic moments in an emerging movement. You can listen to the audio from this historic session at http://www.itconversations.com/shows/detail275.html.)

Podcasting has continued to grow, and much of its "history" is still being written. In fact, we hope that someone reading this book will soon deserve a place in this text the next time it is updated. As we press on, let's not lose sight of one thing: podcasting is not simply a new way to distribute audio recordings, it's a form of expression, of interaction, of community building. Through the unique dialogue that is a podcast, communities of enthusiasts are built, tools are created, and products are sold. Podcasting is a vibrant and exciting new world—one that we have only just begun to explore.

So, the question probably on your mind right now is, "What exactly *is* podcasting?" We'll answer that next.

What exactly is a podcast and why is it so darned great?

Simply put, a **podcast** is audio content available on the Internet that can be automatically delivered to your computer or MP3 player. Strip away all the upcoming potential confusion of feeds, aggregators, subscriptions, and so on, and what's left? Audio on the web.

So, what's the big deal? We've had "Internet radio" on the web for over a decade. RealAudio, QuickTime, and Windows Media have all promised in their own way to revolutionize the way we enjoy "radio." Yet the revolution never happened with these products. All of these formats offer audio playback on demand via the web, but none has taken hold the way that podcasting has. Why? Because there is nothing "sexy" about sitting at your desk, waiting for a sound file to buffer—that is not much of a revolution. Many listeners, tired of waiting for the audio to finally sputter to life, ended up turning the radio back on and getting on with their lives.

Why is podcasting different? How is it that *this* promise of audio over the web is so superior to its predecessors? Why are thousands—millions, perhaps—of people every day enjoying the fruits of the podcasting revolution? The sections that follow answer these questions by examining the main advantages of podcasting in some detail. To summarize quickly, podcasting is **automatic**, it's **easy to control** by the listener, it's **portable**, and it's **always available**.

Automatic

Podcasts can be downloaded, automatically, onto your computer. Once you know which shows you like, you don't have to go looking for them—they come to you. Like a digital video recorder (DVR) recording your favorite shows by subscription, you have the benefit of being able to subscribe to your favorite podcasts. Once you've found a podcast you'd like to listen to regularly, you can simply subscribe to the feed. Using simple software called a **podcast aggregator** or **podcatcher** (such as iPodder Lemon, iPodderX, or iTunes), each new show listed in the feed will download automatically into your computer or portable MP3 player as it becomes available. No hunting around the Internet; no time wasted visiting several websites to listen to your favorite shows. The podcasts simply come to you.

So that there's no confusion, we'd like to emphasize that subscribing to podcasts doesn't cost anything. When we talk about "subscriptions" and "subscribing" to a podcast, we're merely referring to setting up your system to receive the RSS feed and to automatically download any new shows that are posted (more on that soon). As of today, the overwhelming majority of podcasts are delivered free of charge. In fact, podcasts that cost money are a rarity, though they are starting to appear as people try to grasp the business models podcasting can support. (We discuss ways to make money with your podcast in Chapter 11.)

Easy to control

Podcasting puts the listener in control. Unlike e-mail distribution, where the sender decides who will get the files whether the recipients want them or not, podcasting lets the listener decide. Because you control your list of subscriptions, if you no longer want to receive a show, you just unsubscribe. The shows stop coming—it's that simple. No opt-out requirements or begging to be removed from a list. Also, you don't have to worry about keeping your identity secure, as much like listening to the radio, subscribing to podcasts is anonymous. No one will know that you're listening unless you decide to tell them. Finally, you don't need to worry about spam or viruses. RSS essentially forms a "trusted channel," where you know the only content put into the feed is that which the publisher has decided to add. Again, if you ever decide you no longer wish to receive what the publisher is including in the feed, simply unsubscribe. You're in complete control.

Portable

Podcasts are predominantly MPEG-1 Audio Layer-3 (MP3) audio files. The MP3 file format has been instrumental in making audio on the Internet such a success. In fact, among many Internet users, MP3s are quickly replacing compact discs in the same way compact discs replaced audiocassettes and vinyl in the 1990s. While there is some loss of fidelity with MP3, if you use care when compressing the audio, the quality can still far exceed that of both AM and FM radio. Because of the relatively small file sizes of podcast MP3s, they're perfect for downloading from the Internet and transferring to a portable media player. Or, if you like, you can burn them as an audio CD to take anywhere and share with just about anyone. You are no longer trapped at your desk, chained to a stuttering stream from one of the popular media players. Podcasts provide clear, steady audio that you can take with you and listen to whenever and wherever you like.

Always available

The fact that you can listen to podcasts whenever you like is another important part of the growing success of podcasting. This aspect of podcasting has caused many people to compare it to DVRs such as TiVo. Podcasts are, in essence, radio shows on demand, time-shifted to fit into *your* schedule. You don't have to worry about missing your favorite show, because it will be there, on your hard drive or portable media device, whenever you want to listen to it. Podcasting frees you from the appointment-based listening dictated by traditional radio. Have a meeting during your favorite show? With radio, you're out of luck. With podcasting, subscribe to that show and it will be waiting on your portable media player, ready for you to play it when you like.

In a nutshell

The sound fidelity of MP3 encoding, the ease of subscribing and downloading, and the portability of these files make podcasting an important advance in the distribution and enjoyment of audio content. With each passing day, more and more podcasts are being created, produced, uploaded, and downloaded around the world. Shows on every imaginable topic are available, right now, for free. Amateurs, skilled hobbyists, and seasoned professionals are putting together new and beautifully produced content every day, and it is all there for the listening. Communities are springing up around the most obscure topics, information is being exchanged, and theories are being discussed on every imaginable subject. If you have a hobby, an interest, or a curiosity about anything, chances are there is a podcast for you. If not, there soon will be—or perhaps *you* should start a podcast of your own. You'll soon find you aren't the only one looking for a podcast on Nepalese goat herding.

How it all works

Downloading podcasts via subscription is a simple process that requires only three elements: the podcast itself, the RSS feed, and a podcatcher (such as iPodder Lemon, iPodderX, or iTunes).

As we said before, the podcast itself is an MP3 file, ranging on average between 5MB and 30MB in size (roughly a megabyte per minute for most music shows, and about a megabyte per two minutes for most talk shows). That may sound like a lot to download, but now that broadband access (such as cable and DSL) is so widely available, it takes far less time to download a file than you might expect. If you are still using a standard dial-up modem, then you will really appreciate the benefits of podcasting. You can set your podcast aggregator to download the podcasts you desire overnight. No more endless waiting for files to download—your aggregator will do it while you sleep or when your computer is sitting idle. Now *that's* efficient!

> *We are about to talk briefly about computer code. We would like to take this opportunity to make something very clear before we proceed:* **You do not now—nor will you ever—need to fully understand or be able to write code to listen to or produce your own podcasts. We promise.**

The second element is the RSS feed, which is a simple bit of eXtensible Markup Language (XML) code stored on the web as a raw text file. The code includes vital information about the podcast, including when the last show was added to the list, its title, and a brief description of that edition. RSS is the same code used to supply the news feeds for My Yahoo!, Bloglines, and other online news readers with up-to-date headlines, articles, and comic strips. In the case of a podcast, along with the code tags for the title and last date of publication of the feed, is an <enclosure> tag. This is the bit of magic that makes it all possible. The <enclosure> tag contains information about the location, size, and type of file associated with the feed. The feed does not contain the file itself; rather, it stores the web address, as a URL, of where the MP3/podcast is stored on the Internet. With this information, your podcast client knows where to go to retrieve the associated file.

Here is some sample code to give you an idea of what an RSS feed looks like—confusing at first glance to the non-geek, to be sure. After staring at it for several minutes, the bits and pieces start to reveal themselves, and it becomes clear exactly how simple Really Simple Syndication really is:

```
<?xml version="1.0" encoding="utf-8"?>
<rss version="2.0">
  <channel>
    <title>Podcast Solutions Podcast</title>
    <link>http://www.podcastsolutions.com</link>
```

```
    <description>Everything you need to know about podcasting.  Based
on the best-selling book, Podcast Solutions.</description>
    <generator>
        Feeder 1.0.3 http://reinventedsoftware.com/feeder/
    </generator>
    <docs>http://blogs.law.harvard.edu/tech/rss</docs>
    <language>en-us</language>
    <copyright>Copyright 2004, 2005 Michael Geoghegan
and Dan Klass </copyright>
    <managingEditor>pill@podcastsolutions.com (Michael Geoghegan
and Dan Klass)</managingEditor>
    <webMaster> pill@podcastsolutions.com (Michael Geoghegan
and Dan Klass)</webMaster>
    <pubDate>Wed, 06 Apr 2005 20:26:38 -0700</pubDate>
    <lastBuildDate>Wed, 06 Apr 2005 20:26:38 -0700</lastBuildDate>
    <image>
        <url>http://podcastsolutions.com/logo.jpg</url>
        <title>The Podcast Solutions Podcast</title>
        <link>http://www.podcastsolutions.com</link>
        <description> Everything you need to know about podcasting.
Based on the best-selling book, Podcast Solutions </description>
    </image>
    <item>
        <title>#1: Welcome to The Podcast Solutions Podcast!</title>
        <description>
            This is the first edition of our new podcast, to serve as an
            ever-updating addition to our book, Podcast Solutions.  If
            you have any questions or comments, or you just want to
            say hello, please drop us a line.
        </description>
        <author> pill@podcastsolutions.com (Michael Geoghegan
and Dan Klass)</author>
        <pubDate>Wed, 06 Apr 2005 20:26:38 -0700</pubDate>
    <enclosure url=http://www.podcastsolutions.com/podcasts/PS05_04_05.mp3
                    length="14830355" type="audio/mpeg"/>
    </item>
```

When you check your subscriptions (a matter of clicking a button), the software checks each feed for new podcasts. If a new podcast has been added to any of the feeds you subscribe to, the new MP3 is automatically downloaded. The software simply checks RSS feed addresses for new files, and when it finds them, it downloads them (see Figure 1-1). This process is, however, invisible to the subscriber. All you do is click a button and wait while the latest podcasts from your active list of subscriptions download.

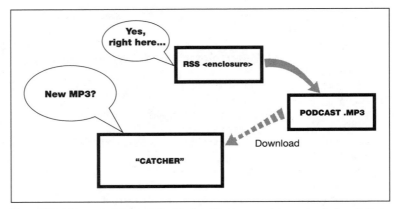

Figure 1-1. The podcatcher checks the feed for new enclosures, and when it finds them, it downloads the files at the address in the feed.

Summary

As you can see, there's no hidden magic to podcasting. When you break it down, in fact, it's rather straightforward. As with most exciting creations, the ingredients were there all along—it just took some people willing to experiment to pull all the pieces together. Since we know you are anxious to get started, this chapter marks the end of the general podcasting overview. From here on out, it's nothing but details, examples, and explanations.

We've worked hard in this book to walk the line between leaving nothing out and bombarding you with too much information. Any less and we'd feel like we might be leaving out that tiny bit of information that makes it all click for you. There are as many ways to produce podcasts as there are podcasters. This book was written with the hope of giving people the information they need to enjoy podcasting on their own terms. There is no right way, there is no wrong way—there is only *your* way. Our sincerest hope is that within the pages of this book is the way that works for you.

Next, we're going to bring you up to speed on how to set up your podcast client and start receiving and enjoying some of the great shows that are available.

2 LISTENING TO PODCASTS

  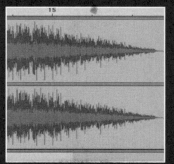

You may be getting anxious to get started on your podcast, but before you take a stab at creating one of your own, it's a good idea to first spend some time *listening*. One of the best aspects of learning to podcast is to sample a variety of the available podcasts. Not only is this fun, but it's a great opportunity to get "plugged into" the podcast community—to *really* find out what is available and what void may be left to fill. Your experience listening to podcasts will help tremendously when it comes time to create your own show. By listening to an assortment of podcasts, you'll get a sense of what you like and dislike. You'll also start to form some ideas on how you want to do your show. As with most anything else, you can learn a lot from the people who are currently producing podcasts. Above all else, you'll have fun.

Soon we'll get into the mechanisms involved in getting podcasts to download effortlessly. Getting set up for this will involve using some new software and becoming familiar with a few new terms. So, before we get into all the potentially mind-boggling stuff (it isn't actually mind-boggling), let's agree on one thing: *you want to listen to some podcasts*. If you're anxious to get a taste and aren't sure you want to plow through a directory or set up software, check out a couple of the podcasts we've included in the Resources section of the book. We've provided a nice cross-section of our favorites, categorized for easy sorting. Enjoy a few, and then let's get you set up.

Finding and "auditioning" podcasts

Before enjoying podcasts in the comfort of your own car, headset, stereo system, or whatever, you'll (obviously) need to find some podcasts to listen to. Finding podcasts is relatively easy, thanks to the tightly knit podcasting community and the ingenious web technologies that help keep information about active podcasts accurate and up to date. This is a wonderful time of exploration, as you dig deep into the podcasting treasure trove. You may even find that you're drawn to podcasts you never thought you'd be interested in. So, take your time, enjoy the journey, and do plenty of auditioning.

Once again: *YOU DON'T NEED AN iPOD*. All you need to enjoy podcasts are

- A computer with an Internet connection
- A web browser or "podcatcher"
- Headphones or speakers

Depending on your tastes and the type of programming you're looking for, discovering a podcast that you think is a gem may take you all of ten seconds, or it may take several days. You never know. Some people just check out a top ten list and have more than enough to listen to. Others have to dig. Finding the right podcasts for you may be like finding a needle in a haystack. Luckily, most of the podcasting haystacks are well explored and meticulously mapped. The best way to get to the needle is to dive right in and start going through the hay.

You can approach auditioning podcasts in several ways:

- Listen to samples/shows at a podcast directory.
- Go to podcast websites to read about/listen to a few episodes.
- Seek recommendations from podcasters.

Directories

Podcast directories are an indispensable tool for finding new podcasts. Most are well categorized and easily searchable, so finding podcasts of the type and tone you're looking for is pretty straightforward. The directories are usually web based, but each of the standalone podcatchers have built-in directories to make searching and subscribing a one-stop affair.

iPodder.org

iPodder.org is perhaps the mother of all podcast directories, spawned directly as a result of Adam Curry's original iPodder software. iPodder.org is an exhaustive directory of podcasts, with categories ranging from agriculture to technology, travel, storytelling, comedy, sports, religion, sex, movies, and music. (You get the idea—there's a podcast for everything!) Each category (or **node**) is maintained by an editor who keeps the category up to date. Many podcatching applications actually integrate iPodder.org's directory, shown in Figure 2-1, into their own subscription directories.

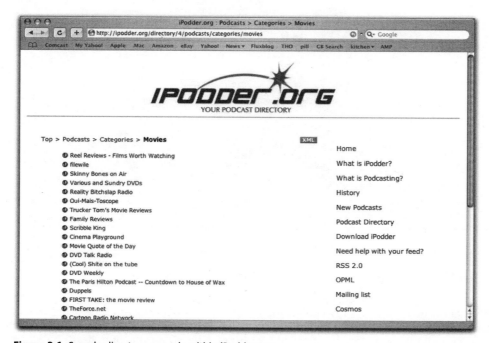

Figure 2-1. Sample directory or node within iPodder.org

iTunes

Before the release of Apple iTunes 4.9, a few more steps were involved in finding, down-loading, and getting podcasts into iTunes if you so desired. But no longer. With the release of version 4.9, iTunes provides all of the functionality of finding, subscribing, and down-loading podcasts within the program itself.

You can search for podcasts by name, host, or genre (comedy, politics, film and television, etc.), and you can listen to shows right from the directory by simply clicking the name of the podcast. The directory isn't as complete as iPodder.org, but it is a lot more fun to look at (see Figure 2-2). Each podcast is represented within the iTunes Music Store in much the same way an album from one of your favorite artists is. To subscribe to a given podcast, simply click the Subscribe button.

Needless to say, when iTunes 4.9 was released, it sent a shockwave of excitement through the podcasting community. Apple's wholehearted embrace of podcasts is a clear signal that podcasting is going mainstream.

Figure 2-2. The Apple iTunes Music Store podcasts section

Podcast Alley

Another notable web directory of podcasts is Podcast Alley (www.podcastalley.com). What causes Chris McIntyre's Podcast Alley to stand out from the many other independent directories is its place at the center of the podcasting community. Not only does it include a robust listing of podcasts, but the site features a monthly ranking of podcasts based on votes, interviews with prominent podcasters, and several podcast forums ranging in topic from listening to podcasts, creating podcasts, equipment recommendations, and more. Podcast Alley's Top 10 and Top 50 listings have become a first stop for many people looking for something new to listen to.

Other directories

Find a directory you like and start clicking names and subjects that you find intriguing. It doesn't cost you anything but a few moments of time. You never know what you might find. Other directories worth checking out:

- Podcast Central (www.podcastcentral.com)
- Podcast.net
- Podcasting News (www.podcastingnews.com)
- Podcast Pickle (www.podcastpickle.com)
- Podfeed.net

Most directory sites make it easy to audition or listen to entire podcasts straight from the directory listing. The podcast directory game is serious business. Each site strives to find that unique feature that'll keep people coming back. Several have their own audio players built in that will load the entire back catalog of a podcast, and stream it for you right there. Each directory is going to give you most of the info you need on a podcast: the name, titles of past shows, the feed info, links to their website, and even ratings.

Listen at the site

An ideal way to get to know a podcast quickly, aside from listening to a couple shows, is to visit the show's website. With few exceptions, all podcasts have their own site that will give you an immediate take on who the podcasters are and what they're all about. Photos, blog posts, and descriptions of each installment of the podcast are going to provide you with insights into the program, where it's been, and where it's headed. Also, you can easily check out several of a site's podcasts by simply clicking links on the site. The podcast MP3 will open in your browser or media player, and away you go.

Seek recommendations from podcasters/other podcasts

Want to find great podcasts? Then go to the great podcasters. Well, at least go to podcasters you like. Who better to steer you toward material that you might like than the very podcasters you already enjoy? These may be out-and-out recommendations, they may be mentions, or they may just be promos played on the show. Every podcaster who has been around for any length of time has developed their own list of favorite podcasts. Podcasters love to talk about other podcasts almost as much as they like to talk about themselves, so you'll never have to wait long to get an opinion on who's doing what.

Listen to find out who your favorite podcaster is listening to, is friendly with, or is talking up. (If you don't have a favorite yet, check out "Reel Reviews—Films Worth Watching" and

"The Bitterest Pill." Those two guys seem to be know-it-alls, but they should be able to suggest something decent.) You will be drawn to podcasters you feel you have something in common with, whether it's a sense of humor or a distaste for the Emmy awards. The podcasters that you feel simpatico with are a good source for providing leads to other podcasts that might appeal to you. See where we're going with this? If a podcaster whose show you really enjoy is constantly referring to another podcast, *check out that podcast.*

Podroll

See if your favorite podcast's web page has a **podroll**, a list of podcasts they enjoy and recommend. Podcasters support each other by linking to each other's websites. This can be of huge benefit to you in your search for something to listen to. You can usually find the links along the side bar of the podcast site (if the site is in the classic two-column blog style) or on a separate links page.

Figure 2-3.
A podcast badge

If you've ever wondered what all those tiny little badges are on podcasters' sites (see Figure 2-3), they are usually links to other podcasts. Click a couple, and see where they take you.

Promos

Everybody needs to promote their show; newer shows are constantly sending promos to or calling into more established shows, in hopes of tapping into a bigger audience. Very often you'll hear a caller to a listener line, cracking wise on a recent topic. You'll also notice that the caller always seems to mention a podcast URL. *They are plugging their podcast.* Now, if the caller is funny/informative/inspirational/whatever-you're-looking-for, take note of their URL. Maybe you'll end up listening to their show instead. This is a great way to audition podcasts without even trying. Just keep your ears open and a pen handy (unless you're really good at remembering URLs) and you're golden.

By sifting through category listings, and browsing through rankings and website recommendations, you're going to soon amass a list of podcasts you'll want to audition. You'll probably even found a couple you're not sure you can live without. You might even find yourself wondering, "Hey, I wonder when they're gonna upload the next show?" Well, well, well, you may already be hooked.

Podcatching

Whether it was the titles that peaked your interest ("The Rock n' Roll Geek Show," "Verge of the Fringe"), or the subject matter ("The Mysteries & Myths of Nepalese Goat Herding"—OK, we made that one up), you soon realize it's time to get set up to receive podcasts automatically. Now, this is where it gets good. Please, stick with us. This is where we start talking a little (and just a little) about computer code and things you should know about, but won't be tested on. Ever. We just want to make sure you have a basic understanding of how the whole thing works before we get too involved. It'll make setting up your podcast that much easier when we do.

The podcast client

While you can easily find and listen to podcasts with just a web browser, what you'll really want to do is have the podcasts automatically come to you. Instead of going from web page to web page, clicking links, you will soon just click one button and, boom, there they are. Well, there they are after they download.

Early in the development of podcasting, people began calling the software used to receive podcasts, **podcatchers**. It was a fun way to personify the two sides of the equation: the show creator would "cast" the show and the listener would "catch" it. Of course, in computer geek-speak, these podcatchers are **podcast clients** or **podcast aggregators**, software designed to make finding and subscribing to podcasts simple. Best of all, they help manage the flow of podcasts from the Internet to your computer and ultimately onto your portable media player.

Are they difficult to use? No. Are they tricky to set up? Not really. Do we promise to never call them "aggregators" again? You betcha.

Lots of choices

There are plenty of podcatchers to choose from, regardless of what platform you're using and what budget you're working with. They all serve the same basic function: looking for and downloading new podcasts. How they handle finding, downloading, and saving the shows to your hard drive varies slightly from one to another, but the examples we give will most likely hold true for all the others. Each has a simple approach to subscribing to and managing feeds, as well as monitoring the progress of downloads. Most are also supported by robust online forums to help troubleshoot any problems you may have in running or configuring the software. Don't worry; help is always a couple of mouse clicks away, but you won't need it, trust us.

As we talked about before, iPodder was the first podcast client, its creation being, if not the official birth of podcasting, at least the beginning of labor. Shortly thereafter, teams of people started developing podcatchers based on the original iPodder concept.

IPodder Lemon (Windows/Mac OS X/Linux) and iPodderX (Mac OS X) emerged quickly in the early days of podcasting and continue to be two of the top podcast clients available (see CD for demo versions). Other podcatchers were close behind, most notably Doppler (Windows), jPodder (Windows/Linux), and Nimiq (Windows). Since the release of iTunes 4.9, with podcatching features built right in, downloading and transferring podcasts to an iPod has never been easier. At this point in podcasting history, podcast clients are already made for Windows, Macintosh, Linux, Pocket PC, smartphones, and even Palm devices. Can a wireless unit with a catcher built into your car be far off?

In addition to standalone podcast clients, many RSS aggregators or newsreaders now offer automated podcast downloading too. Since podcasting is simply a component of RSS with the enclosure tag added (see Chapter 1), soon all RSS newsreaders will most likely support automated podcast downloading.

Time to subscribe

Now that you have found some podcasts you enjoy, it's time to automate the process of receiving new shows. This is accomplished by **subscribing** to the podcast. Remember, subscribing doesn't cost anything. No little prepaid postcards in the mail, no monthly bills. It simply means you're subscribing to the RSS feed and setting up your podcatcher to download new shows to your computer. The process is simple. As mentioned earlier, most podcast clients have a built-in directory, so if you know the name of the show it's easy to add the feed to your subscription list.

Whether it's done manually or automatically, you subscribe to a podcast by adding the web address of the RSS feed into the catcher. That's it. You'll either click a button, cut and paste a URL, or hit the Add button, and you're done (see Figure 2-4).

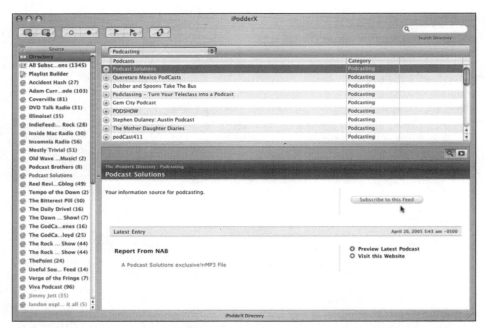

Figure 2-4. The directory in use in iPodderX

Most podcatchers give you various download options when subscribing to shows, so when you find one that sounds interesting, you can subscribe to download just the most recent show, the three most recent, or all of the shows available (see Figure 2-5).

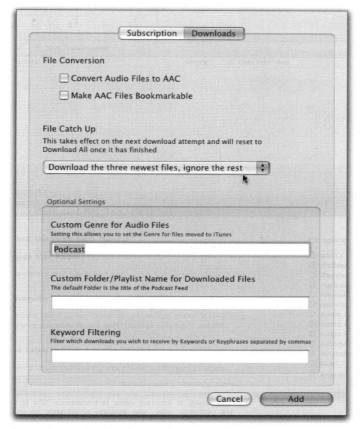

Figure 2-5. Setting download preferences (in iPodderX)

Be forewarned: a podcast that has only been around for a couple of months could have as many as 60 or more podcasts available online. A long-running show can have hundreds of available episodes, and given the new file hosting service plans that are available, most of those hundreds could still be online. Some RSS feeds may only contain a half dozen or so of the latest shows in a podcast series, while others may contain the most recent 50. There is no standard for this. Therefore it's *NOT* recommended to hastily subscribe to download the entire catalogue of a podcast you're not completely infatuated with. After subscribing and listening to several shows, you may decide to go for it, but before you do, consider sticking to 1-to-3 podcasts to start from for any one show.

As an example, let's find and subscribe to a podcast or two using iPodder Lemon. We chose iPodder Lemon because it supports both Windows and Macintosh machines, and odds are good you will too. Better yet, it's free.

Also, iPodder Lemon requires that you put the feed information in manually, as opposed to iPodderX and iTunes that both require a simple click of the subscribe button. By doing it now the hard way, you'll have a better understanding of what the feed is for later on, when you're producing your own podcasts.

Find iPodder Lemon on the *Podcast Solutions* CD (it's easy to find on the CD menu), install it on your computer, and launch it.

Click the Podcast directory tab along the top of the main window

If you already know what podcast you want to subscribe to, and you know their feed info, simply type or cut-and-paste the feed address into the text field next to the Add button. If you're looking for a podcast to subscribe to, click the folders and begin poking around. The Podcast Alley Top 50 and the iPodder.org category listings are a great place to start. When you find a podcast in the directory you want to subscribe to, click the name, and iPodder Lemon will automatically add the feed to the Add field for you (see Figure 2-6).

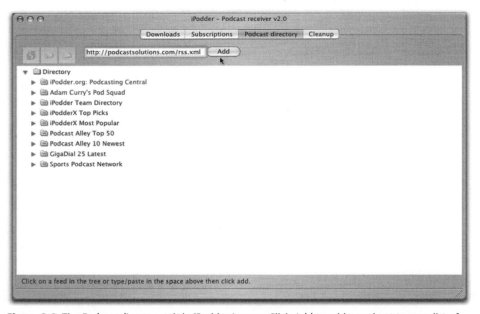

Figure 2-6. The Podcast directory tab in iPodder Lemon. Click Add to add a podcast to your list of subsciptions.

Click the Add button, and the podcast is added to your list of subscriptions, and a list of available podcast episodes appears in the window below, as shown in Figure 2-7. Highlight the name of your new entry and click Check Selected Feed to start downloading.

Your downloaded podcasts can automatically be moved to iTunes or Windows Media Player and into a playlist generated by iPodder with the name of the corresponding pod-cast (see Figure 2-8). Now, you're ready to go. Of course, as we mentioned earlier, you can even use iTunes itself nowadays to subscribe to podcasts!

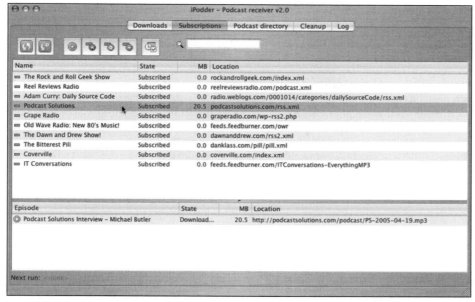

Figure 2-7. The iPodder Lemon Subscriptions tab. Click the Check Selected Feed button to download podcasts.

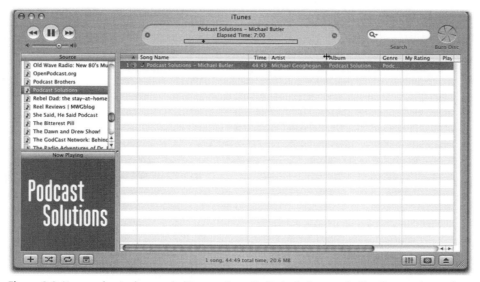

Figure 2-8. Your podcasts show up in iTunes automatically, in their own playlist. Now you're ready to roll!

Summary

To truly appreciate a podcast, you should listen to it "your way." With a podcast, you're not bound to your desk or your car radio. People listen to podcasts everywhere and anywhere. So download a couple of shows and transfer them to your portable media player, burn them to a compact disc, do whatever it takes to listen to it *where you want to listen, when you want to listen*. You'll find there is something incredibly empowering about having information and entertainment come to you, instead of having to go to it. The commute will feel that much shorter. Your time on the treadmill with change completely. You'll actually wish your dentist would keep you waiting a little longer so you can enjoy the end of a really great story. We didn't make that up. Someone actually wished that wish while catching up on her podcasts. Do you dare even get involved?

3 **PODCASTING HOW-TO**

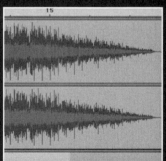

So, it's finally time to do it yourself. You've listened to a few shows, gotten yourself all worked up, and now it's time to hit that mic and start a podcast. Right? Well, not quite.

You could just jump right in, fire up whatever audio software you may find lying around on your hard drive, hit record, "blah, blah, blah," then upload and hope for the best. Frankly, for some people that might be the best approach. However, we want you to slow down, plan ahead, and set yourself up to really enjoy the experience, not just the first time, but every time. We want your podcast to be the best it can be. More importantly, we don't want you to have to go through some of the mistakes the so-called pioneers had to suffer through to get everyone to this point.

For most of the rest of this book, we're going to be talking in detail about the different aspects of making a podcast. So, we thought it would be best to give you a quick overview of the entire process before we start, so that when you get to the details, you'll already feel like you're in familiar territory.

In simple terms, making a podcast consists of recording a sound file, and then going through a few steps to prepare to get it out to the world. That's it. If at any time you feel like we're throwing too much at you, just remember your new mantra: "It's just an audio file I'm gonna upload, it's just an audio file I'm gonna upload . . ."

Here's what we'll be covering in the next set of chapters. Each chapter will include generalized information that will apply to most any situation, and then present more specific examples of how those techniques are applied with specific pieces of software or hardware. We'll cover these topics:

- Developing your podcast conceptually
- Preshow preparation
- Recording
- Editing and mastering
- Encoding to MP3
- Uploading
- Updating your feed

Depending on how much experience you've had with recording and editing digital audio or uploading files to the Internet, you may feel like this is an awful lot to go through. It's not. Besides, we're here to help guide you through the process. As you tackle each step along the way, you may experience that unsettling feeling you get when you do something for the first time—"Am I doing this correctly?" you may hear yourself say. Just remember, it's only your first time once. The steps we outline in this book are straightforward, and the book will always be here for you to refer back to. This may seem like a lot now, but with a couple of podcasts under your belt, the process will become as familiar as backing down your own driveway.

Developing your podcast

They love to use that term in Hollywood: *development*. They'll say, "We're developing a sit-com about a former superhero who's now a stay-at-home dad." What that means is they're "making up" a sitcom, working it out, and planning for its full gestation over several seasons. That's what you're going to do with your podcast. We'll help you make sure you know what you want it to be about, how you want it to sound, how you want it to "feel." We'll talk about creating a format for your show, so that each unique edition feels like it's part of the series of shows. Most importantly, we'll look at how you want your podcast to grow over time and where you'd like to take it in the future.

3

Preshow preparation

Show preparation ("prep") is different from development. Show prep is getting ready before each show so that you can record your podcast. You may need to get some sound effects ready, cue up a voice mail recording to play, or do some research and get some facts straight about real estate investments in Guam. Show prep is also about setting up your studio and checking to make sure everything is working properly, that you have enough hard disk space to record to, and that you can properly monitor your recording through headphones.

Setting up your studio and recording

We'll cover selecting a studio setup that's right for you and configuring that setup to work best while you're recording. We'll talk about the different types of microphones that pod-casters use, and why some mics may be better for you than others. We'll talk about the craft of proper mic technique, and the art of "talking to one person at a time." "What does that mean?" you ask? Keep reading.

Recording and saving your podcast with good recording levels is essential. We'll talk about some of the industry standards you can easily adhere to in your home studio, making your podcast sound as professional as possible.

Editing/Mastering

Another classic Hollywood expression is, "Don't worry, we'll fix it in post!" *Post* being postproduction. In the case of podcasting, postproduction means editing the raw sound file into the show you want to podcast, and doing any kind of processing to the file you need to get the type of sound quality you're looking for. There are plenty of software plug-ins, filters, and hardware processes you can use to make your tiny home setup sound like the biggest FM station in town.

Encoding to MP3

This is where you take your new work of audio art and compress it down to a fraction of its original size. The compression process can mean the difference between a slight loss in sound quality and turning your masterpiece into a potential form of torture. We'll discuss *podcast standards* for encoding, and suggest a few different approaches to encoding that'll keep your workflow flowing.

Uploading

There are actually several ways to upload your podcast to the Internet. We'll talk about various methods of getting your podcast online and help determine which works best for you. Whether you end up using an FTP client (a simple mechanism that allows easy and secure upload of files to the Internet) or upload through the website of your service provider, we'll get you uploaded and online.

Updating your feed

You guessed it! You will soon have one of those fancy RSS feeds we keep mentioning. We know, all this talk of feeds can get a bit old, especially when you're not sure you've ever even used a feed. Not to worry. Whether you update the code by hand (a simple matter of cutting and pasting), use a standalone RSS application (easy, easy, easy), or use the RSS functions of your blog (effortless and automatic), we'll get your feed updated and your podcast downloadable without a hitch.

Summary

Prep, record, edit, encode, upload, update. Pretty straightforward. Remember, if you ever have a question about what something means, there's an exhaustive glossary in the back of this book that'll give you the meaning of anything we mention. Well, let's not put things off any longer. It's time to unearth that hidden podcast and get it out into the light. Shall we begin?

4 PLANNING YOUR PODCAST

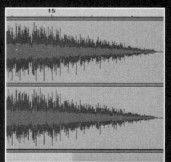

So you want to do a podcast, huh? Well, we're not going to stop you. In fact, we'll help you! But, before you begin, we advise taking a hard look at why you want to podcast.

Your motivation to podcast is going to be what keeps you committed to producing your show. When you are clear on your motivation, you will be free to let your enthusiasm for the subject matter shine through. Ultimately, it is your enthusiasm that will "sell" your show. Most podcasters are producing podcasts because they are genuinely enthusiastic about their subject matter. Whatever the topic is, they love it—passion for their show is spilling out of them, and they will spend much of their free time and disposable income to get the enthusiasm out of their bodies and into the mic. If you have no enthusiasm for your planned show—no true love of it—don't start. It will be too much work to manufacture the energy to do a show week after week, and trust us, listeners can hear a phony from a gigabyte away.

We know that's not you—you're excited and enthusiastic, right? Then let's get to it. In this chapter, we're going to take a look at the following topics:

- **Developing your podcast**: Who, what, how often, and how long
- **Formatting and structuring your podcast**: The freedom of confinement, working clean, and defamation
- **Using music legally in your podcast**: The Recording Industry Association of America (RIAA), indie artists, and the benefits of Creative Commons
- **Incorporating other elements into your podcast**: Voice mail messages and live phone calls from listeners, segments from other podcasts, and other elements

Developing your podcast

Somewhat ironically, there are likely hundreds of pages on the Internet—no, probably thousands—dealing with the topic of producing and distributing podcasts: what mics to use, what mixer is preferable, what directories to get listed in, and so on. However, there is almost no information available about how to create and develop a concept for a podcast. No information on how to make it the best, most effective podcast it can be.

It could be a matter of ego; everyone likes to think they can pull that kind of stuff off without assistance. Perhaps people are in such a hurry to get their podcast online that they want to just hit the Record button and hope for the best. There was a time in the not-so-distant past when, as a podcaster, you could afford to stumble around a bit before you really "found" your show. Nowadays, there are too many listeners, too much attention, and too much at stake to jump into the pool without at least first thinking about how to swim. You may have an idea for a show you've been dying to do. If so, do it the honor of letting it gestate and form fully before you release it into the world.

As you plan your podcast, to ensure its success and longevity, you need to take some time and really consider the following questions:

- Who are you and why should we listen?

- How will you and your listeners benefit from focusing on a specific topic?

- How long a podcast should you try to put together, and how often can you do it and keep it interesting?

Who are you and why should we listen?

When people talk about podcasts and what they like about them, there is a single concept that comes up over and over. It's more than the lack of commercials and more than the wide array of subject matter. One element of a good podcast seems to be universal, whether it is a religious podcast, a comedy podcast, or a music podcast: connection.

> *A fact of human nature is that people would rather listen to something they connect with that is poorly produced than something that sounds like a million bucks and is, to them, a complete bore.*

Honest connection with other human beings seems to be the linchpin in a successful podcast. Not that you have to tell your deepest, darkest secrets, admit your fascination with Ricky Martin, or give out your ATM pin number. You just have to be honest about who you are, what the podcast is all about, and what your intentions are. If you start doing a podcast about movies, but you aren't really *that* big a movie fan, your podcast will wither on the vine. If your heart isn't in it, your tiny audience will soon smell a rat. Also, if you're trying to sell your listeners a book, a diet plan, or a set of steak knives, don't try to fool them into thinking they're listening to anything other than a sales pitch. Podcast listeners are smart, savvy people who easily spot a fraud. If you're honest with them, they'll connect with you and your show. If you don't break that connection by betraying their trust, they'll stay connected to your show for the long run. It's essential to choose a topic that fascinates, inspires, and excites you, and it will fascinate, inspire, and excite others.

Respect your audience. You're asking your listeners to find, subscribe, download, transfer, and listen to your show. That requires some effort on their part. In return, give them an honest presentation. You have the privilege of whispering in their ears, following them from their homes to their jobs and schools, and accompanying them on their daily walk, and they want someone they can trust to join them on these journeys. You'll create a relationship in which you present them with thoughts and ideas, and they listen, respond, and interact.

Of the utmost importance is to decide what exactly your podcast will be about. What is it you're trying to accomplish with your podcast? Are you hoping to expose listeners to great undiscovered musical talent from your hometown? Perfect. Are you trying to create a support group for people who must maintain a low-carb diet for health reasons? Great. Do you just want to sit on the floor in your underwear taking about Dungeons & Dragons? Well, hey, who are we to judge . . .

> *Listeners = Community*

When listeners subscribe to your podcast, you and they are entering into an agreement of sorts. They agree to download your podcast on a regular basis, in the belief that you will be podcasting on a consistent basis on the topic they've come to expect from you. This is an important point; you need to do your best to uphold your part of this bargain.

Also, the listeners agree to download the kind of podcast they heard the first couple of times they listened. They expect that each podcast in the "series" will be new and yet similar to the previous shows, much like watching a new episode of their favorite TV show. So, if you've been doing a simple, tight cooking show, and then you suddenly go off on a rant on your views of privatizing public schools, you're violating the trust you've established with your audience. To avoid doing this, it is imperative that you be very clear about what podcast you're producing, so you can continue to produce the show your listeners expect. This isn't to say that you can't do a show on whatever happens to be on your mind—you just need to let listeners know that is what your show is about. Essentially, you need to manage the expectations of those who subscribe.

Narrowcasting: The benefits of a well-defined concept

You may be thinking, "A Dungeons & Dragons podcast? Are these guys serious?" Sure. D&D, badminton, chewing rocks, whatever subject you like. This is the age of **narrowcasting**, or making programs available that may appeal only to a small percentage of a total potential audience. But, for those the program appeals to, that appeal is immeasurable.

We hate to be the ones to break it to you, but you are not completely unique. Sure, you're unique in that technical, "every snowflake is different" kind of way. But as far as humans go, you're not completely singular. Other people have the same interests and hobbies that you have. It may seem like you're all alone in your curiosities, depending on just how curious they are, but plenty of fellow *whatevers* are out there. If there's a podcast that you think you'd like to listen to, then that is the one for you to produce.

Not everyone is going to want to listen to a podcast about playing badminton. Actually, it might happen that very few people do. But, to those few people who do want to listen to that kind of show, it might be to them the greatest show ever made in the history of sound recording. Where else are badminton fanatics going to get information and entertainment revolving around the game they love? Certainly not radio. Yet a podcast about badminton, or any other narrowly defined subject, is more than just an audio recording: it is potentially the center of a community. A well-defined podcast is going to get immediate interest from people who share the same interest. As the podcast grows, so does the listener base. Soon the listeners and the podcasters are all sharing stories, tips, and information about that subject matter. Before you know it, a podcast you thought only a handful of listeners would enjoy is indispensable to an entire subculture.

Determining your podcast's length and frequency

The length of your podcast and how frequently you make a new one available can have a major effect on your podcast's appeal, especially if you don't know what you're getting yourself into.

Show length and the law of diminishing returns

Once they get over the initial growing pains of the first podcast or two, most podcasters feel they could talk on and on for hours. But a longer show is not *necessarily* a better show. Trial and error has shown that between 15 and 30 minutes is about the optimum length for a solid podcast. If you are going to err, err on the side of brevity. A shorter podcast has a higher likelihood of being listened to regularly, as compared to a longer one. Also, by making a show that is too long, you are weakening "the brand." People's attention will wander during an hour-long show unless it is rock solid. And, if it is rock solid, break it into two separate podcasts. You'll reduce the chances of losing the audience while building anticipation for the next installment. Odds are that if you're recording for an hour, you could stand to cut it down. You won't regret it.

You're never locked into a set length for your podcast. Just because your first one is 25 minutes, that doesn't mean you have to make every one 25 minutes, especially if you don't have 25 minutes worth of content. The length of each show is up to you and should be determined by the amount of material you have for that podcast. Remember, this isn't radio.

Show frequency and the law of diminishing returns

Doing a daily show sounds exciting at first. You sit down at the mic every day, pontificate for 25 minutes, and you're golden. Heck, you're doing your listeners a favor by giving them something to listen to every day. The downside, of course, is that you don't have much to say every day. Or, if you do have something to say every day, your listeners probably don't have time to listen that often. Now, that being said, there are several great daily podcasts, the most notable being Adam Curry's "Daily Source Code." But Adam Curry has decades of experience as a broadcaster, and he also has the entire podcasting community supplying him with information, promos, songs, and so forth to fill his show. A "normal" podcast will not have this luxury. You would need to come up with new material every day that's fresh and tight enough to require its own show.

If you are doing a new podcast, you may need to edge another show off a listener's subscription list to get listened to on a regular basis. There are only so many hours in a day, and only so many of those can be devoted to listening to podcasts. The best way to get new listeners to subscribe to your show is to not overwhelm them up front. Sometimes it is true that "less is more." Give listeners a tight, well-put-together taste and no more. An age-old, but still valid cliché from the entertainment world applies here: "Always leave them wanting more." (Not less . . .)

Find a schedule that works for you. When I first started doing "Reel Reviews - Films Worth Watching" (www.reelreviewsradio.com), I established a pace of roughly two to three movie review podcasts per week. That was great in the beginning, but I soon realized that pace was too optimistic. In addition to watching the film (often more than once), listening to commentaries, reading, doing research, recording, editing, and posting, I found that I also had to spend time running the site, responding to e-mails, and taking care of other general podcaster responsibilities. All of that plus running a business and spending time with my family proved to be too much. I ended up finding a sweet spot at roughly one "Reel Review" podcast per week. Now I do not feel rushed and I can devote the time necessary to produce a solid show. In the long run, I know that the show content benefits from the extra time, and ultimately that is only thing that matters. Remember, content is king.

—Michael Geoghegan

Formatting and structuring your podcast

One of the attractive aspects of doing a podcast is that there are no rules. The Federal Communications Commission (FCC) doesn't tell you what you can and cannot do. There is no programming director or group of shareholders to tell you what to say or what to play. As long as you don't infringe on anyone's copyright, you're set. You're your own podcaster, ready to take on the world however you see fit. To hell with the old way, you're going to reinvent the wheel and roll, baby!

In a lot of ways, before you can break the rules, you have to make the rules. We strongly suggest you create a format for your show, which will be the wheel on which you ride.

People in the radio industry actually use the analogy of a wheel or a clock to determine when to do things, what to play when, and so on. At the top of the hour (wheel), they play an upbeat new hit, then they play another song, and then at quarter past the hour they go to a commercial break. After the commercial break, they play another big hit, followed by an old favorite, and so on. The entire day is formatted by this wheel, with different songs, commercials, and promos being plugged in at the appropriate times.

Since your podcast doesn't go on and on all day like a radio station, maybe it's best to see your podcast in a linear fashion, with a beginning, middle, and end. Every good book, every classic movie, and every song you've ever liked has had this beginning, middle, and end format. So should your podcast. Think about how you want to begin and end each podcast, and how you should order the various segments in between. Audiences love structure. They especially love to see a tried-and-true structure applied in a new and surprising way. Why do people watch episode after episode of the same sitcom for years, sometimes decades? Because they love seeing the same characters butt heads in the same ways over new problems every week. The structure of the show never changes, but how that structure is lived in each episode is what is so fascinating.

This may sound a bit binding at first. It isn't. Advertising legend David Ogilvy was famous for saying "Give me the freedom of a tightly defined strategy" (or something to that effect). If you leave yourself too much freedom (no format), you will flounder around show after show, unsure of what to do next. Worse, you will quickly frustrate your listeners. But, if you give yourself total freedom within a tight format, you will never stop thinking of ways to use that structure.

Here are a few examples of how you might format a 15–30 minute podcast. You'll soon see what we mean when we say there is freedom in constraint.

Example format for a talk show:

- Intro music
- Greetings and thanks
- Listener mail
- B topic (short)
- Listener voice mail message
- A topic (long)
- URL/phone number
- Outro music

Example format for a music show:

- Show ID
- Up-tempo song
- Slower song
- "Back sell" first songs, give URL/phone number
- Up-tempo song
- Requested song
- "Back sell" with album information, promote next show
- Last song

Example format for a technology show:

- Voice mail message
- Intro song
- Tech news and reviews
- B topic (short)
- Question from mail/voice mail
- Promote upcoming show
- Phone interview with expert guest on topic A (long)
- Outro music

These are just a few examples to give you an idea of what we mean by **format**. Do you have to do exactly the same thing every time? No, but your format will be there when you need it, like a security blanket. You can deviate from it as much as you like, change it, destroy it, and put it back together. If you start with a structured format in mind, you will never regret it. Remember, before you can break the rules, you need to know what the rules are.

> *A perfect example of a show with a good structured format is the "The Dawn and Drew Show!" (www.dawnanddrew.com). While the show has a somewhat free-form feel, which Dawn and Drew acknowledge to anyone listening, it always ends with a segment of feedback from people who have called the show's comment line. You can always count on it. Because Dawn and Drew always include the caller feedback segment in their show, they end up receiving a lot of calls on the comment line. It is a great way to get listeners involved with and ultimately part of the show.*

As you are developing the format for your show, keep in mind that your show is a podcast, not a radio broadcast. People who rely too heavily on radio as a model find themselves breaking up segments with musical segues and then reintroducing their guest or topic, as is always done in radio. They do this in radio because radio is live, so listeners don't necessarily hear every moment of the program. Podcast listeners are there from the beginning of the program to the end, so reintroducing guests or topics is not necessary. Actually, it is painfully annoying.

Start strong, finish big

You don't have to be brilliant from the first word to the last in your podcast. Actually, you don't ever have to be brilliant. What you should be, to stack the deck in your own favor, is strong out of the gate. Start strong, and they will keep listening. The best comedian in the world will lose an audience immediately if he flounders in the first moments on stage. The audience members start shifting their feet, stirring their drinks, and checking their watches to see how long this clown has to go before he gets off stage. They're stuck in the club and have to either wait the guy out or leave. As a podcaster, you don't have the luxury of a captive audience. While a live comic has a chance to get the audience back on his side, if you lose your listeners in the first moments of your podcast, they are gone with the press of a button. Off to another podcast they go, perhaps never to return. Your listeners have thousands of podcasts they could be listening to. Make them feel like they're in good hands right away.

Lead with your strength. Be upbeat and get into it. Dragging your feet and waiting to get up to speed is risky business with several thousand other podcasts waiting in the wings. Make sure the opening of your show reflects the tone and pace of the show. If you have a trademark opening that works, stick with it. The theme song of your show, a familiar sound effect, and a catchphrase all can help kick-start each podcast and help build that initial momentum.

Even more important than starting strong is finishing big. The old showbiz adage of "Save the best for last" holds true for podcasts. Save some of your strongest material for the end. If you leave people with a message that really resonates with them, that is what they will remember. They will forgive all the missteps and missed cues, all the bad jokes and awkward transitions, if you leave them with your best stuff. This goes for comedy, information, sales, you name it: finish big.

As a side note, consider putting longer segments toward the end of the show. If you start with one long segment, and you then do several shorter segments, the podcast will seem top-heavy and unsteady. People are used to what they're used to. "But podcasting is about breaking the rules?!" you may scream. Yes, it is. It's about breaking the rules of content and the rules of business. It's about reexamining the way broadcasting has failed, and it's about making podcasting better. It is not, however, about fighting human nature. Humans inherently, for whatever reason, have come to expect certain story structures. Don't fight it. Embrace it and use it to your advantage.

4

Working "clean"

Podcasting means no FCC—only pure and unbridled free speech for as far as the ear can hear. *You're free to say exactly what you want.* But should you? Is using adult language the only way to achieve your desired effect? This is something you need to make a conscious decision about before you start.

There is and always will be an audience for adult material. There's a feeling of exclusivity, of freedom, when listening to something kind of dirty. Sure it's childish, but there's something thrilling about listening to something your parents wouldn't listen to—that you could never listen to at school or in the office, but might excitedly whisper about to someone else in the halls. If your target audience is young adults, you may feel that using adult language is required. If you must, you must. But don't do it if it's not natural. Nothing sounds worse than awkward swearing.

If you decide not to swear, you need to stick to it (see the previous section for more about your audience's expectations). However, if you do decide to "work blue," just be aware that you're potentially alienating just as many listeners as you may be attracting. You'll certainly reduce the number of listeners who may want to listen to your show at work or when the kids are around. This may not sound like a big deal, but depending on your target audience, using adult language could deal a sizable blow to your potential listener base. If your show could be listened to by people in an open area, don't go blue—it's not going to get played. The office is out. School is out. Carpool is out. Sure, listening to a podcast is an individual thing, done by many people wearing headphones. But not everyone wears headphones. If listeners don't feel comfortable listening to your podcast in public, your show won't be played in public. That means missed opportunities to reach new listeners. Oops. Is it that important?

> *I was a stand-up comedian for many years, performing in clubs and coffeehouses all over Los Angeles. And, frankly, I worked "blue." Swear, swear, swear. As far as I was concerned at the time, the swearing was not gratuitous. The bad words all fit in with the rhythm of the jokes, with my persona, with the venue. All my favorites had been masters of adult language: Lenny Bruce, Richard Pryor, Bill Hicks, Chris Rock . . .*
>
> *When I first heard about podcasting, I immediately realized it was the perfect way for me to get back into doing comedy without hanging around clubs until all hours of the night. Because it was podcasting, I could say anything I wanted to. But I didn't. I was tempted to. Frankly, I had to fight the urge to swear with all my might. Even now, there are many times I stumble around for a word to substitute for the swear word in my head.*
>
> *I made the decision not to swear because I was greedy. Greedy for listeners. I admit it, I didn't want to do anything to turn anyone away. So, I plowed ahead, "clean."*
>
> *I realized that most of my new material was about being a husband and a father, and that many of my listeners would be family types, too, who would want to be able to listen to the show around the kids.*
>
> *It got frustrating. I felt like I was stifling myself. I talked about it on a podcast and quickly found out that the listeners didn't want me to swear. The content didn't require it. I soon realized that the material actually hadn't been suffering because of my working clean. I was talking about exactly what I wanted to, but using innuendo and malapropisms instead of curse words. I have continued to keep the show as clean as I can ever since.*
>
> *I have never received an e-mail or a voice mail message from anyone saying they wished I would swear more. I have received countless messages saying how glad people are that I don't.*
>
> *—Dan Klass*

Your decision to use adult language or not should really be dictated by the show you're trying to do. If it's a family show, a business show, or an informational/educational show, adult language is going to hold you and your podcast back. Many podcasters attract listeners by labeling their shows "work safe" and/or "kid safe." That way, listeners know they won't be embarrassed (or worse) by listening to the podcast in a public place.

Consider, too, if down the line you're going to try to attract sponsors or advertising. Do you need to limit yourself to the kinds of advertisers who will pay for an adult-themed show? Or is that exactly the market you'd be looking at? Let the future of the podcast dictate this.

A few words about defamation and slander

We don't really know where else to put this in the book, but we thought we should throw in a fact or two about slander. **Slander** is the oral communication of false or malicious statements about or charges against someone that are injurious to that person's reputation, business, and so on. If you are new to broadcasting/podcasting, you may have never even considered the legalities of what you may and may not say. If you did say something slanderous about someone, it would not be difficult for the person's attorney to get hold of a copy of the slanderous podcast. Be careful! Podcasts are not a small discussion among trusted friends; they are publicly available audio content just like radio and TV, and some of the same rules will apply.

Generally speaking, there are three defenses to an accusation of slander:

- The statement is true. This is often referred to as an **absolute defense**, meaning if it is true it can't be slander.
- It is a statement of opinion.
- The person referred to in the statement is a public figure, or it is "fair comment on a matter of public interest."

Of course, there are other defenses, and protecting yourself against accusations of slander is more complicated than just following a set of rules. Even though the preceding are defenses, you can still end up spending tens of thousands of dollars "defending" yourself. Please keep in mind that we are *not* lawyers—we are podcasters—so be sure to check with your lawyer before speaking out too frankly against someone.

Using music in podcasts

Welcome to the minefield. Including music in podcasts is the area of podcasting most fraught with danger, confusion, and potential liability.

Almost every podcast has music in it, whether it's in the form of entire songs or short, ten-second segues. The amount of music you'll use is something to consider up front, because using music in podcasts can legally be a tricky situation. We're living in an era of file-sharing paranoia on the part of major record labels and a "music should be free" mentality on the part of many Internet users. Let's be very clear up front: *music is not free.* Music costs money to produce, to promote, and to distribute. The writers of the songs spend a lot of time, and the record labels spend a lot of money, to get that music written, recorded, and out into the world. So, to protect that investment, they all closely control the use of that music and the rights to reproduce it. Everybody wants to get paid and protected, and rightfully so.

To cut to the chase: *if you use music in a podcast without the express permission of the persons/entities that own that music, you are in violation of copyright.*

It's true that most unknown, independent artists would be more than happy for a little podcast exposure, and very few would come looking to sue you over playing one of their songs. But just as you may not want people freely giving away your podcast to anyone who will take a copy, you can't assume that a recording artist (or any artist, for that matter) is OK with you using her work, even if she has songs available on the Internet for free download. The recording artist may want to reserve her "right to copy."

To distribute a musical work you did not create and do not own legally, you need to get permission from the writer of the song, the performer of the song, and the owner of the master recordings.

Composers' rights

The **composers' rights** of musical works are handled by any one of three rights organizations: the American Society of Composers, Authors, and Publishers (ASCAP, www.ascap.com), Broadcast Music, Inc. (BMI, www.bmi.com), and the Society of European Stage Authors and Composers (SESAC, www.sesac.com). These organizations track the use of a composer's works in radio, television, film, and other media, and collect payments to the composer for such use.

On January 1, 2005, ASCAP introduced its "Non-Interactive Experimental License Agreement for Internet Sites & Services - Release 5.0" license, which is designed to handle the needs of webcasters and web developers using ASCAP music where the song segment is less than 60 seconds in length. *Clearly, this does not apply directly to podcasters.* Assuming that it's the closest license we have to go by as a guide, and that BMI and SESAC have similar licenses, a podcaster would be required to pay an annual fee of US$300.00 for ASCAP, another US$300.00 annually for BMI, and approximately US$170.00 for SESAC, and that's only covering the written element of the song. (Actually, it's only covering the written element of the song if you're webcasting, which hasn't yet been defined to include podcasting.)

Performers' rights

So, assuming you've secured the composers' rights from ASCAP or BMI (assuming that you need to), you are only cleared to perform the song yourself or have someone perform it for you (on a webcast). If you are hoping to use an existing recording of a song, you still need to secure the **performers' rights**, which are controlled by the record labels. Two separate elements are required to license the performers' rights: the mechanical license and the master use license.

The **mechanical license** covers the right to reproduce a performance of a particular song on a song-by-song basis and is handled by the Harry Fox Agency. The Harry Fox Agency explains very clearly under what circumstances someone is required to option a mechanical license on its website (www.harryfox.com):

> "If you are manufacturing and distributing copies of a song which you did not write, and you have not already reached an agreement with the song's publisher, you need to obtain a mechanical license. This is required under U.S. Copyright Law, regardless of whether or not you are selling the copies that you made.

> "You do not need a mechanical license if you are recording and distributing a song you wrote yourself, or if the song is in the public domain. If you are not sure if the song you are looking to license is in the public domain, and therefore does not require license authority, we suggest you use the search on www.pdinfo.com."

The issuing and the costs surrounding a **master use license** are controlled completely and solely by the owner of the master recordings, which is usually the record label. The label will determine the licensing rate based on how popular the song or artist is, how current the work is and, frankly, how much it thinks it can get for the license. Now, the label is under no obligation to issue anyone a license to use any song. If the label sees podcasting as a potential avenue of lost revenues, it simply will not grant you permission, or it will set the licensing fee so high as to make it impossible for you to license the work.

To keep the licensing fees for Internet use in check, SoundExchange (www.soundexchange. com) was created to act as the licensing entity for the record labels. According to SoundExchange, the group has "been designated by the U.S. Copyright Office to collect and distribute statutory royalties to sound recording copyright owners and featured and nonfeatured artists." Although SoundExchange has set a relatively low annual fee for Internet use of RIAA music, the wording of the licensing agreement is such that it *does not actually apply to podcasts*, but rather (as is usually the case) applies to streaming media.

Using mash-ups and remixes

The mash-up trend is in full swing, with more mash-up DJs popping up every week, and more radio stations playing mash-ups on a regular basis. A **mash-up** is a song created out of pieces of two or more songs, usually by overlaying the vocal track of one song seamlessly over the music track of another. A classic example is the infamous "Ray of Gob" put together by mash-up genius Mark Vidler (www.gohomeproductions.co.uk), which expertly combines bits of several songs by the Sex Pistols with Madonna's "Ray of Light." The song got worldwide attention and radio airplay (by none other than Steve Jones of the Sex Pistols), and Vidler got legitimate remix work with Madonna.

Mash-ups are incredible fun and a fascinating way to reexperience some of your favorite tunes. What mash-ups are not is **podsafe**. "Podsafe" is a term you'll hear quite a bit when talking about using music in podcasts. It means "music that is safe to include in your podcast, legally." Mash-ups are the opposite of podsafe. Just because you've heard mash-ups and remixes on other podcasts doesn't mean they're legal. If using one copyrighted song in your podcast is considered a copyright infringement, then distributing a mash-up would be violating the copyright of several songs at the same time! Just because a song is remixed, or mixed with another song, doesn't mean it suddenly falls into the public domain. Mash-ups are a legal nightmare, which is why you won't see a mash-up compilation CD at your local record store anytime soon. Radio stations can play them, because radio stations pay ASCAP, BMI, and so forth for permission to broadcast. Remember, we're not in that game.

Using music legally

So, now that your mind has been boggled, you're most assuredly asking yourself, "So, how do I use RIAA music in my podcast?" The answer seems to be "Very carefully." To be frank, nobody is crystal clear about exactly how to go about getting approved music from major labels without opening themselves up to potential liability. There is no precedent at this time to indicate whether securing a mechanical license and a master use license would be enough. Rest assured that there are very few—if any—podcasters who have the financial resources required to fight the major record labels if one of the labels decided to make an example of them and sue them for copyright infringement.

Your best bet is to find music anywhere else but in your CD collection, unless of course your CD collection is made up only of independent artists who would be willing to grant you all rights to use their music . . .

Brian Ibbott produces and hosts "Coverville" (www.coverville.com), one of the most widely listened to independent music podcasts on the internet. On "Coverville," Ibbott plays, as you might imagine, nothing but cover songs, performed and recorded by major label and independent recording artists. He has made every effort to include the music that he wants to on his show legally. Here is what Brian has to say about ASCAP, BMI, and the state of the music podcast.

Podcast Solutions*: How soon after starting did you realize you might need to get "legal" about it?*

Brian Ibbott*: Oh, it was the first show. I knew that what I was doing probably wasn't that different from what Sean Fanning was doing with the whole Napster deal, even though, all right, I'm neatly packaging five, six songs into a nice little 30-minute MP3, but it's ending up as an MP3 on somebody else's desktop.*

Around the middle of October [2004], I started calling ASCAP and BMI and saying, "All right, here's what I'm doing, here's this thing called podcasting, what kind of license do I need for this? Is it something that is licensable?" And I spent about an hour on the phone with each of them. And they said, "All right, we'll just fit you into a web stream- ing license; that's close enough." They were really lax about it and said, "Webcasting license, close enough. Here's a bill for two-hundred and fifty bucks, go ahead and get started . . ."

I kind of suspected that was only half of the equation. It was pretty much later in October when I did a little more research and found out about the whole mechanical rights side of it, with the RIAA, SoundExchange, and Harry Fox and all that.

I've talked to the RIAA, I've talked to SoundExchange and Harry Fox, and they're all aware of podcasting, and they're all aware of what I'm doing, so it's certainly no secret. But, until there's a way, until there's a method for me to pay for the mechanical rights, I do as much contacting of the artists as I can, which is a lot easier with the smaller groups, and in the other cases I just play it and cross my fingers.

Every quarter I put together a list (for ASCAP and BMI) of all the songs I've played, and I have to put down on what date, what show it appeared on, and who the performer was, and who the songwriter was. And they basically take the two-hundred and eighty dollars or whatever it is that I pay for a license, divide it by the number of songs I play, and send out a check to each of those songwriters.

I had a call (recently) from the RIAA. Driving to work, the cell phone rang, and it's the RIAA on the phone. It's one of those moments, like, "OK, is this the guy I left the message for . . ." He was really knowledgeable about podcasting—I didn't have to explain anything, this guy had really done his homework. He said that the big "sticky wicket" is that users end up with an MP3 on their computer, and unfortunately it is very easy to get some cheap software to split that up into individual songs if they want.

He basically implored upon me and said, "Hey, let's see what we can do about this together. Let's have some conversations about this and get some other podcasters together who want to play licensed music, and let's figure out a way to make it so that either the user doesn't end up with an MP3 they can split apart, or we figure out some way to discourage the possibility that they could split it apart." I'm thinking of things like what I do on the show already, talking over the beginnings of songs, talking over the ends of songs, segueing between different tracks so that if they were to try to break it out, they wouldn't get a clean copy.

I don't think we'll get to a point where the user doesn't end up with an MP3 on their computer—that's the whole basis of a podcast. But there are some things we can do to make it less possible for them to break it out into individual tracks.

PS: *What would be your advice to new music podcasters?*

BI: *My advice would be, play what your passion is, play what you're excited about, play what you're enthusiastic about. I don't do an all RIAA show, or an all independent show intentionally. I play what I enjoy and the songs that I'm hearing that I like, and I think that's what—this sounds really cheesy and sappy now that I'm saying it—it's what's going to make your show that much more credible, and it's probably going to keep you doing it a lot longer than if you aren't playing something that you're enthusiastic about.*

"Fair use"

"But I'm just using about ten seconds of this song for my intro . . ." Doesn't matter.

Many people still believe in the myth of "**fair use**"—that if you use only a small portion of a song, or use it as part of a review, a news story, or a parody, that it is legally without liability. Guess what, that's just not the case. Perhaps it should be, but it isn't. Corporate owners of intellectual property are very protective these days (as you learned in the preceding section), and they are as inclined to control the use of small sections of their properties as they are the use of complete works.

Even if it is just a short snippet of music for the intro or closing of your show, it needs to be music that you have permission to use or that can be used freely without the need to pay royalties.

Public domain

Using music that is in the **public domain**, due to the copyright of that work expiring, is just as tricky a situation as using the work of a major label artist. The public domain status of a work is often difficult to establish, and that status can be challenged at any time. Under current laws, the character Mickey Mouse will soon enter into the public domain. Needless to say, the Walt Disney Company (and its corporate brethren) is spending millions of dollars to have the guidelines of the public domain changed, or at least muddied, to protect their invaluable icon (even though their greatest earlier films were based on works in the public domain). If you feel you know a work is in the public domain, and you use it, you may find out the hard way later on that you were quite mistaken. Especially as podcasting grows, the eyes and ears of the legal departments at all the major record labels, movie studios, and the like will be keeping close tabs on the shows flying around the Internet. Unless you are planning to use a sound that is widely accepted as being in the public domain (none spring to mind), be very cautious about including supposedly public domain music in your podcast.

Getting your hands on an original copy of a work in the public domain is usually quite a feat. If you simply go down to the music store and start buying discs of old music, you may still be violating copyright if you use those songs. If a public domain work has been extensively restored, the restored version of the work (the version you'd most likely find on Amazon) could be copyrighted. The underlying work is in the public domain, but not the version you just purchased. Be careful.

Creative Commons

Some music on the Internet is not necessarily copyrighted in the traditional sense, but is protected by what is quickly becoming a popular means of restricting some rights while allowing others to intellectual property: a Creative Commons license. The Creative Commons organization was founded in 2001 to create a simple, straightforward way for content creators to protect their works, while giving clear and concise information on how those works can be used and redistributed by others.

A Creative Commons license can be applied to work in any medium: sound recordings, videos, films, photographs, and written works. There are hundreds of hours of songs under Creative Commons license that you can freely use, as long as you adhere to the license guidelines of those works. These guidelines grant or restrict the right to build upon the work and sample the work, or indicate whether or not a work can be used for commercial purposes (see Figure 4-1). Most songs and podcasts are licensed under the "Attribution-NonCommercial-NoDerivs 2.0" license, which states that others are free "to copy, distribute, display, and perform the work" (podcast), as long as the creator is given credit for the work, the work is not used for commercial purposes (sold), and the work is not built upon.

> As a side note—and we are surely getting ahead of ourselves here—you might consider licensing your podcast under a Creative Commons license.

COMMONS DEED

Attribution-NonCommercial-NoDerivs 2.0

You are free:

- to copy, distribute, display, and perform the work

Under the following conditions:

 Attribution. You must give the original author credit.

 Noncommercial. You may not use this work for commercial purposes.

 No Derivative Works. You may not alter, transform, or build upon this work.

- For any reuse or distribution, you must make clear to others the license terms of this work.
- Any of these conditions can be waived if you get permission from the copyright holder.

Your fair use and other rights are in no way affected by the above.

This is a human-readable summary of the Legal Code (the full license).

Disclaimer

This page is available in the following languages:
Català Deutsch English Castellano Suomeksi français hrvatski Italiano 日本語 한국어 Nederlands polski Português 中文(繁)

Figure 4-1. A Creative Commons "Attribution-NonCommercial-NoDerivs 2.0" license

The Creative Commons "Sampling License" allows you to use excerpts of a work, but not the entire piece. This is perfect for remixes and mash-ups, and it may also be a perfect license for a podcast. Other producers would be able to repurpose small sections of your program (which would be great promotion for you), but they couldn't legally use the whole thing.

Finding Creative Commons music is as simple as using the search tool built into the Creative Commons website (www.creativecommons.org) or Yahoo's Creative Commons Search (http://search.yahoo.com/cc). Also, Internet Archive (www.archive.org) is a valuable resource for finding Creative Commons (and reportedly public domain) works, either through independent artists or through **net labels** (i.e., music labels that make their catalog available under Creative Commons license on the web).

Indie artists and easily licensed music

Luckily for podcasters, not all bands are signed to major labels, and not all music is as closely regulated and licensed as the music of major recording stars. Before most singers, songwriters, and bands become major recording stars, they are usually unknown recording artists. They pour their hearts and souls into their music, playing live and recording their songs in the hope that people will appreciate their work. They may not all want to be on a major label or be a famous face on MTV, but rest assured that most of them would like their music to be heard.

The Internet is full of websites promoting independent recording artists and their music, and most of these artists would be thrilled to have their music featured on a podcast. The one thing we can't stress enough is that by looking to independent recording artists, you are not compromising the sound of your podcast. Actually, upon beginning your search for music by independent artists, or **indies**, you will soon realize that the music being put out today by "unknown" bands is just as good, if not better than, the stuff you're sick of hearing on the radio. In terms of production quality, sheer songwriting/singing talent, and musicianship, there is a nearly endless supply of music that is of major label quality.

One of the easiest ways to begin looking for music to incorporate into your podcast is to look into websites specializing in independent music, such as GarageBand, IndieHeaven, Magnatunes, and 15 Megs of Fame. GarageBand alone represents a community of thousands of independent artists and their work in dozens of genres, and it offers a free "Webcasters/Podcasters License." You can search for music by song title, band name, and genre, or you can use the "band sounding like" or "song sounding like" search features to find the exact sound you're looking for. By obtaining the free license, you are able to include any song you choose from the GarageBand catalog in your podcast at no charge. With the other sites, it is prudent to contact the artists directly to obtain permission to play their songs.

Even though making a song available for free download on a website would seem to constitute "tacit consent" to distribute, it is better to err on the side of caution. Dan has been sending out requests for permission to play music on his music podcast, "Old Wave Radio," and has, as of this writing, never been turned down. The artists want to be heard. Just get permission before you use their music.

Association of Music Podcasting

The Association of Music Podcasting (AMP) is a collective of podcasters and independent labels that want to promote new and undiscovered music legally through podcasting. Member podcasts run the gamut from alternative rock, down-tempo, punk, new wave, hip hop, and jazz. Part of the AMP's bylaws states that all podcasters agree to only play "RIAA-free" music, with direct or indirect (in the case of blanket agreements like GarageBand's license) permission to use the music in podcasts.

The official AMP website (www.musicpodcasting.org) launched in April 2005 and is a valuable resource for information on bands and artists who recognize the power of podcasting. Whether you end up becoming a member or not, browsing through the site and listening to the podcasts will give you a nice sampling of artists that you might approach yourself. AMP has a well-designed and well-implemented "Music Submission Area," where bands can upload music directly to the AMP servers for consideration by members. The legal copy accompanying this page may be a valuable bit of text for you to adapt to your needs when sewing up your music permissions. The submission form ends with the following legal text, created by Chris MacDonald of IndieFeed (www.indiefeed.com):

COPYRIGHT DISCLAIMER: In order to submit your works to the Association of Music Podcasting, either for sale or for promotion on an AMP Podcast, you must first agree with our copyright disclaimer:

1. I agree that all works I submit to AMP are my property, and that I own the rights to these works. I grant the Association of Music Podcasting permission to distribute my mechanical production of song or songs within a Podcast, for promotional purposes, and I indemnify and hold harmless AMP from any additional claim of interest related to these songs for this express purpose.

2. I agree that all submitted works contain no recordings, lyrics, copyrights, or other elements that are the copyright of any other artist, except under the limited provisions of the Creative Commons License Agreement http://www.creativecommons.org.

3. I agree that although I may have recording contracts with RIAA, ASCAP, BMI, or other recording industry entity, my contract states that I retain ownership of my works, and I am free to distribute, broadcast, or sell these works at my discretion, and waive any rights to royalties, fees, or payments related to Podcast play on AMP.

If you agree to the terms above, and electronically submit to us, or send us copies of your CD for Podcast play, online store sales, or both; this constitutes an agreement that you understand and agree with the terms above.

The right artists will be anxious to get exposure on podcasts. Be sure to protect them—and yourself—by getting specific and implicit permission up front. You'll never regret it.

Royalty-free music

Nothing is this world is free, even royalty-free music. Well, some of it may be free, but most of it you pay for, at least once. Still, beautifully produced royalty-free music can be found in just about any style you can imagine, and at any length, so finding something that suits your needs is a snap. The fees are reasonable (much more reasonable than being fined for copyright infringement) and each service offers differing licensing plans to suit your preference. Freeplay Music (www.freeplaymusic.com) charges a small annual fee per individual song, while Sounddogs (www.sounddogs.com) goes with the à la carte method, but it charges only a one-time usage fee and you're set.

Because each music service is so different, it's imperative that you read the service agreements carefully. Some services require annual renewal, while others don't. Some charges are based on listenership, while some involve flat, one-time fees. There are as many ways of going about it as there are services, so be careful and read the fine print.

Make it or buy it

After all this talk of music licensing, it may be refreshing to know that there's one way to use music that doesn't require any kind of license or fee: make the music yourself. Sure, you're not a musician. If you were a musician, you would have skipped over this entire section on music rights. But, since this is the computer age, making music for your podcast may be as simple as sliding around some samples. Apple's GarageBand software (no relation to the GarageBand site mentioned earlier) or similar software for Windows make creating music out of royalty-free loops easy for even the most tone-deaf wannabe producer.

Or, if that seems like too much time and effort, remember this: if you hire someone to record a music track for you, you own that track. You own it, you control it, and you can use it whenever and however you would like. Looking in your area for a small independent record producer may unearth the all-in-one writer/musician/producer you need to put the ideal theme song together. This kind of all-in-one arrangement can work for fast, cheap, and amazing results.

Voice mail messages and phone calls

We've said it before and we'll say it many times over: one of the best things about podcasts is the interaction you have with listeners from around the world. A great way to incorporate this interaction into your show is to drop voice mail messages or incorporate "live" phone calls into your podcast.

Voice mail messages

You might be surprised to find out just how easy it is to include voice mail messages in your podcast. Several free and pay services are available that will give you a phone number where listeners can leave messages, and those messages can be sent to you via e-mail. The sound quality varies based on the service, but even the worst free service is better than nothing.

Perhaps the most widely used of the free services is K7 (www.k7.net). Although the sound quality is somewhat poor (especially if your listener is calling from a cell phone), the audio can be cleaned up nicely with noise reduction software like BIAS's SoundSoap (www.bias-inc.com/products/soundsoap). Of course, now you're buying software to clean up free voice messages instead of paying for a service where the sound quality is better (and doesn't need to be cleaned up). Weighing the pros and cons is up to you. Some people would rather buy software and get the calls for free. Others don't want to bother with the software and would rather just pay for the service.

Before you commit to any service, be careful to read the entire service agreement. There can easily be hidden limits on calls and call lengths that can end up costing you more than you expect.

Phone calls

You may decide that playing prerecorded phone messages just isn't enough, and you want to take some "live" callers. Well, given the prerecorded nature of podcasting, unless you tell your listeners ahead of time exactly when you'll be recording, most of your "live" calls will be outbound. Recording phone conversations can be a tricky affair that requires extra software and/or hardware to make it happen. Sure, you can just "MacGyver" it and set up a microphone next to your speakerphone and hope for the best, but that isn't necessary. Like many other areas of podcasting, you can spend as little or as much as you'd like to get phone conversations into your podcast. From free Internet telephony technologies like Skype, to simple Radio Shack adapters (US$20.00 to $30.00), to professional-grade digital hybrids costing hundreds or even thousands of dollars, there are plenty of ways to go about it. We'll delve deeply into the mechanics of the various options when we talk about equipment in Chapter 5.

4

Other elements

You may also need to plan playing sponsorship announcements and advertisements or segments of other people's podcasts during your show.

Sponsorships and advertisements

You'll need to plan ahead before including sponsorship announcements or advertisements in your podcast. We'll talk more about the specifics of these in Chapter 11, but for now make sure you know whether you're reading live announcements or playing a prerecorded element. Also, give thought to where in your podcast to play these announcements. Most podcasters tend to get them out of the way early on, so once the show starts, it can flow without interruption. Others like to play or read sponsorship announcements or ads during a transition in the middle of the show, once things have gotten off to a clean start. Really, any time is worthwhile, except at the end. If you leave the plug until the end of your podcast, your sponsor or advertiser may feel like you're burying their announcement where people can too easily stop listening.

Segments of other podcasts

You never know, you may want to play segments from other people's podcasts on your own, whether you're reviewing their show, recommending their show, or ridiculing their show. Regardless of your intentions, get permission from the other podcaster to use the segment. The other podcaster will most likely be flattered that you thought of him and could end up becoming a valuable friend and ally later on (more on this topic in Chapter 10).

Summary

Wow. If you've gone through all the development and planning we've talked about in this chapter, you're just about ready to roll. Get yourself together, find a theme song, get permission to use it, and sit down for your first show prep session. You've done well, Grasshopper. Congratulations.

But you're not ready to podcast just yet—you haven't set up your "studio." If you're into looking at and buying electronic equipment in the least, the next chapter should be a lot of fun. If you are *not* into equipment, or you have an aversion to anything that plugs into a wall, don't fret: we have some suggestions and recommendations for professional-quality, inexpensive equipment that will get you set up and sounding great with little to no stress.

5 PODCASTING TOOLS

  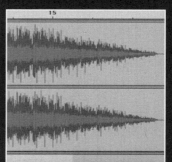

It's time to do some soul searching and some serious shopping. It's time to put together your podcast studio. Now, as we said before, the price of entry is relatively low. You can record and prep your podcast with nothing more than a microphone and a handful of free software applications. On the other hand, you can very easily spend thousands of dollars on a "power podcaster" rig to ensure you have broadcast-quality sound.

When you first begin to consider all the possibilities—all the hardware and software options—it can be a bit overwhelming. Fear not. In this chapter, we'll discuss everything, from the different kinds of cables you may encounter to what type of microphone to use, and we'll give you insights into the various tools you'll need to record, edit, mix, and master your podcasts. We'll cover the following topics in depth:

- Microphones
- Pop filters
- Headphones
- Mixers
- Cables and connectors
- Balanced and unbalanced audio
- Computer connectors
- Hardware processors
- Audio interfaces and sound cards
- Phone patches and digital hybrids
- Digital recorders and mobile rigs
- Audio recording software

We'll also present the "Podcast Studio Buyer's Guide," which outlines our suggestions for complete hardware and software packages. These packages range from a very basic single microphone to an elaborate high-end recording setup. The Broadcast Supply Worldwide (BSW) was so impressed with our podcast studio suggestions that the company now carries them at a great discount on its website at www.bswusa.com/podcastsolutions. Check out the BSW site for great savings. We've purchased a lot of equipment from BSW, and we're thrilled that the company has chosen to offer these packages to our readers.

The equipment required to podcast spans the gamut from simple to complex. As an interesting note, in fall 2004, Duke University equipped the entire incoming freshman class with a "podcasting kit" (whether the students knew it or not). Many read about the fact that the students all received Apple iPods, but what didn't receive quite as much attention was that they also received a Griffin iTalk, which allowed them to record on their iPods (see Figure 5-1). That is all it takes to turn an iPod into a voice recorder. Simple solutions like that, or the Personal Audio Recorder software for Palm devices (included on the companion CD) enable you to get some basic voice recording done. In fact, many of the Duke University students ended up using their new setups to record field notes for their classes.

Figure 5-1. Apple iPods with a Griffin iTalk and iTrip attached
(Photo © 2005 Jason Niedle)

Let's take a look at the equipment that it takes to set up a quality podcast studio for you to record your new show.

Microphones

Many would argue—and rightfully so—that the microphone is the single most important piece of hardware in an audio toolbox. The weakest link in your audio chain is going to determine your recording's sound quality. That being the case, why start out with a weak link?

Before trying to determine which mic might be best for you, let's go over some microphone terminology, so you have a better idea of what you're getting into.

Types of microphones

Microphones generally pick up sound waves and convert those waves into a form that can be used by electronic equipment in one of two ways.

Dynamic microphone

A **dynamic** microphone uses a wire coil and a magnet to create the audio signal. A diaphragm is attached to the coil, and as sound waves hit the diaphragm, they move the coil back and forth past the magnet. As you may remember from your junior high science class, a wire coil moving within a magnetic field generates an electrical current in the wire. This electrical current travels through the mic cable to the other equipment in the audio chain, where it may be saved as a recording or sent to a device, such as a loudspeaker or headphones, which can convert the electrical signal back into sound waves.

Dynamic mics are great general-purpose microphones, and because they have very few moving parts, they're rugged and durable. They generate their own current, so no external power source is needed.

Condenser microphone

A **condenser** (or **capacitor**) mic produces an audio signal when sound waves hitting the diaphragm cause two plates within a small capacitor to vibrate, creating variations in the voltage between the plates. When the plates are close together, a charge current occurs. When they are farther apart, a discharge current occurs. What does this mean? As with the dynamic mic, the variations in the electrical current can be reinterpreted as sound waves by the receiving electrical equipment.

A condenser mic needs a power source to work, since it requires voltage across the capacitor. The power is usually supplied by a small battery within the microphone or by external power known as **phantom power**.

> *Phantom power is a direct electrical current, usually between 12 and 48 volts, that supplies microphones and other equipment power through audio cables. Forty-eight volt phantom power is the most common and is often supplied by mixers and mic preamps.*

Condenser mics are sensitive and very responsive, and they create a much stronger signal than dynamic mics. This makes them an ideal choice for studio work, where you may want to pick up subtle shades of vocal tones in speech. However, they are less durable than dynamic mics.

Pickup pattern

Just as mics vary in the ways they capture a sound wave mechanically, they also have differing **pickup patterns**. The pickup pattern establishes exactly from which directions the mic will and won't pick up sounds. In the sections that follow, we'll describe the pickup patterns mics fall into: omnidirectional, unidirectional, and bidirectional.

Omnidirectional

Omnidirectional mics pick up sound from all directions equally (see Figure 5-2). They are best suited for recording more than one or two people at a time with a single mic, but they will also pick up all the sounds around those people while they are talking. Also, they pick up too much extraneous sound for use in a studio (unless you want your audience to hear everything that's going on). Since you're capturing sound equally from all around, the resulting recording may be too unfocused for your use.

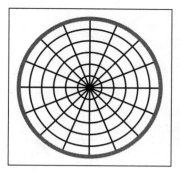

Figure 5-2.
This **polar pattern** is used to illustrate the directional properties of a microphone. The gray circle around the outside shows an omnidirectional pattern.

Unidirectional

As its name implies, a unidirectional mic will pick up a clear sound wave from only one direction. A unidirectional mic gives the best isolation of sound, since its pickup pattern is so finite. Unidirectional mics include the **cardioid** and **hypercardioid**.

Cardioid is a very scientific-sounding way of saying heart-shaped (see Figure 5-3). Sounds are picked up predominantly from the front, but with some pickup on the sides. This pattern is good for recording podcasts in the studio, since it is well suited for isolating the speaker's voice, while still giving a little latitude in the pattern for side-to-side movement while speaking. For example, you can shift in your seat a little without affecting the level at which your voice is being recorded.

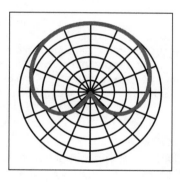

Figure 5-3.
The heart-shaped pattern of a cardioid microphone

However, there are some drawbacks with cardioid mics. They tend to suffer from the **proximity effect**, in which the mic becomes more sensitive to low-frequency sounds as the sound source gets very close. If you're within a few inches of a cardioid mic, you may get excessive lows and "boominess." You may like that sound, but it's not natural or accurate. Also, because off-axis frequency response varies, if you use a cardioid as a handheld mic for a roving reporter–type interview, you'll get a distracting whooshing sound as you move the mic back and forth from person to person. That is why most reporters' handheld mics are omnidirectional.

Our general recommendation is to use a cardioid mic (unidirectional) in the studio and an omnidirectional mic for roving-reporter work. We'd like to emphasize that this is a "general" recommendation—there are exceptions to it, some of which we've noted in this chapter.

Hypercardioid is a more extreme version of the cardioid, with the sides of the pattern drawn in to form a narrow sweet spot (see Figure 5-4), making this pattern much more directional and rejecting almost all sound outside its pickup pattern. Hypercardioids are used in the movie business to record dialogue, and their typically long, thin design has earned them the moniker "shotgun mic."

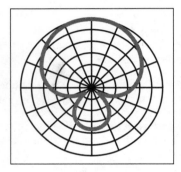

Figure 5-4.
A hypercardioid pattern. Notice the narrowed sides and the extra area of pickup in the back of the mic.

Some of the top voice-over talents in the country use hypercardioids in their home studios. There is some debate about whether this is really the best way to go for podcasters, however, as a hypercardioid rejects so much sound that the recording can sound cold and unnatural. Only a very practiced voice artist can pull off using a shotgun mic to do voice-over work, as it requires that the artist never stray from that narrow pattern. We can't, in good faith, recommend going to a hypercardioid for your home studio. You'd just be begging for trouble.

Bidirectional

Although we haven't seen many of these, there are bidirectional mics with a double cardioid pattern that looks like a figure eight (see Figure 5-5). This might make a good mic for a two-person podcast, if the podcasters were dead-set against using separate mics.

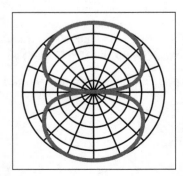

Figure 5-5.
A bidirectional pickup pattern

Microphone recommendations

The microphone you buy will depend largely on your budget (as so many things in life do). The entry level for a decent mic starts at about US$100. As you might imagine, beyond that the sky is the limit (Neumann sells a broadcast mic for around $4,000!). We can't recommend going overboard, but do keep in mind how important your mic is. In a way, your microphone is the first step in the portal to your listeners. Much like a bad camera lens can cloud or distort a photograph, a bad mic can ruin your audio.

> *Please note that all prices listed in this chapter are approximate— though the prices were correct at the time of this writing, they are, of course, subject to change. All prices are in U.S. dollars.*

Just starting out

Many podcasters have started out with a USB-type headset mic similar to those used for gaming or dictation. These can be found at most computer or office supply stores. USB mics are generally **noise canceling**, meaning they actually subtract the sound hitting one diaphragm from the sound that hits another. (Many broadcast headset microphones are also of this type.) So the only sound that gets through is sound that is louder to one diaphragm than the other. These can be particularly advantageous in noisy environments. Use of headset or head-worn mics is also advantageous during interviews with guests with bad mic technique, since the distance between the mic and a person's mouth stays fairly constant. A $50 USB headset for a podcaster who is going to be outside of a controlled (quiet) environment and who will be recording himself or herself directly to a laptop is a good solution. That said, if you find yourself getting addicted to podcasting, we suggest you invest in a quality mic that will last for the long haul.

In the sections that follow, we'll recommend some microphones in each of a few budget brackets.

The $100 zone

You should probably start looking for a mic in the $100 range. You'll likely be disappointed with the sound quality if you purchase a mic for less than $100. Dan used a $50 mic he had lying around his house for over 40 podcasts, but he had to struggle to work within its limits (he could never touch it while he was recording, or it would make a horrible sound). Michael was smart enough to get a decent mic early on, and it shows in his sound quality.

Plenty of mics are available in this price range, and for someone just starting out, the mics we suggest here will serve you very well. Should you later decide you have a need for a "better" mic, you can then make the choice to upgrade.

We recommend the Audio Technica AT2020. It is a great-sounding **side address** (meaning you talk into the side instead of the top) electret cardioid condenser mic with a clean and bright sound, and it has many of the same features as its siblings in the AT30 and AT40 series.

Another great find, recommended to us by Paul Figgiani of PodcastRigs.com, is the KEL Audio HM-1 (www.kelaudio.com). Available only from KEL, it is a small and rugged mic with a warm, round tone, and it's perfect for adding some character to thin or edgy sounds. Check out the KEL website to hear samples of various voices and instruments recorded with an HM-1.

One of the mics in this price range most commonly used among podcasters is the Marshall MXL-990, which retails for around $60 to $70. Its reasonable price and the included carrying case and shock mount make it very attractive to budget-conscious podcasters. Strangely, the MXL-990 wasn't designed for vocal use, but it has somehow managed to catch on among podcasters anyway.

The mics just listed are all for studio use and require phantom power. If you are looking for a rugged handheld mic for on-the-go interviews, check out the Electrovoice 635A. It is a great omnidirectional dynamic mic that is also extremely durable. Another mic to take a look at for double-duty studio work and fieldwork is the Sennheiser E835.

The $200–$300 zone

In this price range, we recommend the big brothers of the Audio Technica AT2020: the AT3035 ($200) and the AT4040 ($300).

For out-in-the-field interview work, take a look at the Sennheiser MD46 ($180). (Yes, we know it is a cardioid mic and therefore contradicts our earlier recommendation of cardioids for the studio and omnidirectionals for the field, but trust us, this is the exception that proves the rule.)

For headset fans who want a professional-level combination of noise-canceling mic and headphones (think sportscaster and live event commentary), take a look at the Beyerdynamic DT290 ($240). When ordering, make sure to ask if it has XLR and TRS connectors added for the mic and headset. The DT290 used with the handheld Sennheiser MD46 makes for a great live event interview and recording setup.

The $350–$400 zone

Without a doubt, the big boys of podcast recording are the Electrovoice RE20 ($400) and the Shure SM7B ($350). These are both professional-level dynamic cardioid microphones used extensively in broadcast and recording studios around the United States. Both are known for their relative lack of proximity effect. Because they are dynamic mics, they require no phantom power. The downside is that they need to be used with powerful and extremely quiet mic preamps. Careful selection of equipment to complement these impressive mics will yield superior audio quality.

Over $400

If you're looking to spend more than $400 on a microphone, you're on your own. Frankly, if you're willing to put that kind of money into a mic to record audio that will be compressed to an MP3, you're crazier than we are. Let us know what you get and how it sounds.

Pop filters

You'll also need a **pop filter**, for when you're "popping your p's." A pop filter is a wind-screen or foam filter that helps reduce popping noises created by breath or speech when a person says a plosive such as "p" or "b." A **plosive** is a consonant that is pronounced by completely closing the lips or air passage and then releasing air suddenly. Without a pop filter between you and your microphone, your listeners will feel like they're being bar-raged by popping explosions—not a relaxing listening experience. You can use the foam version that fits snugly over your mic or the screen version that is suspended between you and the mic. Either way, use one.

Headphones

Besides your mic, the next most important piece of gear for your podcast studio is your headphones. You have a great many headphones to choose from. Make sure the ones you select are comfortable, as you'll wear them not only when you record, but also when you edit. If you don't already have a set, take a look at the bargain-priced Sennheiser HD 202 ($20), or the favorite among broadcasting professionals, the Sony 7506 ($100). These headphones come highly recommended, and with them you'll be able to clearly hear what's going on during recording and editing. You'll also find us reminding you at every opportunity to make sure you connect your headphones as far along in the audio chain as possible so you can hear the cumulative effect of all your audio gear.

5

Mixers

Some podcasters, depending on their setup and the software they're using, opt to not use a mixer or any external audio sources such as CD players, MP3 players, and so forth. They record on to their computer as the computer plays any additional audio. We'll discuss later on how that all works. However, unless you are using a USB microphone, we strongly sug-gest you use a mixer, particularly as it will allow you to use many of the microphones listed in the previous section.

For the most part, podcasters use mixers to combine ("mix") the sounds from their micro-phones with other audio sources while they are recording. A mixer allows you to have independent control over each of these various inputs as you combine them in your audio chain. As an example, a mixer allows you to have two different mics set at different input volumes. This may be helpful, for example, with a husband and wife podcast, where the husband may naturally speak, well, louder. The mixer can be used to adjust for this. A mixer will give you multiple inputs, each with its own volume adjustments and, in some cases, equalization controls. Also, a good mixer will supply phantom power should you choose to use a condenser mic. Finally, many mics don't have enough output to drive a PC's mic input on their own—a mixer solves this problem. The bottom line is that you should use a mixer.

Using a mixer, you can play your intro music and adjust its level while you begin recording your voice, and then perhaps you can add in a recorded comment or another song as you record. Or you can use the mixer simply as an interface between your computer and your audio equipment.

Since you will most likely be recording on your computer, we need to note that many computers don't come with the perfect audio inputs needed for recording. That is why you need to be aware of how you will connect your mixer to your computer. Some of the mixers we recommend have connectors built right in, while others require a bit of outside assistance. Also, you need to make sure that your sound card enables you to record sound at top quality (16-bit/44kHz).

In addition, you'll need to give some thought to whether or not you want to use external dynamics processors such as compressors, limiters, and gates. We'll get into what each of these actually does in the next chapter, but for now just understand that dynamics processors help make your recording more even and polished-sounding. Some dynamics processing can be done with software plug-ins, but other processes are best handled during recording by hardware. If you want to use hardware processors (we know, it's a bit early to determine that now; hang in there), you'll need a mixer than has channel inserts. We'll talk more about channel inserts in the upcoming "Cables and connectors" section.

The main things to look for in a mixer are

- Quiet mic preamps (that raise the level of the mic signal)
- Enough microphone inputs for your needs
- Channel inserts (if you will use external processors)
- Phantom power (if you are using a condenser mic)

Recommended mixers

Now let's look at a few mixers we recommend for podcasting in the different price ranges.

Under $100

The mixer known by many as the "podcaster's best friend" is the Behringer UB802, also known as the Eurorack 8. This is a basic mixer with two mic preamps and six total inputs. Best of all, you can find it for around $60.

Under $200

A number of nice mixers are available in this price range. Take a look at the Yamaha MG10-2 ($129) or the Tapco Blend 6 ($149). Our personal favorite is the Alesis Multi Mix 8 USB ($199), which features four mic inputs and eight total channels, and EQ. Best of all, it provides a means of communicating with your computer via USB. We have heard good things about this mixer from many of the podcasters using it.

Over $200

In this price range, you're paying for the number of channels and the quality of components. Michael uses the Mackie Onyx 1220 (around $640). The Onyx series by Mackie is used by a number of podcasters who have taken the studio route (e.g., "Reel Reviews," "Grape Radio," "IT Conversations," and "The Point Podcast"). They include boutique-quality preamps, Perkins EQ, and all kinds of nice features, including the ability to add a 24-bit/96kHz multichannel FireWire output card. Overall, it's a very nice unit.

Cables and connectors

Things may start to get a bit confusing if we don't talk for a moment about the different cables and connectors you will encounter as you are planning, purchasing, and setting up your podcast studio. You may not end up using each of the audio equipment connectors mentioned in the sections that follow, but it is good to know what they all are.

RCA connector

RCA connectors are the small, nonlocking mono connectors (see Figure 5-6) you've been using all your life on your stereo equipment to attach turntables, tape decks, and CD players to your amplifier or receiver. Red for the right channel, white for the left channel, and yellow for video.

Figure 5-6. RCA connectors

1/4" phone jack

The "phone" in "phone jack" relates to *gramophone*, not *telephone*. These are the large, 1/4" connectors commonly associated with guitars and headphones (well, old-school headphones). Phone jacks are used for mono signals and stereo signals, as well as channel inserts to connect hardware boxes to mixers. At a glance, all phone jacks look the same, but they are not. Depending on the type of tip a phone jack has, and the way that tip is wired, the phone jack will serve very different functions (see Figure 5-7):

- **Tip-sleeve (TS)**: This is a mono phone jack, where there is a connection on the tip of the jack and one on the sleeve. These are used for unbalanced audio.

- **Tip-ring-sleeve (TRS)**: This is a ¼" plug with three connections (the tip, the ring, and the sleeve). It is used for balanced audio (see the section "Balanced and unbalanced audio" for more information). The same type of plug, with different wiring, is used for stereo headphones.

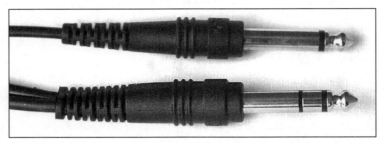

Figure 5-7. Two types of phone jacks: tip-sleeve (top) and tip-ring-sleeve (bottom)

Channel insert cable

This is a special Y-shaped cable (see Figure 5-8) used to connect effects processors such as compressors and gates to your mixer. Using a channel insert cable isn't the only way to connect these items, but it is by far the easiest.

A single TRS phone jack is connected to the mixer channel insert jack, offering three separate connections. The cable then connects to the effects processor after splitting into two TS phone jacks: one to input the signal and one to send it back to the mixer. In this way, the signal goes from the mixer, through the effects processor, and then back to the mixer, to be combined with other audio elements.

Figure 5-8. A channel insert cable sends a signal from the mixer to an effects processor and back.

1/8" mini plug

The most common 1/8" mini plug is a tiny version of a TRS phone jack. It's used for post–Walkman era stereo headphones and other input/output devises. Mono (TS) versions also exist. It looks just like the TS plug shown in Figure 5-7, only smaller.

XLR connector

XLR connectors are the large, professional-grade connectors you'll see on pro and semi-pro audio gear (see Figure 5-9). They are locking connectors that can carry a balanced audio signal and phantom power. If you have a choice between using an XLR cable to connect your mic to a mixer and a 1/4" TRS phone jack, choose the XLR cable—it is more rugged, and it will produce a cleaner, stronger signal.

Figure 5-9. XLR connectors

XLR/phone combo jack

We're starting to see combo jacks on more and more audio equipment, especially the newer, smaller home studio computer interfaces. Small and versatile, these combination jacks work with either 1/4" plugs or XLR plugs.

Balanced and unbalanced audio

Balanced audio is a way of greatly reducing noise and interference from your cables, resulting in cleaner recordings. Long audio cables make wonderful antennae, and they pick up all sorts of stray signals floating around in the air: radio waves, radiation from computer monitors, and interference from electrical currents.

In an unbalanced cable, two wires are used to carry the signal. The one that carries the sound is the **hot line**, and the other is the **earth** or **ground line**. These cables are fine for short distances and consumer electronics. As soon as you get into longer cables and pro gear, preventing potential noise in the line becomes a concern. Also, because mic signals are at a much lower level, balanced audio is almost always necessary.

Balanced cables have three wires: two hot lines and one ground line. Using an XLR connector as an example, pins 2 and 3 carry the opposite sides of the signal. The audio is the difference or the voltage between the two hot lines. Let's call them, for example, Ground, A and B. The audio is A-B—that's what you get if you connect a voltmeter or any other device across the two wires. The ground is only for shielding; it carries no signal. Cut the ground, and you still get the audio. It shields noise because the A and B wires are twisted together, and if any noise or hum gets into one, it tends to get into both. So if you have noise on A and the same noise on B, the A-B (difference) between them tends toward zero.

Computer connectors

In the following sections, we'll take a look at the most common computer connectors used with audio gear.

USB

Universal Serial Bus (USB) was designed to replace the array of serial connectors and parallel ports, and attach everything from mice to printers to your computer quickly and easily (see Figure 5-10). USB provides a serial bus standard, which makes hot swapping of devices possible, without restarting the computer. USB connectors offer transfer rates well above what is needed to push audio into your computer; therefore, they have become a very common means of connecting PCs with mics, mixers, and audio interfaces.

Figure 5-10. Universal Serial Bus (USB) connectors

FireWire/IEEE 1394

FireWire started as a way for Apple engineers to achieve high-speed transfers to and from their internal hard drives, while simplifying the cabling system. It was a great idea that didn't work out as the company had planned. Instead, Apple realized that its "FireWire" was much more useful for connecting to external drives and peripherals. Apple took its new technology to the Institute of Electrical and Electronics Engineers (IEEE), and in 1995 the official FireWire specifications were released as IEEE 1394. Running at speeds of 100 Mbps, FireWire made it possible for Windows and Mac users to connect high-speed, high-load devices to their computers, and it essentially made the digital video revolution possible (Sony refers to their FireWire as **iLink**). FireWire (see Figure 5-11) is now used to connect PCs with video cameras, hard drives, scanners, webcams, and audio mixers. Yes, mixers. FireWire offers fast, clean, all-digital transfers of audio to your computer.

Figure 5-11. A six-pin FireWire connector (aka IEEE 1394 or iLink)

Audio interfaces and sound cards

Now that you know all about mixers and computer connectors, you need a way to get the audio from your mixer into your computer. Sometimes it's as easy as plugging the mixer directly into the computer, as with the Alesis mixer, which has a built-in USB connection. Usually, though, it's not quite that straightforward. While many computers come equipped with some sort of audio connection, a dedicated "quality" audio interface will probably serve you best in the long run. If your computer has USB inputs (and many do), a straightforward USB audio interface will do the trick nicely. If not, you may want to dive in and get a pro or "prosumer"-level sound card.

In this section, we'll start off by looking at the most basic interfaces, and then we'll move on to cover the more high-end solutions.

USB audio interfaces

A USB interface acts as a fairly simple bridge between your audio equipment and your computer. The audio equipment plugs in on one end of the interface, and the interface plugs into a USB port on your computer. It's that simple.

The most pared-down version of a USB interface is probably the popular Griffin iMic (www.griffintechnology.com, $40), which accepts 1/8" stereo inputs at either line or mic level. It also supports line-level outputs for connecting your iMic to speakers or another recording device. According to Griffin, using the iMic will give you sound superior to what you would get using a built-in sound card. We've used the iMic and found it to be a very handy and reliable interface.

The Edirol UA-1EX Audio Interface (www.edirol.com, $100) offers component-quality sound to and from your computer. The Edirol uses RCA inputs for superior sound, and it includes optical output to transfer digital signals to digital recorders and a headphone jack for monitoring the sound going to the computer.

The M-Audio MobilePre (www.m-audio.com, $150) is a USB-powered preamp and audio interface with three kinds of audio inputs and outputs, including two microphone/instrument preamps for crisp 16-bit/48kHz sound. For his very first podcasts, Michael paired this unit with a Radio Shack 33-3001 Pro-Unidirectional Dynamic mic and got very acceptable results.

The Edirol UA25 ($250), while somewhat expensive, comes highly recommended. It has a pair of XLR/TRS combo jacks with phantom power, S/P DIF optical I/O ports, and MIDI IN/OUT ports, as well as a built-in analog limiter. We can't recommend the UA25 enough.

As a side note, if all you will ever need to do is simply record from one or two mics, and you will do all your "mixing" (such as adding music) in postproduction, any of the units just mentioned (Edirol or M Audio) will work perfectly and take the place of your mixer.

FireWire-capable audio interfaces are also available. They can be rather expensive, but you have some high-quality choices. If you're interested, check out the PreSonus FIREBOX ($400), the M-Audio FireWire 410 ($300), or the MOTU Traveler ($895).

Sound cards

Whereas the audio interface is an external bridge between the computer and the audio equipment, a sound card is installed directly into the body of the machine to extend the audio capabilities of your PC. (Keep in mind that generally speaking, an external interface will be superior to an internal sound card.) The card includes digital-to-analog converters for audio outputs and analog-to-digital converters for audio inputs. The inputs/outputs are often mounted to the card itself and end up giving you convenient connectors right on the side or back of the computer. Other times, the card connects to an external hub that houses your inputs and outputs. Either way, the goal is to get crystal-clear sound into and out of a PC that originally couldn't accomplish these tasks on its own.

SoundBlaster (www.soundblaster.com) from Creative Technology (maker of the Zen Micro MP3 player) was the sound card that started it all back in 1989. The current incarnations offer not only above CD-quality input/output, but even support home theater standards such as DTS-ES and Dolby Digital EX, as well as beloved THX certification, for the ultimate in home theater and gaming sound.

Phone patches and digital hybrids

To record phone calls, you need to find a way to patch the audio from those calls into your mixer. To do this, you can use either a simple and inexpensive phone patch or a rather expensive, but completely professional, digital hybrid.

Phone patch

A **phone patch** or **tap** is a simple bit of hardware that takes the sound from your phone line and sends it directly into the mixer. The signal is not processed in any way, so what you record is every sound going through the phone: the caller's voice and your own. While this is not ideal, it certainly works. Check out the Radio Shack Recorder Control ($26).

Digital hybrid

A **digital hybrid** is a rather expensive piece of professional hardware that strips out the host's voice, leaving the caller's voice in isolation. The hybrid is connected to your mixer so that you can use your microphone for your side of the conversation and record the caller's voice on a separate channel. While there is still some bleed-through, it can easily be cleaned up in postproduction. For our phone interviews for *Podcast Solutions* (www. podcastsolutions.com), we used a Telos One ($895). Telos (www.telos-systems.com) makes some of the best hybrids on the market. Another popular manufacturer of hybrids is JK Audio (www.jkaudio.com).

> Here's a tip that applies to using hybrids as well as any time you have an interview with two main sources. Record each on a separate track or channel. For example, record your mic track on the left channel and the hybrid audio on the right channel. That way, you can tweak and adjust the channels separately prior to a final mixdown. This would be impossible if you recorded the two channels as a combined audio signal. By following this advice, you can repair all kinds of audio "sins" that would otherwise be impossible to fix. This is how all the Podcast Solutions (www.podcastsolutions.com) phone interviews were recorded.

Double-ender

There is a way to get around having any hardware to break out the sound. If your callers are also set up to record themselves, you can try a technique referred to as a **double-ender**. (This method is perfect for recording other podcasters, since they are already set up to record.) Here's how it works: while you talk to your guest on the phone, you record your end of the conversation as you would any podcast by speaking into your microphone. Have your guest do the same from his end. When the call is finished, you and your guest will each have a pristine recording of your own side of the conversation. Now, simply edit the two "ends" together by laying one on top of the other and syncing them up. Voilà! It sounds like you had a live, in-studio guest, even though the other person could have actually been located miles and miles away during your conversation.

Of course, recording and mixing a double-ender every time you want to take a caller may end up being more trouble than it's worth, and not every caller will have the necessary equipment or skills to make the audio sound good.

Stand-alone digital recorders and mobile rigs

We've assumed up to this point that you're recording sound to your computer. Actually, that isn't necessarily the only solution. It's an incredibly practical one, as odds are good that you already own a computer and don't have any other means of recording digital audio, but a number of noncomputer options are worth investigating, particularly if you're planning to do some recording in the field (i.e., on location). Lugging a laptop around to interview people at a political rally may not be the best approach, either for your podcast or for your equipment. We recommend looking into using a digital recorder for this sort of task.

Another reason to investigate a digital recorder is to avoid the likelihood of losing a podcast due to a computer crash or hard drive "hiccup." Most podcasters have lost at least one recording to a system failure. Now, this is not to say that digital recorders are foolproof, but since they're designed solely for the purpose of recording and playing sound, they're far less likely to die on you mid-show. Let's face it, isn't it a bit much to expect one machine to record, edit, encode, and upload, *and* balance your checkbook, retouch your photos, play Tetris, and catalogue your DVD collection?

Some very small player/recorders that have taken podcasting by storm are the iRiver 700 and 800 series. They are compact and easy to use, and they record to a proprietary high-quality MP3 format (to their internal memory) that you can easily convert to standard MP3, WAV, or AIFF format. Recording to MP3 is never the best way to go, but considering the size of the iRivers and their incredibly reasonable price, it may be worth the sacrifice.

For those who don't want to skimp in any department, there is the Marantz PMD670 Professional Solid State Portable Recorder. Marantz has been a leading name in portable recording units for about as long as we can remember, and it is leading the field in professional digital recorders. The Marantz machines record WAV, BWF, MP3, and MP2 format files to inexpensive CompactFlash cards, with over 40 assignable quality settings. These units have RCA input/output and XLR inputs, so you can connect professional microphones directly to the recorder—even condenser mics that require phantom power. The Marantz PMD670 is such a solid machine that we even recommend it as a tabletop unit for in-studio use.

The Podcast Studio Buyer's Guide

In this section, we'll outline several potential podcast rigs for you to check out and compare. For each item, we include information on its current "street price" (as opposed to the much higher manufacturer's suggested retail price, or MSRP), but each of these podcast studio setups is available as a discounted package from our friends at BSW (www.bswusa.com/podcastsolutions).

We'd like to point out up front that our gear suggestions come from hard-won experience. We've discovered (the hard way) that the most inexpensive gear usually gets replaced very quickly, causing you to spend more than if you had just bought the right piece of equipment up front. You can acquire most of these packages piecemeal over time as you build your podcast studio. First, we'll showcase our picks for various studio setups, and then we'll present some options for podcasters on the go.

Just A Mic

If you're just looking for a microphone, we recommend the following:

- Samson C01U USB Codenser Micropohone ($79)

Just plug it in and go. This USB mic is immediately recognized by your PC or Mac and is ready to record.

Podcast Starter

These are our recommendations for those just starting out:

- Audio Technica AT2020 Studio Cardioid Condenser Microphone ($100)
- Alexis MultiMix 8 USB Mixer ($150)

The AT2020 offers unsurpassed sound for the price. There is no need for an additional audio interface, since the Alexis MultiMix has a USB connection built in.

Podcast Veteran

Here's what we recommend for experienced podcasters:

- Audio Technica AT3035 Cardioid Condenser Microphone ($200)
- Yamaha MG 8 Mixer ($150)
- Edirol UA-1EX ($100)
- dbx 266XL Dual Compressor/Gate ($150)

The AT3035 offers the clear tones you'd expect for Audio Technica at twice the price. The Yahama mixer is a great piece of equipment, with very quiet preamps and channel inserts to enable proper connection to the dbx 266, a wonderful entry-priced professional compressor/gate. The 266XL accepts "dual" inputs, so you can use it with two separate mic inputs. The mixer connects to your PC or Mac via the Edirol UA-1X.

Podcast Professional

Now for the professionals out there:

- Electrovoice RE20 ($400) or the Shure SM7B ($350)
- Mackie Onyx 1220 12-Channel Mixer ($640)
- dbx 1066 Compressor/Gate/Limiter ($400)
- Add the Portable system mentioned in the next section or connect directly to an audio interface such as the Edirol UA-1EX ($100)

The Mackie Onyx mixer is strong enough and quiet enough to push these fantastic broadcast mics, and the dbx 1066 offers top-notch signal processing. This podcast studio will never disappoint and is perfect for the podcast entrepreneur (see Chapter 11) or businesses that want quality audio to use in their podcasts.

Portable Podcast Professional

This is the same gear that Michael used when Disneyland brought him in to host and produce the Disneyland 50th Anniversary celebration (see Figure 5-12):

- Marantz PMD 670 ($699)
- Sennheiser MD46 Interview Microphone ($170)

The Sennheiser MD46 performs flawlessly in high-noise environments where many on-the-go interviews are recorded. The Marantz PMD 670 allows for a total portable recording solution direct to CompactFlash. Take this setup home and connect to any of the previously mentioned packages and you have a perfect dual-purpose digital recording solution.

Figure 5-12. Marantz PMD 670 and Sennheiser MD46 mic
(Photo © 2005 Jason Niedle)

Ultra Mobile Rig

Finally, for those looking to record unobtrusively, take a look at this nice portable setup
(see Figure 5-13 for a photo of the mic):

- iRiver 899 ($179)
- Giant Squid Audio Lab Omnidirectional Lapel Microphone ($55)

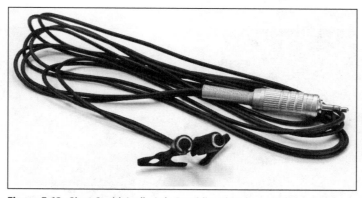

Figure 5-13. Giant Squid Audio Lab Omnidirectional Lapel Microphone

The iRiver 899 and the Giant Squid Audio Lab mic (www.giant-squid-audio-lab.com) are
so small, no one will even notice that you're podcasting. Sometimes, that's a good thing. In
addition to this setup being a superb stealth rig, you can get some great audio out of it.
Thanks to our friend Geoffrey Kleinman from DVDtalk (www.dvdtalk.com) for this great
recommendation. Geoff actually uses this same setup to record press event interviews of
movie and DVD releases for his website. His whole mobile recording "studio" fits in his
pocket.

Podcast studio setups

Figures 5-14 and 5-15 show podcast studios employing some of the gear outlined in this section.

Figure 5-14. Michael's home podcast studio, which is set up in the corner of his home theater where he does his "Reel Reviews"
(Photo © 2005 Jason Niedle)

Figure 5-15. The "Grape Radio" studio
(Photo © 2005 Jason Niedle)

Stringing it all together

So, how does all this equipment fit together? It's pretty simple, actually. Audio signals flow like water, so we'll talk about the setup in terms of the direction that the sounds flow from your mouth to the recording device.

Here's how to set up a standard configuration:

1. Connect your microphone to the mixer's mic inputs, using XLR cables.

2. Connect external sound sources (CD player, iPod, keyboard, etc) to the mixer's line in inputs using phone plugs. You may need to get adaptors/connectors to make this work (RCA to phone adapters, mini stereo to phone, etc.).

3. If you are using hardware compressor/gates, use special channel insert cables to connect your equipment to the channel insert jacks. The sound will flow from the mixer to the external boxes and then back into the mixer. See the mixer's documentation for full details.

4. Connect a cable from the phone jack of your "main out" to the audio interface plugged into your computer or recording device, whether that is an external USB interface (e.g., iMic, Ederol, etc.), a stand-alone recorder (e.g., Marantz PMD 670), or a sound card with RCA inputs.

5. Monitor your sound using headphones plugged into the headphone jack on the mixer.

It is imperative that you monitor the sound through headphones plugged into the mixer, not the computer. Monitoring the sound from the computer headphone jack will feed that sound back to your ears a split second or two after the sound actually occurs. For instance, you will speak, and then a fraction of a second later, you will hear yourself speak in the headphones. This effect is called **latency**, and it's a killer. When you can hear yourself instantly in your headphones, you can monitor your mic position, your breathing sounds, and so forth. When there is latency, your brain is so busy trying to get your ears to catch up with your mouth that you end up slurring your words like a freshman at a keg party. You will inexplicably elongate all your vowels.

Monitoring through the computer's headphone output is very tempting, especially if you're adding live software effects to your voice that you want to hear in your headphones. Don't do it. Listen to yourself when you're finished recording. You'll sound sober.

Audio recording software

The audio recording and editing software you choose, as much as the hardware you choose, will determine the experience you have recording and editing your podcasts. And, to be clear, you're not just going to be recording—you'll going to be recording, editing, processing, mixing, and mastering. It sounds like a lot, and it is. Depending on exactly how in depth you want to get with each level of this process (and we'll get into all of it in the following chapters) will to some extent determine what software you use.

The amazing thing about recording to your computer is that it's all digital—1s and 0s. If we were still recording and mixing using analog equipment, there is no way a new podcaster could afford the equipment needed to get the kind of sound quality we can all get now through digital recording.

Now that the sounds are digitized, they can be viewed as a **waveform** (a graphic representation of the dynamics of a sound) and in turn can be cut, copied, and pasted just like graphics or text. We can rearrange the sounds, add echo, reduce noise, change stereo to mono, and increase volume, all without degrading the sound or losing data.

In this section, we'll look at several audio recording applications, each available at a different price and with a slightly different set of tools. Keep in mind that even the simplest, least expensive recording software will deliver great sound, as long as the sound going into the computer is good (digital crap in, digital crap out). The major differences between the packages relate to how many features are built in and how well the packages may (or may not) handle certain production and postproduction tasks. Not every package listed here does everything you'll need. By the same token, you'll hardly need all of the features of many of these more robust applications.

> *Much of the software mentioned in the sections that follow is available on the companion Podcast Solutions CD.*

Sony Sound Forge

Sony Sound Forge for Windows (see Figure 5-16) is an audio powerhouse that can open and edit WMA, WMV, WAV, MOV, AVI, PCA AIF, and MP3 files, and can record at up to 24-bit/32-bit 192kHz files.

Audio Hijack Pro

For the Mac OS X, you can easily set up Audio Hijack Pro (www.rogueamoeba.com/audiohijackpro; see Figure 5-17) to record the audio from one application (e.g., iTunes) or from all applications currently running by using its Record System Audio setting. This feature has made it an invaluable tool for Mac users, especially those who want to record their voice, music, and live callers all at the same time. At the time of this writing, Audio Hijack Pro has no editing functions, but it does a great job handling plug-ins, so you can easily add dynamic processing as you record.

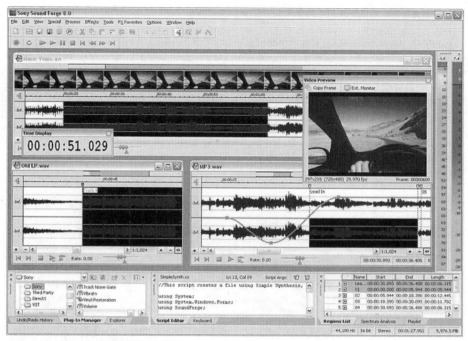

Figure 5-16. Sony Sound Forge

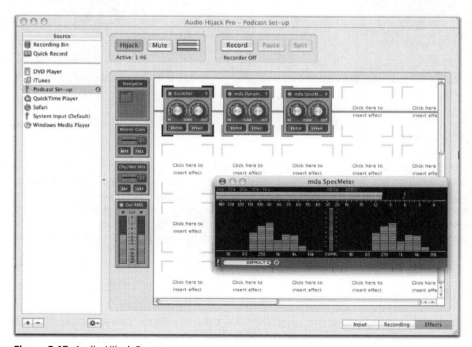

Figure 5-17. Audio Hijack Pro

BIAS Peak

BIAS Peak (www.bias-inc.com/products/peak) is an industry-standard stereo audio recording, editing, and processing application (see Figure 5-18) for the Macintosh OS. It is the ideal audio utility for podcasters, and audio professionals and enthusiasts. In addition to fast and powerful audio editing, Peak integrates a wide variety of effects and signal processing tools to create custom fades, adjust audio gain, repair digital audio spikes, add real room ambience, change pitch and duration independently, and more, all while offering additional real-time effects such as parametric EQ, compression/limiting, reverb, dozens of other special effects, and access to third-party VST and Audio Unit plug-ins, or additional solutions from BIAS, such as the highly acclaimed SoundSoap family of audio noise reduction and restoration tools.

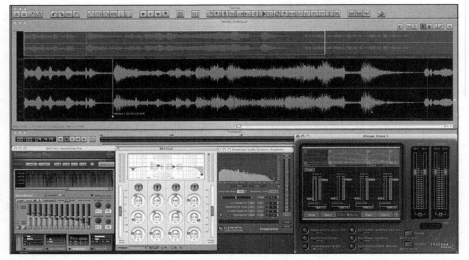

Figure 5-18. BIAS Peak

DSP-Quattro

DSP-Quattro (www.i3net.it/Products/dspQuattro) is a professional creative tool for audio editing, plug-in hosting, and CD mastering. It includes a whole host of recording and editing features to ensure that output is recorded just as you hear it and edited to perfection using editing functions and digital effects. It also supports plug-ins, both included effects and third-party plug-ins (from Akai, Roland, Yamaha, and many others). Finally, it also boasts many CD-creation facilities, including fully programmable playlists and effect chains.

CastBlaster

CastBlaster (www.castblaster.com), the brainchild of Adam Curry and Ron Bloom's PodShow, was developed for podcast production and gives the user the ability to play audio files while recording. Songs, promos, phone messages, and more can be preloaded into memory. During the recording session, these sounds can be played and recorded along with the podcaster's voice. CastBlaster acts essentially like a software version of an external mixer: each audio "input" has its own level controls and is mixed with the mic inputs to then be recorded.

Two-track vs. multitrack

Please remember that there is a big difference between two-track and multitrack software. As we have pointed out, some of the software we have mentioned is two-track only, which is great for recording two tracks, editing, processing, noise reduction, all that stuff. But you can't mix in music and so forth. For that, you need multitrack software. The sections that follow provide a few suggestions for multitrack software.

Audacity

Audacity (http://audacity.sourceforge.net) is a free, open source recording and editing application that features multitrack capabilities (see Figure 5-19). This means you can record one track, stop, and then record or paste in another separate track over the first. Multitrack capabilities are very useful for adding music and sound effects after your initial recording take. Since it is not financed and maintained by a commercial concern, Audacity seems very bare bones, but actually it does most everything you need and, considering the price, it is great. It can handle even professional VST plug-ins, with the use of Audacity VST Enabler (http://audacityteam.org/vst). You can't use plug-ins to process sound as you record with Audacity, but they can be used for mixing and mastering.

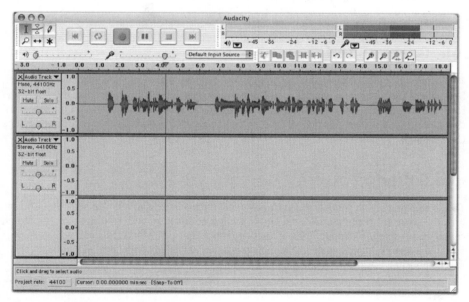

Figure 5-19. The Audacity workspace

As a side note—and this may seem a bit blunt—but you get what you pay for. Many people we know (present company included) who use Audacity have lost at least one recording session to a crash of the application or system. That said, we still think Audacity is a great starter application, but we suggest always having a backup. When possible, record to a separate hard drive from the one running the operating system and applications. This will help to avoid many problems, and this advice applies to all audio editing and recording software.

Since Audacity is free and is available for Windows, Mac, and Linux, we'll use it for many of the tutorials and screenshots in upcoming chapters.

Adobe Audition

Adobe Audition (www.adobe.com/products/audition/main.html) is a full-featured professional-level multitrack audio editing application. It offers advanced mixing and editing as well as support for effects processing. Many podcasters use the versatile and powerful Audition application as their sole audio editing software.

n-Track Studio

n-Track studio (www.fasoft.com) is an affordable multitrack audio-editing application that has more than enough power for the professional podcaster. n-Track Studio allows you to record and play back an almost unlimited number of independent tracks, limited only by the speed of your computer. It also allows you to apply real-time effects to each track. Support is available for multichannel 16-bit and 24-bit sound cards with sampling frequencies up to 192kHz.

Apple GarageBand

This application is included in the iLife suite on all new Apple Macintosh computers. Before looking elsewhere, give GarageBand a try if you are a Mac user. It has a great, easy-to-understand user interface and is more than capable enough for all but the most demanding podcasters. Some of the most successful podcasts are produced using GarageBand.

Apple Soundtrack Pro

This is the perfect solution for multitrack recording and editing on the Mac. Soundtrack Pro is a powerful professional-level audio-editing application with multitrack support and repair and restoration capabilities. It includes more than 50 effects plug-ins as well as over 5,000 sound effect and music loops. You can build your own intro and outro music and a full audio effect studio with this one application.

Voice Over IP

We weren't sure where to put this section, so we're including it here. Many podcasters use software called **Voice Over IP** or **VOIP** to record phone calls placed over the Internet. With several software packages available for VOIP, you can essentially have endless Internet phone calls with people and record them for your podcast. While the quality is not quite up to the level we would like, the price is right—it's often free.

> *Because with VOIP the voice signals of the callers are carried as packets of data over the Internet, and audio takes up quite a large file size, you need a decent connection speed to run VOIP applications. We'd recommend at least 512 kbps, preferably 1 mbps.*

The most popular service for podcasters is Skype (www.skype.com), which is available free of charge for multiple platforms. Using a free Skype account and some of the following software you can easily record local and international calls for use in your podcast.

Windows users should check out HotRecorder (www.hotrecorder.com; around $15 without ads, free with ads), Total Recorder (www.highcriteria.com; around $36 for the professional version), or Replay Radio (www.replay-video.com/replay-radio; around $50). For the Mac, try Ambrosia Software's WireTap Pro (www.ambrosiasw.com; $19). It takes almost no setup and has an idiot-proof one-button interface.

When you use software such as this, you are asking your computer to do a lot: run the operating system, the VOIP software, and the recording software, as well as all those background applications that keep your computer humming along. When possible, to avoid audio recording problems, we highly suggest using an external recorder. Your computer will thank you. Also, as you can imagine, doing so helps you avoid asking your interview subject to redo the interview because your overtaxed computer just froze and ate the recording.

Audio plug-ins

We talked briefly and vaguely about dynamics processors—compressors, limiters, gates, and so forth—in this chapter. Now, we know we haven't explained in detail what each of these does (we really get into it in the next chapter), but we do need to mention now that dynamics processing can be handled by stand-alone hardware (e.g., dbx 266XL) or by software plug-ins.

Each of the recording applications we mentioned can handle processing using plug-ins, either in real time as you record or afterward when you apply them as you might apply a filter in Photoshop. Check each application's documentation to see exactly how it handles the plug-ins and where they need to be stored on your hard drive. Once the plug-ins are loaded properly, you have the software equivalent of thousands of dollars of audio hardware at your disposal.

If the application you end up using doesn't have many plug-ins preinstalled (e.g., Audacity), you can download a great group of free mdaVST plug-ins from `www.mda-vst.com` (click VST Effects).

Summary

A tricky and sometimes nerve-racking part of the podcast setup process can be determining what the right tools are for you. The good news is that we've supplied you with some great starting points and lots of information to mull over. Sift through the software on the companion CD and try each one that sounds appealing. Each usually has a timed trial period. Or, start out using Audacity until you feel the need to upgrade. It's harder to sample the hardware, but if you end up purchasing something that doesn't work out for you, you can always either return it or sell it on one of the many podcasting forums.

For more information on podcasting hardware and software, be sure to check out Paul Figgiani's PodcastRigs.com site (`www.podcastrigs.com`), as well as his superb podcasting forum. Paul does an outstanding job of keeping up to date with all the developments in hardware and software, not only for use in podcasting, but for video and film production as well. It's well worth stopping by his site with any questions you might have on hardware, software, setting up equipment, and finding great deals.

Once you have at least your first studio set up, you'll be itching to record. Well, that's what Chapter 6 is all about—not just recording per se, but preparing to record, learning about all that processing we talked about earlier, and developing your voice talents like a pro. Take a deep breath, relax, and settle in. Up next, it's time to say "Hello."

6 RECORDING YOUR PODCAST

  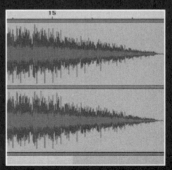

Now, here's where the fun stuff begins. It's time to slide on those headphones, clear your throat, and begin. But before you hit the Record button, let's first go over a few things about recording audio, using the microphone, and making sure your recording is clear with good "levels." The podcast you record today may still be getting hundreds of downloads in six months, so let's ensure you'll still be proud of the sound quality that far down the road. Still being proud of what you said is completely up to you.

Introducing the waveform

Figure 6-1 shows a **waveform**. Actually it shows two waveforms. A waveform is a visual representation of a sound recording with the magnitude ("loudness") of the sound being plotted vertically over time. The top waveform represents the sound recorded on the left stereo channel, and the bottom waveform represents the right stereo channel. You'll notice that along the left side of the window are numbers decreasing from 1.0 to 0.5 to 0, and then increasing back up. When you look at a waveform, know that 0 is silence and 1.0 is "as loud as possible." Knowing this, you can begin to "read" a sound file. This will be helpful when you record, and it will be essential when it's time to edit your podcast.

> *This waveform measurement scale varies depending on your audio editing software. In some editing software, the scale will be between -∞dB and 0dB, with 0dB indicating "as loud as possible." Another popular application uses the scale 0 to 100, with 100 representing the limit for peak audio. To avoid confusion, read the instructions that came with your chosen audio recording/editing software to understand the scale used.*

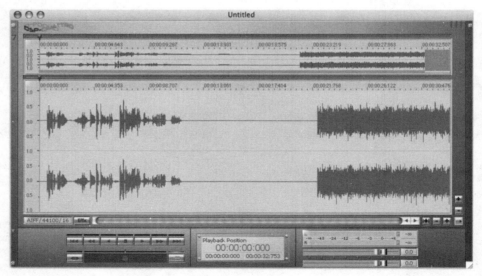

Figure 6-1. Sample waveforms, with a section of speaking, a section of silence, and a section of loud music (in the application DSP-Quattro)

In the samples in Figure 6-1, the very beginning of the sound recording is of a person speaking. The dynamics of the voice create unique peaks and valleys in the form. The speech is followed by several seconds of silence, represented by the straight horizontal line at the 0 marker. After the silence is continuously loud rock music, with very little variation in the loudness of the track (it's all just plain loud).

Recording levels

Now, before we go any further, we would like to state that we aren't sound engineers, and if you share with a real sound engineer the following information, they'll think we're crazy. Audio engineers work within strict broadcast standards that we, as podcasters, don't have to adhere to. Now, that being said, we'll talk about broadcast standards and give you some insight into conforming to them enough so as not to limit your podcast's future. In the meantime, we're going to stick with what seems to be working for many podcasters.

To generalize, the goal of a good recording is to get relatively consistent levels of sound while allowing for an adequate amount of dynamic range and a total avoidance of **clipping**. This allows listeners to hear both the loud and soft portions of a recording without having to adjust the volume to compensate. Clipping occurs when you go above 1.0 on the scale in Figure 6-1. Once you exceed that limit, you are pushing too much sound into the recording software or device, and the recording will sound terrible. In fact, once you exceed this maximum limit, you will lose the audio portion at the top of the waveform (hence the term "clipping"). Once this digital sound information is lost, it cannot be retrieved. Remember, your final file will depend in large part on the quality of your original recording. The clipped parts will take on a sound not unlike scattering shards of glass on a concrete playground. Nothing sounds worse than a podcaster who continues to clip—it is downright irritating. Definitely not what you're looking for.

If your recording levels are so high that you're experiencing clipping, you're losing sound that you'll never get back. That horrible glass-cracking noise won't go away. You can make it less loud, but that sound will be a permanent part of your recording. The only way to get rid of it is to cut it out (along with whatever you were saying or playing at the time).

It's better to record with your levels lower than you'd like than too high. If your recording levels are low, there are several ways to increase them, to bring them up to your desired volume. However, there are compromises here as well. Keep in mind that as you increase the volume of the sound, you're increasing the volume of everything: speech, background noise, and hiss. Obviously, the best solution is to record with good, solid levels from the start. You need to find that balance of a high enough level to get a strong signal but without clipping. It's the Goldilocks approach: not too loud, not too soft—just right. Now you can see why sound engineers earn a good living.

To get more technical about it, you should monitor your sound levels not by looking at the waveform, but by watching your meters during recording/playback (see Figure 6-2) and listening through a pair of reliable headphones. Your meters should give a fairly precise reading of the amount of sound coming in or going out, measured in **decibels** or **dBs** (pronounced "dee bees"). Your headphones will tell you (obviously) what it actually sounds like. A professional sound engineer will tell you that your recording should maintain levels between −12dB and −6dB, with 0dB being the point at which the sound will degrade. Never go above 0dB, no matter what! In visual terms, you want your meters every now and then dipping into the red section; however, if they are always in the red, then you are recording too "hot."

Do a test recording, and check your levels as you go. When you've finished recording the test, see how the levels look on playback. If they're too high and you're clipping, adjust your input/output levels accordingly.

Remember, as we mentioned in Chapter 5, your headphones should be plugged into your audio chain as late in the process as possible. This way, you'll catch as many potential problems as possible while recording. And, you should *always* monitor your sound while you're recording. If you think you look too dorky with headphones on "in the field" (on location), use a pair of discreet ear buds. Just use *something*.

Important audio terms and concepts

Even with your levels at perfect output, at this point your recording will probably sound a bit thin. It's not because your voice is that much weaker than everybody else's, it's just that you aren't yet using as many of the tricks of the trade as the pros are in the form of **dynamics processors**. By processing your sound, you will make your thin, hollow recording sound like it's from a big budget studio.

Before we go much further, let's go over some basic (and essential) audio processing terms that will help in our discussion. As with all things audio, entire books have been written on each of these individual components and processes. We aren't aiming to give you a comprehensive education in dynamics processing, but instead to give you a basic idea of what each component and process does so that you will have enough knowledge to know whether it applies to your situation.

Some of these terms will seem familiar, since we touched upon many of them briefly in the equipment chapter (Chapter 5), but now let's quickly discuss how each of these tools and techniques will affect the quality of your sound.

- **Dynamics**: This term refers to the variations in magnitude in a sound. If a sound has many variations in volume, it is said to have a large **dynamic range**.

- **Loudness vs. voltage**: Loudness is not determined by the peak levels in the waveform—that is the voltage. If a waveform is very "fat," meaning that there is not much difference in volume between the highest peaks and the lowest, it is termed "loud." The quiet parts almost have the same magnitude as the loud parts. See the part of the waveform for rock music in Figure 6-1, for example. Although its voltage is lower than the spoken section, it is louder. Loudness equals "power."

- **Compression**: Compression takes the loudest parts of the audio (only) and reduces their magnitude, compressing the overall signal and thereby decreasing the dynamic range. When using a compressor, you can specify the amount of compression to apply. For example, 3:1 compression will cause an increase of 3dB in the original audio signal to only output a 1dB gain in the finished recording. This can be very useful, particularly on the human voice. After compression has been applied, you can then increase the overall volume or magnitude of the track, making it "louder." Compressing your audio will start to give it that professional "broadcast" sound. When compression is done correctly, you end up with a pleasing average level for your entire audio file. Compression can be used during recording or in mastering.

- **Limiting**: Limiting is kind of like an extreme version of compression—it keeps the louder passages of your recording from exceeding a set level. Limiting is similar to compression, as it lowers the overall magnitude of the sound, but there is an appreciable difference in approach: limiting keeps the sound from exceeding a certain level, as opposed to compressing it to meet that level. Look at compression as pushing down against the louder portions and limiting as setting a barrier that cannot be moved. Limiting can be used during recording or in mastering.

- **Gain**: Gain is the fancy audio way of saying "volume." Most compressors/limiters will have a gain setting. Increasing the gain just means that you are building in an increase of volume to the effect.

- **Expander**: An expander is the opposite of a compressor, and it's a useful tool for noise reduction. When the signal volume drops below a certain level, it's automatically reduced even further by the expander. This cleanly accentuates the quiet and alleviates background noise, room noise, and even breathing sounds. When the person being recorded stops talking, the expander smoothly reduces the input level and then increases it again when the speaking resumes. For example, think of someone who has her hand on the input volume dial. As the person speaking into the mic stops speaking, the person manning the dial turns it down even further so that background noise is not heard. When it becomes obvious the person is speaking again, the person manning the dial turns the dial back up again.

- **Gate**: A gate is a noise-reduction tool (it's often called a **noise gate**). Gates are the extreme version of expanders. Imagine a real gate, swinging in the wind. When the wind blows enough, the gate opens. When the wind dies down, the gate closes, not yielding to the softer breeze. An audio "gate" works in exactly the same way. When there is enough sound going into the system, the gate opens, allowing the sound to be recorded. When the sound level dips too low, the gate closes, not allowing unnecessary room hiss into the recording. This is another method for excluding background noise, such as general room noise, the sound of air conditioners, and so forth. Be careful: settings that are too extreme can create more problems than they solve.

- **Attack**: "Attack" is the term used for the amount of time an effect takes to engage once it's triggered. You'll see attack settings on your hardware and software compressors, limiters, expanders, and gates. Depending on the sound you are going for, you adjust the "attack" and "release" up and down. If the attack is too slow on your gate, for instance, the gate will clip the beginnings off of each spoken phrase. If it is too fast, the ends of words will be cut off. Not good. Finding the sweet spot on the gate's attack will keep the room hiss at bay, and make the opening and closing of the gate undetectable to the listener.

6

- **De-esser**: This is a very specific mode of compression that reduces the harsh tones of human speech in the sibilant frequencies by increasing the amount of compression of those frequencies. De-essers are used during recording, but they can also be applied during the mastering process.

- **Normalizer (or peak normalization)**: A normalizer is not actually a dynamics processor. A normalizer simply increases the volume of a track to its highest level or a percentage thereof before clipping occurs. Almost every piece of digital audio software has some kind of normalizing built in. Most sound engineers will tell you to never use it, but it is a very common postprocess for podcasters (see the earlier "Recording levels" section). Normalizing is done during the mixing and mastering stage.

- **RMS normalization**: This is a form of normalization that normalizes the apparent loudness of a sound (more on RMS normalization in Chapter 7). RMS normalization is also done during the mastering process.

- **Equalization (EQ)**: Equalization allows you to alter the overall emphasis of different frequency bands. As an example, you may want to reduce audio frequencies below 120Hz as they may add too much rumble to your spoken word podcast. Alternatively, you may want to boost the frequency in the "presence" ranges to add sparkle or emphasis to your voice. Whole books have been written about EQ. Chapter 7 deals with this subject in more detail.

Once you have your studio set up and are about to record a few tests, get to know the different dynamics processors, and get a feel for what you like and how you'd like your voice to sound. Whether you apply the processors live as you record or in postproduction, giving the sound a going over with a compressor/limiter will give your podcast a professional, big-budget feel.

> Be aware that most dynamics processing is like salt: a little can improve some things, but a lot ruins everything.

As an example, Figures 6-2 and 6-3 present a sample recording before and after compression, respectively.

An important point is to develop your own recording standards. And listen. Listen to your recordings, listen to the recordings of others, and determine what it is you like and don't like about yours in comparison. Try not to overtweak your sound file. Each time you process the sound, you are distorting it and leaving behind artifacts (like the "jaggies" you get from overenlarging a digital photo) that you won't be able to get rid of.

When you experiment with different settings in your software, it is critical that you keep notes. Remember that compression will affect two files differently if the files were recorded at different levels. As such, you need to have a grasp on your settings going down the whole chain, from input to output. This way, if you ever need to change your setup for a different kind of recording or editing, you also have the guide to get everything back to your default standards. This may not seem terribly important right now, but trust us—nothing is worse than losing "your sound" and not knowing how to get it back. (For suggestions on basic settings, see Chapter 7.)

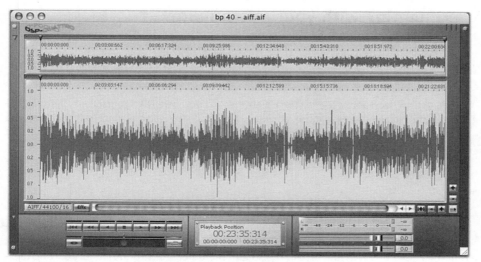

Figure 6-2. A sample of a raw recording before processing

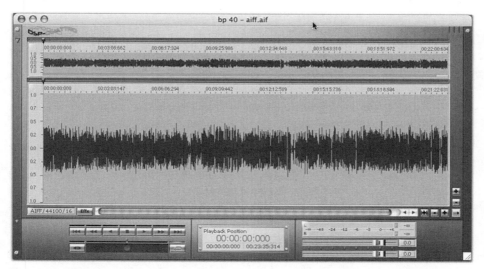

Figure 6-3. The same recording as shown in Figure 6-2 after compression. Notice that the waveform is now much more consistent.

Recording yourself

OK, it's finally time to hit the mic. Phew! Now, let's be honest, recording yourself is half science and half art. Luckily, we've covered most of the science by now, so let's get to the really good stuff.

Experimenting with your microphone

> *"Hey, buddy, how do you get to Carnegie Hall?" "Practice . . ."*

Unless you've had some experience behind the mic, you owe it to yourself to spend a little time goofing around. Yes, goofing around. The world can wait for your first podcast until after you've had a little quality time with your mic and become good buddies. If you've done your homework, the microphone you're using is going to suit your needs for many, many podcasts to come. So why not take the time to get acquainted with it and learn how to best work with it?

Hopefully, you've taken our advice and found yourself a unidirectional mic (we're assuming for the sake of this discussion that you're recording alone, in your new studio). If so, your microphone wasn't designed to record sound evenly from every direction. The great benefit to this is that it won't pick up unwanted sounds from all around your studio. This is particularly helpful if your studio is also a home office/guestroom/laundry sorting facility. Take another look at the pick-up pattern of the mic, and make sure that the mic (especially if it's a side address model) is facing the right way and that you'll be talking into the right end/side.

As covered in the previous chapter, set up your equipment so that audio picked up by the mic is being routed to your headphones. Put your headphones on, clear your throat, and do a great, rock concert–style "Check, One, Two . . . Check." Didn't that feel good?

Hopefully, if you're set up properly, you hear your sound check in your headphones loud and clear, with no lag time (**latency**) between the time you spoke and the time you heard yourself in your headphones.

To find the optimum mic/mouth position to use when recording, sing yourself a little embarrassing nonsense song (OK, you can sing or say whatever you like) while slowly moving your head and mouth up and down and from side to side in front of the mic. It should immediately become evident at exactly what point in space the microphone is picking up your voice with the clearest sound. That is the place at which you need to speak into the mic; that is the sweet spot.

Adjust your mic, your chair, and/or your sitting position so that you naturally sit at the microphone in a position where your voice will hit that sweet spot when you're recording.

Developing voice technique

You don't have to speak loudly into the mic. If you find yourself yelling, perhaps you need to turn up the volume of your headphones. The converse is true, too: if you are speaking softly but it still seems to come through loudly, turn the cans down.

Relaxation is the key to good vocal technique. Relax your voice, not your body. You need to find a way to relax your voice but maintain good energy. This is why most voice-over artists record standing up. Doing so helps your energy, breathing, and blood flow.

I have done voice-over work for TV, radio, commercials, and movies. When you go into the recording booth, there is always a mic (of course), a music stand for your copy, and a pair of headphones. But there is never a chair.

—Dan Klass

Once you can relax and let your voice come from you naturally, you will hear an amazing improvement over your earlier recordings. "How do I relax?" you may ask. The answer is to spend time recording. The more time you spend recording, the less "new" it becomes. You'll get used to speaking into your mic's sweet spot and hearing your own voice played back to you in the headphones. In fact, you'll get used to the whole process.

We're used to hearing our own voices, but not as other people hear them. Other people hear only the sound that makes it from our mouth to their ears. What we hear of ourselves is a mix of what is coming out of our mouth and the sound of our voice as it resonates in our chest and throat. That's why a lot of people say they hate the sound of their own voice when it is recorded. It's because their voice sounds different from how they perceive it—they've never heard it isolated enough to get used to the sound.

Don't be afraid to talk with your chest. Some people talk with their throat. Some people talk through their sinuses. The voice-over guy who everyone says has such "great pipes" doesn't get the sound from his windpipe or his vocal cords. He gets it from his chest. Goof around with dragging your voice down into your chest and listen to the difference it makes. We're not suggesting that you should try to record yourself forcing your voice into your chest, but if you can relax enough, you will learn to allow your voice to resonate in your chest a little. It will give your voice a fuller, richer sound, effortlessly.

Talking to one person at a time

Part of your goal as a podcaster should be to speak clearly, convincingly, and (somewhat) professionally. You don't want to sound like a DJ from the 1950s, and you certainly don't want to sound like one of those overly enthusiastic guys who seem to always be pitching a new kitchen wonder on late-night infomercials. By contrast, you may not want to sound like an exhausted college kid from the local university FM station, either. Your goal should be to sound like yourself. Or at least the polished, credible version of yourself you'd like to introduce to your audience.

You can spend thousands of dollars on voice-over classes if you'd like, and invest hours of your free time going over advertising copy and public service announcements, hoping someday to learn the tricks to sounding natural behind the mic. Or we can just tell you the big voice-talent secret. It's up to you. Practice makes perfect, as we eluded to in the earlier Carnegie Hall line, but you need to make sure you are practicing the right way. There is one technique that, above all others, will help you sound simultaneously like a professional voice-talent and a real living and breathing human being:

Talk to one person at a time.

6

You do not want to try to talk to your entire audience at once, because you do not want to sound like you're giving a speech. Imagining yourself talking to a group will make you start to sound like a politician or one of those infomercial people (what's the difference?). People who talk to groups sound vague or fake. Their speech patterns become so rhythmic or so annoying that you can't bear to continue to listen. Most of their message is lost in the method. They are not truly connecting with anyone in the audience.

Speak as if you are speaking to one person. Talk to that person. Really talk. Don't think of what you're doing as podcasting or broadcasting or anything else. It is a conversation. It is a conversation where you are the only one talking, but it is still a conversation. The other side of the conversation comes to you in the form of e-mail, blog posts, and voice mail messages.

You want listeners to feel like you are talking directly to them, whispering directly into their ears. To really fine-tune this approach, here is another trick of the trade you can use that will help you create the specific tone you're looking for with your podcast:

Decide exactly who the one person you're talking to is.

The person you choose does not have to actually be listening. That isn't the point. The point is to give yourself a buddy, a listener, a point of reference. The person you choose to imagine you're talking to will affect the way you deliver every word. By focusing your attention on that person, you guarantee you'll never end up sounding like a political candidate.

Choose wisely. As an example, you may have one friend who, somehow, just makes you funny. Something about talking to him or her brings out the comedian in you. You are smarter, sharper, and quicker whenever the two of you talk. You've even thought to yourself, "Man, if we ever got together to do a podcast, it would be the greatest!" *That* is the person to talk to. If you think this sounds crazy, just humor us and give it a try. You'll see that instead of somewhat cautiously approaching the microphone, you are now not even thinking about the mic. You're thinking about how anxious you are to tell your "funny buddy" your latest story. He or she doesn't have to be in the room with you to be your podcast sidekick. Every show you do can be a show secretly recorded for the person who brings out the best in you.

Odds are good it's not your mother. It may not even be your significant other. The person you deliver the show to could be someone you hardly know, as long as there is something about talking to that person that turns you into the person you want to be in your podcast.

This technique is not by any means restricted to people doing entertainment podcasts. If you are doing an educational program or a sales program, this approach is a must. Who are you educating? Is the person 19 years old or a middle-aged mother of two? New to the subject or experienced in the field? Choose someone to represent the student. Who exactly are you selling to? Imagine you are selling to a former or current customer—someone who seems to completely epitomize your target market. Don't choose an imaginary student or an imaginary sales prospect; choose real people.

Allowing yourself to make some mistakes

You don't have to be perfect. You don't even have to be good. Just do as mom always told you and be yourself. Assume going into this, especially in the early stages, that you'll be editing your podcast before you send it off to the world. Remember, this isn't a broadcast—it's a podcast. You have complete control over what ends up in the final product. If you go into your first recording session knowing that you can take out any mistakes and edit down any incoherent ramblings, you'll be much more relaxed and much less likely to need to edit things. It sounds strange, but it's true.

In our research for this book, we realized something very telling: many well-established podcasters have taken their first podcast offline. The first show is gone—vanished. Podcaster after podcaster, no first episode to be found. Why, you may ask? Because the first one is often . . . well . . . bad. If it's not bad, it's at least not up to the podcaster's standards.

Let yourself make some mistakes. It is better to start and not do as well as you'd like than to not start at all. After completing the initial preparation recommended in this book, you can wait and wait until you feel like you're ready, or you can just jump in. The sooner you jump in and get started, the sooner you'll be past the first show.

This also goes for waiting until you're relaxed enough, prepared enough, rested enough. Don't wait to start because the house isn't clean, or you don't yet have the perfect microphone or the best story to tell. Just jump in and do it.

If you really hate it, don't upload it. There's no podcasting law that says if you recorded a podcast, you have to send it out into the world. Shelve it. Hide it away. Just don't throw it away. Someday you may have thousands of fans who would love to hear a recording of you back in the early days when you were just starting.

6

> *In an effort at full disclosure, we must inform you that some in the podcast community feel strongly about not editing their podcasts. While we would not presume to speak for them, the basic argument goes that podcasting is a means of communication that allows for someone to be completely natural expressing his thoughts and feelings. Practitioners generally take the approach that since things aren't perfect and polished in everyday life, podcasts shouldn't be either. It is not uncommon when listening to one of these podcasts to wait a few seconds as the person recording wanders off to pour a cup of coffee or to take a phone call. Podcasters producing this style generally come from a blogging background and see podcasting as an adjunct or additional way for them to share their thoughts and opinions. This makes complete sense to us, but runs somewhat counter to our idea of a show. If this is the style you prefer, then you need to pay even more attention to levels and processing as you record your show. The beauty of podcasting is that there is room for everyone and every style of show.*

Recording a podcast

For our demonstration of the recording process, we'll use the Audacity audio editor and recorder (http://audacity.sourceforge.net). It's cross-platform (available for Windows, Mac, and Linux), it's easy to use, and it's free. Audacity is also a multitrack recorder, just like some of the higher-end recording packages. This gives you the option of either recording your music and sound effects "live" as you record your voice to one stereo track or mixing the music and sound effects in later by layering multiple tracks of sound, one on top of another. For our demonstration, we're going to record from a single source (the microphone). We discuss adding music and sound effects during podcast production in the next chapter.

Figure 6-4 shows Audacity's main recording window. Note the Pause, Stop (which is also Play—you press the button to toggle between the two), and Record buttons at the top of the window. The playback and recording meters are at the top right of the window.

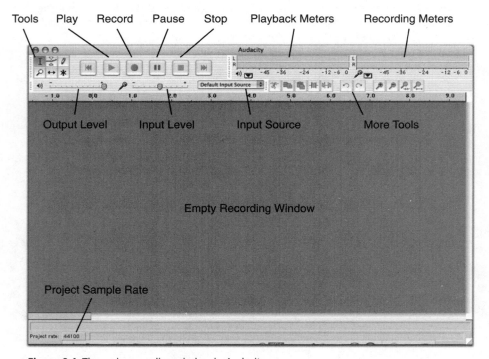

Figure 6-4. The main recording window in Audacity

> If you aren't using Audacity, don't worry. All the concepts we're about to discuss are general enough that they should apply to almost any software you're using.

Setting up the software

First, we need to make sure that the software knows how to get the sound, and at what rate and in what format it should record and save the sound. To do so, follow these steps:

1. Launch Audacity and create a new file.

2. Go to the Preferences window (see Figure 6-5), click the Audio I/O tab, and set the inputs to correspond to your recording setup.

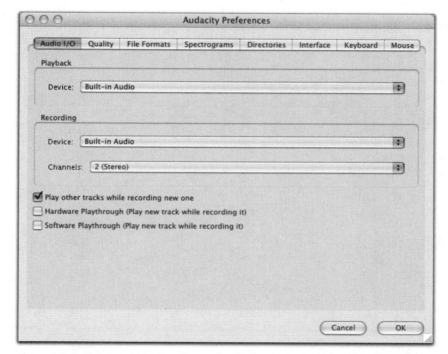

Figure 6-5. Setting the playback and recording devices in the Audacity Preferences window

3. Also in Preferences, click the Quality tab, set your Default Sample Rate to 44100 Hz, and set your Default Sample Format to 16-bit (see Figure 6-6). This will ensure that your recording is of "CD quality," without unnecessarily overtaxing your system. Depending on your recording software, you may have the option of recording in different formats (MP3, Apple Lossless, ACC, WMA, etc.). However, *we strongly recommend recording at 44.1kHz/16-bit*. It is truly the only way to go. Yes, the files are large, but you will thank yourself later when you decide to repurpose your podcast onto disc or broadcast it. Producing podcasts is hard work—do them the honor of full-quality recordings.

Record at 44.1kHz, and encode to MP3 at 44.1kHz or 22.050Hz, because many players can't handle other sample rates. Don't put your podcast at a disadvantage. All current editing software will be able to deal with 44.1kHz/16-bit audio. Some are restricted when editing at higher bit and sample rates. If you do decide to record at even higher bit or sample rates, check that your entire editing workflow can deal with those audio files.

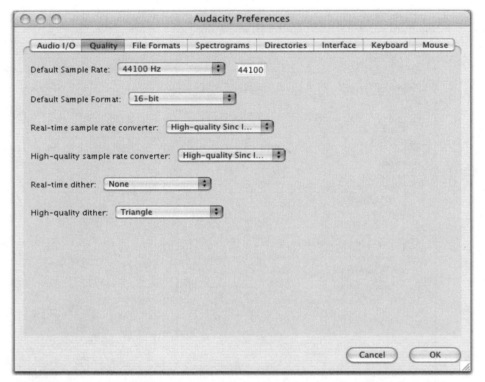

Figure 6-6. Setting your quality preferences to 44100 Hz and 16-bit will give you "CD quality" recording.

4. There's one last thing you should set in the Preferences window. Under the File Formats tab, select either WAV (if you are using Windows) or AIFF (if you are using a Mac) as your desired file format, as shown in Figure 6-7.

5. Finally, click OK in the Preferences window to save any changes.

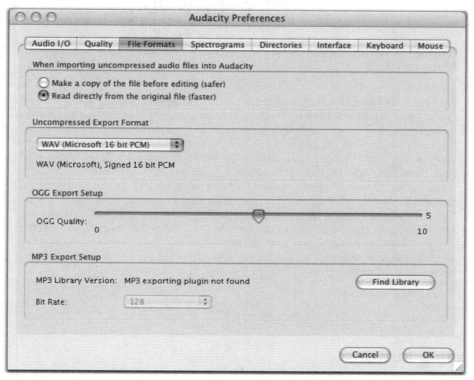

Figure 6-7. Choose your recording format: WAV (Windows and Mac) or AIFF (Mac).

Now you're ready to do a sample recording. One of the downsides of Audacity is that it won't give you readings on your recording meter unless you're actually recording. This makes it impossible to check your recording levels before you record. So do a small sample recording to set levels and then close out the recording without saving it. If you are using another recording application that does allow you to check levels without recording, always do so.

Your audio levels (as mentioned earlier) should normally fall between −12dB and −6dB on your meters. If you are going above −6dB, your signal is a bit too hot. If you are going all the way to 0, you need to turn down your mixer/preamp's output or stop talking so darned loud. If you go "into the red" (up to or past 0dB), you will get that horrible digital, glass-shattering sound. Not good.

Remember to leave yourself some **headroom**, or space between where your meters are hitting and 0dB. Give yourself at least 6dB to spare, or 12dB if yours is a low-noise audio chain. You can always pull the levels up later, but you'll never get rid of clipping.

Of course, if you are recording your podcast using a hardware solution such as a digital recorder, then your main focus will be on ensuring that you have your input levels set correctly. Be sure to refer to your device's instruction manual for complete recording setup instructions.

An additional element to consider when using hardware to record a podcast is that you must be careful to ensure that you have not induced clipping anywhere in the recording chain. As an example, if you are using a freestanding compressor or mixing board, it is possible to induce clipping in one of those items prior to the sound ever reaching your recording device. This happened to me once. I had recorded everything with perfect levels on my digital recorder, but when I listened to the completed recording, I could hear the telltale sign of clipping. It was minor and only happened a few times in the recording, but it was there nonetheless. I racked my brain to figure out how this had happened and why I did not catch it when recording. The answer was rather straight-forward: I was monitoring the audio from a point in the recording chain that was prior to the hardware that induced the clipping. The bottom line was that the output stage of my mixing board had clipped, and I failed to catch it because I was so focused on the levels on the final recording device. Lesson learned: make sure all the levels are correct throughout the recording chain.

—*Michael Geoghegan*

Pushing buttons

The "buttons" on every piece of recording software we've ever seen (and we've seen a lot!) are designed to resemble the buttons on a conventional old-school tape recorder, as shown in Figure 6-8.

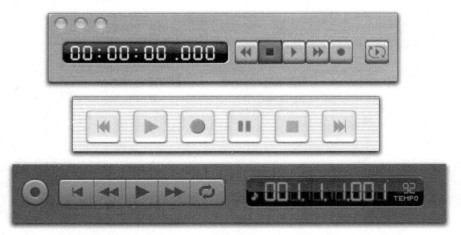

Figure 6-8. Three different control panels: BIAS Peak on top, Audacity in the middle, and GarageBand on the bottom. Notice that all the controls have a standardized appearance.

There are Play, Record, Pause, Rewind, Fast-Forward, and Stop buttons. (Oftentimes the Play button will serve double duty as the Pause button.) Your main focus right now is going to be the Record button. The Record button starts the magic. The Record button has all the muscle. The Record button isn't really your best friend, though. The button to keep by your side—the button that always has your back—is the Pause button.

If you get into trouble, pause. If you forget what you wanted to say, pause. If you stop, you've really stopped. You'll need to most likely reset the recording head (an analog tape term if we ever heard one) to the end of the recording, and start recording again from there. It's going to complicate things more than just pausing. If you pause, you've just paused. Nice and clean.

If you get into trouble, pause.

Record, knowing you can edit later

Do yourself the favor of planning out your recording session. Know ahead of time whether or not you're going to edit your podcast. If your podcast is supposed to be endearing and funny, you may want to leave in any gaffes and fumbles in the name of "character." However, if you're trying to do something a little more polished, you probably aren't going to want to let the rough edges show. If you know you'll be editing a little, record with that in mind. If you mess up, stop talking for a moment, back up your thoughts, and start again, clearly. When you go to edit, you will have given yourself a clean place to cut out the stumble (see Chapter 7 for more details). Actually, by pausing long enough, not only will you leave yourself a good edit point, but also the gap in the waveform will be easy to spot, making editing simpler. There is no reason to rush while you're recording. You'll have all the pieces of the podcast that you need, and you can easily cut out the ones you don't.

Be sure to give yourself a little bit of silence at the beginning of the recording, so you make sure that everything gets recorded. Even if you choose not to edit your podcast, you will most likely want to at least tidy up the ends, so the podcast starts and ends quickly and cleanly.

Click the Record button. Talk. Play some music. Talk some more. Say good-bye and thank you. Click the Stop button.

Congratulations! You've recorded a podcast!

Yeah, it seemed like those instructions might have been longer, huh? Well, what more can we say about what to say? If you skipped the preceding chapters and came straight here, it's no wonder that seems like an awfully flippant way to describe the actual recording of a podcast. If you have read everything up until now, we are confident that you are well prepared to click, talk, and click.

If you forgot to say something (especially if it was the name of the podcast or your URL), start another file and record the omitted material. You will be able to easily cut it into the original recording. And if you decided to add in your music and sound effects after the fact, don't worry. We're about to cover how to handle that in the next chapter. Just remember, this is not a broadcast—it is a podcast production.

Saving your podcast

Obviously, you'll need to save your recording. Since you'll be producing several podcasts, and your master recording isn't the only audio file you'll have to this particular edition, we recommend saving and organizing your podcast files with this in mind. How you do that is up to you. We suggest creating a Podcast directory (folder) on your hard drive, and then making a separate subdirectory for each show. This will give you a specific place to save your master recording, as well as any edited versions or additional elements.

Summary

This has been quite a chapter, but you made it to the end. You've now configured your audio software to record at the highest quality necessary, set your audio in and out settings, and saved your first recordings. You even learned about the keys to presenting your podcast with connection and clarity. You've covered a lot of ground in a short amount of space, and yet, here you are: you've recorded your first podcast.

Don't worry about goofs. Don't worry about the part where you went off on a tangent. You'll fix all that when you edit the show in Chapter 7.

7 PUTTING IT ALL TOGETHER

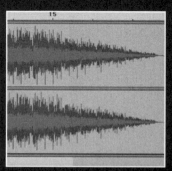

There are probably as many ways to handle the editing of a podcast as there are podcasters. Some podcasters approach postproduction by simply hitting the Stop button on their recording setup, while others labor for hours, fine-tuning their podcast until it is perfect. (Of course, "perfect" is a completely subjective assessment.) The approach you take will depend, like so many other things, on you and your podcast. You may just want to record the show "live in studio" where whatever happens, happens. No editing, no assembly after the fact. Or you may want to assemble your podcast from various individual pieces, weaving the elements together in the editing process.

There are several schools of thought when it comes to producing podcasts. Some believe "less is more." Others believe "the more the merrier." We believe "better is better." You don't want to spend your life editing and remixing your podcasts, only to have them compressed to within a megabyte of their lives. But, you never know what even the immediate future holds, much less what you'll end up doing with your podcast later on. This is why we want you to take the time to get your podcast sounding the best it can, before the big MP3 squeeze. This is something we are really committed to, and it's something we may stress a bit too much, but you'll thank us for it later.

In this chapter, we will discuss the following, in great detail:

- Understanding the basics of digital audio editing
- Editing the podcast recording, including cutting on the silence before the sound, cleaning up the audio, and using a multitrack setup to add sound elements
- Examining dynamics processing
- Adjusting the volume of your podcast

Introduction to digital audio editing

Remember, podcasting isn't radio. There is room for error while you're recording. You're not going out to your audience live, so you have complete control over what the audience will end up hearing. Coughs, "ums," mispronunciations, and mindless tangents can be removed from your podcast with a single stroke of the DELETE key. You are crafting a piece of audio content; the power is in your hands.

> *Sometimes radio isn't radio. Ever wonder how everyone on National Public Radio (NPR) always sounds so darned smart? The broadcasters seem to effortlessly flow from one complicated subject to another without so much as an "ahh" or "um." And how come their guests are just as eloquent? You guessed it: beautiful editing. They record a lot of the interviews ahead of time and edit them before they are aired. If you ever want to sound like a real pro, hire a former NPR audio editor (see www.onthemedia.org/transcripts/transcripts_123104_curtain.html).*

The editing process is the time for you to create your podcast out of the raw materials of your original master recording. Your original recording is like clay, and you are free to mold it any way you like. Elements can be shortened, moved, or removed. Segments can be rearranged to create a better flow or a clearer point.

When examining the various elements of your podcast, ask yourself, "Do I really need that?" If the answer is no, and you don't think it's funny enough, insightful enough, or "whatever" enough, lose it. You can always refine it and then say it again in another podcast at a later date. Just remember, your podcast will be on your server being downloaded for months to come, so you need to be happy with what you put out there.

Be warned that you can labor over your podcast forever, taking out every hiccup, tightening every pause, and cutting and pasting until each segment sings like a bird. But do you need to? And if so, why? Be aware that it's a tempting pitfall. Sure, you want to create podcasts that you can be proud of, but nobody is expecting them to sound like they were produced by pros in a million-dollar studio.

Seriously, it's only a podcast. What's a stray "um" or "like" between friends? Actually, for some podcast listeners, the "ums" and "likes" that would never be heard on broadcast radio are part of the allure of podcasting. Podcasters aren't professional broadcasters, they're real people, and some real people say "um" and "like."

If you're recording a 30-minute show and end up editing that show for three hours, you may want to tighten up your preproduction, to give yourself a break in postproduction. Or rethink the standards that you're trying to live up to. If you want to sound like a seasoned pro and end up sounding too casual, maybe it's because you *are* casual. Is that such a bad thing? If you're editing yourself to such an extent that it's overshadowing the recording, you need to consider accepting what you're doing, instead of trying to live up to something you aren't. It's very easy to fall into the trap of overediting your shows, because it's so darned simple to do.

7

Editing the recording

Let's take a look at the waveform again and see what needs to be done to our recording before we start encoding it to MP3. Figure 7-1 shows the waveform of a friend's podcast recording. Notice the almost flat area at the beginning of the wave; this is a bit of silence at the beginning of the show.

Let's do some cutting. We edit before we do any dynamics processing or start playing with the sound levels. This is because we may be editing out coughs or bangs that would cause spikes in the levels. These spikes, if left in, could have a dramatic effect on the dynamics processing. For instance, if there is a loud bang in the recording, the spike in the wave could trigger a compressor's attack, causing the more even parts of the wave to be compressed unnecessarily. The object is to first cut out everything we don't want and then process the sound we do want to get the best results possible.

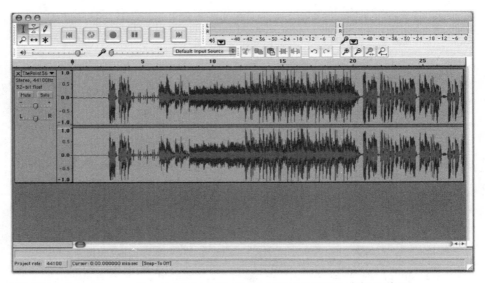

Figure 7-1. A sample recording waveform, with silence at the beginning of the podcast

So, first let's tighten up this file by cleaning up the silence at the beginning of the recording. (For these examples, we'll mainly use the freeware application Audacity; however, the steps are almost identical in any other audio-editing application.)

1. Highlight the segment of silence at the beginning of the recording by placing your cursor at the beginning of the waveform and pressing down on your (left) mouse button. While continuing to hold the mouse button down, drag the cursor to the right, highlighting the entire segment you are going to cut. If you find the segment is too small to easily highlight, use the zoom function to get a closer view of the waveform. When you have finished selecting the silence, release the button. The segment you are hoping to delete should remain highlighted (see Figure 7-2).

2. Click the Play button and listen, just to make sure you aren't about to cut something you didn't intend to.

3. If everything sounds OK (like silence), press the *DELETE* key.

The silence disappears. With this file, we would follow the same process for the silence at the end of the recording. This cleanup process is also useful if you have any unwanted material at the end of a recording.

In the sections that follow, we'll look at different ways in which you can add to, take away from, and manipulate your recording to get it sounding just perfect before you think about encoding it to MP3, ready to be published on the web.

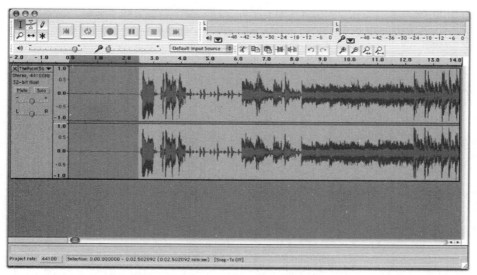

Figure 7-2. Highlight the silence at the beginning of a recording, and then "erase" it by pressing the *Delete* key.

Using the silence

The old adage "Silence is golden" definitely holds true in sound editing. The silent pauses in your recording are the places you will be able to cleanly cut material out, or add material in, without leaving a noticeable blip in the sound file. Since the general "noise" of your recording is going to be fairly uniform, cutting material out between two moments of silence will create almost undetectable edits. As long as the general timbre of your voice is the same and your recording technique is uniform throughout, you will be able to carve entire chunks out of your podcast or rearrange entire passages without anyone ever noticing.

> *Always cut immediately before sounds. Want to remove something? End the cut right at the beginning of the next sound to be kept. If it's speech, then cut immediately before the first syllable. The change in sound (from silence to speech in this example) will mask the edit. The same is true for any type of sound, either effects or music. The more sudden the change in the sound, the more it will mask the edit immediately before it.*

The simple technique presented in the preceding section to edit out some silence is the same one you'll use when you're trying to edit pieces of recorded voice, coughs, "ums," or anything else. The trick is to determine exactly what it is you want to cut and make sure that's all you're cutting.

In this next example, assume you want to cut a stray "um" from your original recording. To do so, you'll want to follow these steps:

1. Highlight the section you want to remove (see Figure 7-3).

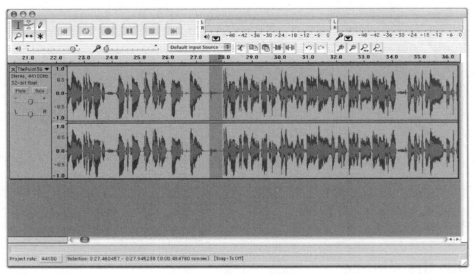

Figure 7-3. Highlight the offending audio ("um") and then delete, copy, or cut this section of the recording (being careful to start and end the selection in areas of silence).

2. Listen to the section by clicking the Play button, just to confirm that it is in fact what you want to cut. Only the highlighted section will be played.

3. When you're confident that you have the right section, press the *DELETE* key.

The offending section will disappear, and the waveform will close up around where that selection *used* to be. Now, listen to your edit. You can always undo the action if you're not happy with the results. If it sounds good and seems to flow well, move on.

> *Be careful not to "overtighten" your show. When people speak, they often pause between words, whether for effect or simply to breathe. We've heard some podcasts where it's obvious the editor was trying to eliminate all the silent sections. Your ear will easily pick up that something just doesn't sound natural—how could a person speak for three minutes without taking a breath? Since audio editing with a computer is so easy, remember to use some restraint. This is why we keep reminding you to listen, listen, listen! You'll be able to tell if you've gone a little overboard in your editing.*

Not only can you cut things out using this procedure, but you can also move things around. If something you really liked about those two seconds was just nixed, and you want to simply put that segment elsewhere, all you have to do is cut and paste it to the appropriate point in your podcast as follows:

1. Highlight the segment you want to move and cut it (Windows: *CTRL+X*; Mac: ⌘+*X*).

2. Find the place in the file where you want to paste in the extracted segment and single-click that spot.

3. Paste the cut segment into place (Windows: *CTRL+V*; Mac: ⌘+*V*).

Voilà! The segment of sound has been moved to the new location. Listen to your new edit to see how it sounds. You can always undo it and try again.

Cutting on sibilant sounds: "S" marks the spot

Words are not always clearly separated in the waveform. When you speak, some words will flow into one another. This makes editing a little trickier, as you are trying to find a way to cut out something without a telltale edit sound (a clicking or popping noise caused by a bad edit). In such cases, you can experiment with cutting on **sibilant sounds**, or **"s" sounds** as they are more commonly known. Although people's voices vary greatly in tone and texture from word to word (or even from sentence to sentence) depending on their mood, delivery, and so on, we tend to always make the same "s" sound. While you could never expect to cut in the middle of a soft "a" or "m" sound, there is something unique about the sonic qualities of the sibilant "s" that makes it very handy in sound editing. As an example, if you said "Mike stands next to . . . ah . . . what was I going to say . . . oh yeah, stands next to the new bike," you might be able to cut together the two sibilant "s" sounds in "stands" and remove the entire "next to . . . ah . . . what was I going to say . . . oh yeah" part.

7

Cleaning up the audio

Sometimes you'll find yourself with audio that isn't quite up to your standards. Audio converted from a tape recording may have that familiar hissing sound. Perhaps the recording levels weren't properly set, and in order to get good audio levels you have to increase the gain so much that you also get a lot of ambient noise. Maybe you're stuck with the dreaded 60Hz hum that video users are so familiar with.

When this happens, you have a number of options. Obviously, you want to do your best to eliminate the noise interfering with your audio. A common solution is to apply what is known as a **notch filter**. This is a way of reducing the amplitude of the offending frequencies. Check the software you're using, as most will provide a tool for accomplishing this task.

Figure 7-4 shows an example of using a notch filter. In this figure, we have applied a notch filter to cause a −18.0dB reduction in amplitude at 10kHz. The Q value of 9.87 is a number representing the amount surrounding frequencies are affected by the filter. A lower Q value causes a wider notch, affecting more surrounding frequencies, and a higher Q value causes a narrower notch. In this case, we have effectively reduced the amplitude of the 10kHz frequency so that we no longer hear the "noise."

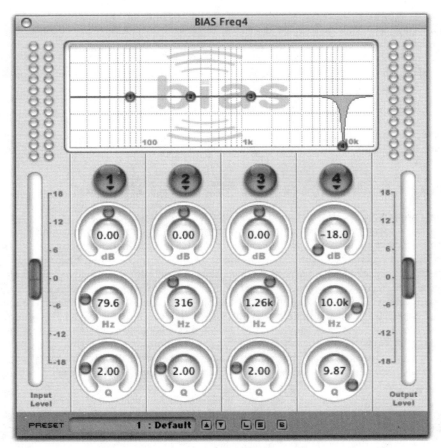

Figure 7-4. A notch filter applied to handle a noise issue occurring at 10kHz using a four-band paragraphic EQ

For more complicated jobs, or to automate the task, many software solutions are available. One of our favorites is from BIAS (www.bias-inc.com). Bias SoundSoap 2 (see Figure 7-5) is a stand-alone application available for both Mac and Windows that does an excellent job cleaning up audio. One of its best features is the ability it offers you to "listen" to your audio and learn the noise profile. This feature makes SoundSoap 2 both quick and easy to use.

> *I was once forwarded a tape recording of an interview with one of my favorite film directors that had been made during the 1970s. Using both SoundSoap 2 and a notch filter, I was able to remove almost all the tape hiss. It turned the whole recording around, so that the interview could be easily heard without noise distractions.*
>
> *—Michael Geoghegan*

Figure 7-5. SoundSoap 2

Using a multitrack setup to add music, sound effects, and comments

We mentioned earlier that you have the option to add music, sound effects, and other sound elements into your podcasts in postproduction using a multitrack recording and mixing application such as Audacity, Adobe Audition, or Apple GarageBand. Before you start adding additional audio elements, you should be confident that the editing process is finished. It's much easier to edit *before* you start adding music and sound effects than after you've added these elements. Also, once you add music and sound effects and do a **mixdown** (i.e., combine all the layers of sound into one), it is nearly impossible to make further edits. Editing after the mixdown makes for nothing but disaster, as you can't cut without completely disrupting the musical elements.

Adding sound underneath your original recording

Music is one of the greatest ways to bring extra life to your podcasts, but sometimes it's tricky to get it cleanly into your show while you're recording. Depending on your studio setup, you may need to add all the musical elements of your podcast in postproduction. This is easily tackled by using a multichannel sound application that will let you record a new audio track while simultaneously listening to the others, or allow you to add another track under your first, into which you'll paste some music.

You can add music as a short intro or outro to give the listener a quick sense of the tone of the show to follow, or as a **music bed**. A music bed is music that plays under your recording or a section of your recording throughout. Adding a music bed to a podcast is a great way to give your program a signature sound.

> Using a music bed is also a very handy editing trick. The underlying music will often mask room noise and can help to cover up some edits. If you find that either of these issues applies to your recordings, first try to rectify the problem, but know that a music bed may be a helpful tool for you. See our interview at www.podcastsolutions.com with Dave Slusher from "Evil Genius Chronicles" (www.evilgeniuschronicles.org) for some related conversation and techniques.

For this example, we'll cover how to add some podsafe intro and outro music to your podcast, again using Audacity:

1. Go to Project ➤ New Stereo Track to create a new stereo track within your podcast project window. You'll paste your musical intro into this track.

2. Open the song/musical piece you want to use as your intro music from within the editing application.

3. Copy the waveform (or at least slightly more of the recording than you intend to use) and paste it into the new stereo track you created in your podcast project window (see Figure 7-6).

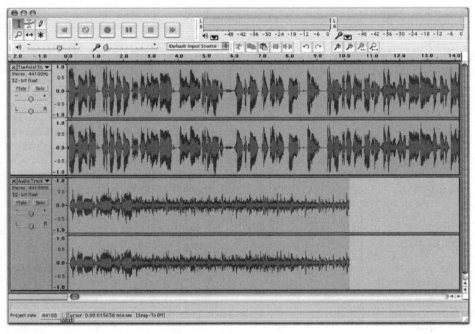

Figure 7-6. Create a new stereo track, into which you can paste some podsafe music.

Fading out your music

Now assume that you like the way the music segment begins, but you want the music to fade out sooner than the original song does. You simply need to use the Fade Out effect to automatically create a fade, as follows:

1. Highlight the section of music you wish to fade. The length of the fade-out (and the speed at which the sound fades) is determined by the length of the selected sound you want to fade. The fade is created by leaving the volume of the beginning of the selected piece at 100% (full volume) and gradually decreasing it to 0% (silence) at the end of the selection.

2. Go to Effect ➤ Fade Out. The effect will immediately begin to process. When it is finished, your selection will have a smooth, gradual fade-out (see Figure 7-7).

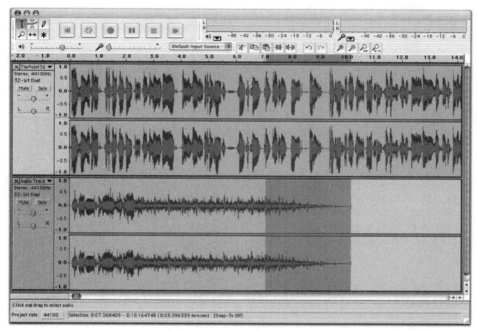

Figure 7-7. The music track after applying a Fade Out filter

3. Use the Time Shift tool to slide the section of music back and forth within the timeline, to position the music where you'd like it. If you want the music to start first and then play for a few seconds before the original speaking segment begins, use the Time Shift tool to shift the spoken-word recording on the upper track (see Figure 7-8).

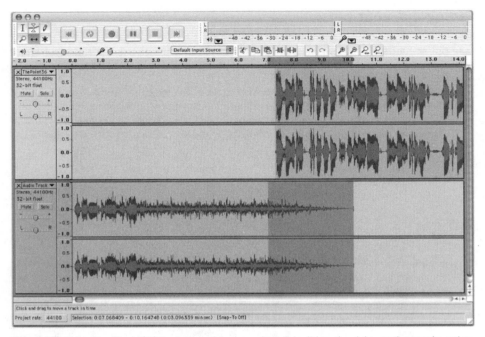

Figure 7-8. Using the Time Shift tool, the original vocal track is slid to the right, so the vocal portion starts after the music begins to fade.

You can apply this method of adding new tracks and pasting in music to sound effects, voice mail messages, prerecorded segments, or anything else that you want to add to your podcast after the initial recording session. Odds are good you're not on a set schedule, so take as much time as you feel you need to put together the show you're aiming for. Since you're the boss, you decide when you're finished.

Locking and backing up your podcast

OK, **locking** is just a cool term we thought we'd throw out there, so you'd know what to call this point in the process. When you're done cutting things out, cutting things in, and evening things out, and you know you're not going to change the actual content of your podcast anymore, you consider your podcast "locked." From here on out, it's just about improving the sonics of the show, not the content—the content is locked down.

But before we move on to discuss the aforementioned sonics, we should say a word or two about backing up your files. We know, we know—ever since your first day on your first computer, you've been constantly reminded of the importance of backing everything up. Saving copies of your podcast as you go through your production process is a must. A *must*. At each level, do your podcast the honor of saving a copy specific to that step in the process, and save that version somewhere that is *not* on your hard drive. When you've finished recording, save that version of your show (show.original_record); when you're done editing, save that version (`show.edit`); and so on until your podcast is uploaded and the RSS is updated. The reasons for this are twofold:

- You never know when you'll want or need to go back a step in the process and start over.
- You never know when your hard drive will die and take its entire contents with it.

> *We speak from experience. We lost the original draft of Chapter 5 of this book in a horrible iBook hard-drive disaster. There was no warning—everything seemed to be humming along nicely. Then suddenly it was all gone. Don't let this happen to your podcast!*

Mastering your podcast

Another great audio-production term is **mastering**. You've probably heard this term used in relation to mastering sound recordings for reproduction on CD or vinyl.

> *For our younger readers, there used to be these things called **record** or **vinyl** albums that were sort of like giant analog CDs . . . it's a long story.*

In the mixdown process (explained toward the end of this chapter), you make your audio sound the absolute best you can in its pure digital form. In the mastering process, you make the audio sound the best it can given the characteristics and deficiencies of your target medium: CD, vinyl, cassette or, in our case, MP3.

Yes, we're dealing with MP3s. For us, then, the mastering process involves making the sound of the podcast as professional and as pleasing to the ear as possible, given the fact that we're about to throw away a large amount of the original sound file for the sake of the file size. (More on that in the next chapter.)

Doing a little dynamics processing

We touched upon dynamics processing in previous chapters when discussing possible studio setups and recording techniques. Just as you had an opportunity to add compression, limiting, sibilance reduction, and other processes to your sound as you recorded, you can also do much of the same processing in postproduction using plug-ins (audio filters). Depending on your system, using plug-ins to process the signal as you record may put too much strain on older or slower computers. Asking one computer to record new audio while also processing that audio and sometimes playing other audio sources can be a bit much. Knowing this, podcasters tend to fall into one of two camps: those who do much of their vocal/audio processing while they record using hardware, and those who do most of it in postproduction using plug-ins.

If you're using a hardware processor, you may not need to do much processing at the mastering stage. Your signal may be just as even and snappy as you'd like. The extent of your postprocessing may just be making sure your levels are where you want them and calling it done. Serious podcasters tend to use a combination of hardware and software processors to get just the sound they're looking for.

As we discussed earlier, there are many wonderful (and often free) plug-ins to load into your system and experiment with. But don't get too filter-happy: when it comes to processing sound, sometimes too much of a good thing is just that: too much. Forget about the Chorusifier filters and the Flanger—those are for music, not for speech. (Unless, of course, you are playing sound effects games to achieve some sonic goal for spicing up your podcast.) Your main concerns will be a compressor, limiter, de-esser, and gate/expander (for an explanation of what each of these does, see Chapter 6). We highly recommend the use of a compressor and a limiter, in that order.

When you first use these processors, our advice is to experiment on a copy of your podcast (just in case), leaving each plug-in at its default settings (look for a Voice, a Speech, or even a Vocal setting). This way, you'll get a feeling for what each one does and how it changes the specific sound of your podcast, and then you can start playing with them. We've found that the best way to get a grasp on how these dynamics processors will affect your audio is to just start adjusting the controls and listen for the differences. That along with a bit of our general guidance from Chapter 6, and you should be on your way. Of course, you can always turn to the Internet if you are looking for exhaustive information on exactly how these processors work and the intention behind each control.

Sometimes the whole is less than the sum of its parts. Huh? Sometimes, listening to each process as it's applied doesn't give a clear picture of how the file will sound once everything has been applied. You might want to listen not to the direct results of these tools, but to how the ultimate MP3 sounds. You might be surprised, for example, at how many digital artifacts are accumulated from all the different steps. Your added compression could actually make the final MP3 sound worse, even though the intermediate version sounds better. Never be afraid to experiment: go back a couple steps, tweak a setting, and try again.

In the sections that follow, we'll discuss some dynamics processing techniques and look at how to normalize a recording.

Applying processing to your recording

Something to keep in mind as you're refining your recording/editing/mastering process is that dynamics processing effects can be applied to the entire sound file at once, or to specific areas or tracks, one at a time. This gives you amazing flexibility when it comes to tweaking your sound. Some sections of your recording may need a little extra compression, while others need none. If you've included a song in your podcast, it may not need any processing (since the producer and musicians probably already spent many thousands of dollars and several sleepless nights to get it to sound just right), while the rest of your recording needs a great deal of smoothing out. By selectively processing your podcast recording, you can maximize the quality of your sound without overprocessing it unnecessarily.

Whichever editing/mastering application you're using, the steps involved in processing your sound are going to be pretty much the same as in any other application: decide what part of the sound you'd like to add an effect to, highlight that part of the sound, and add the effect.

Again, keep in mind that as we go through the following example, the specifics may vary from application to application, but the principles of processing are the same across all applications. We use BIAS Peak in this example.

1. Determine what area of your recording you'd like to process, and highlight that area.

2. Now you'll apply some compression. Highlight the audio section to be processed, and from the Plug-Ins pull-down menu select Insert 1 ➤ VST ➤ BIAS Squeez 1.0 (BIAS Squeez is the compressor included with the application).

3. Set the appropriate settings based on your audio and choose Bounce. (Other applications may use the term Apply or Process for this setting.) This will cause the compressor to process the audio.

You'll see that the variations in the dynamics of the sound wave are now reduced (see Figure 7-9), giving the podcast a tighter, more even sound. The loud sections aren't quite as loud in relation to the quieter sections. This gives your podcast a more professional sound and makes it much easier to listen to, especially through headphones or ear buds.

> For the sake of this example, we've taken the same audio and repeated it three times over so that you can see the differences the processing makes. The first section in Figure 7-9 (left of the first marker) is the raw audio with no processing applied. Notice that it is very dynamic.

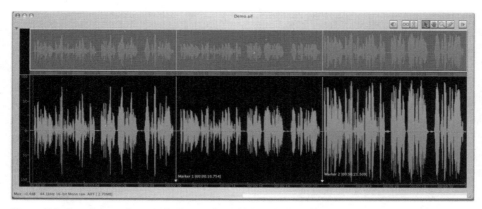

Figure 7-9. Sample waveform. Left: Raw audio. Middle: After compression applied. Right: Final with Gain applied.

As a rule of thumb, dynamics processes are usually added in the following order to maximize sonic quality:

1. Equalization (EQ)
2. Noise gate
3. Compression
4. Limiting

Other effects will typically come in before compression, but sometimes after.

Now we will increase the gain to maximize the benefit of having used the compressor. Highlight the audio to be processed and (in BIAS Peak) go to the DSP pull-down menu, select Change Gain, and set the amount of gain to be applied. In Figure 7-9, the gain applied was roughly 6dB, resulting in a peak of –0.2dB (more on that later). The final section (the rightmost section in Figure 7-9) represents the finished audio.

Remember that each of the three sections in Figure 7-9 is the exact same piece of audio repeated. Notice how the final section peaks at roughly the same level as the original piece, but that the lower-level information has been increased to give the audio a full, rich sound.

Normalizing individual tracks or sections

Normalizing means adjusting the volume or loudness of a piece of audio to a specific level (expressed in dB). This process is incredibly useful when you're putting together a podcast using bits of audio from various sources or from multiple recording sessions where the recording levels may be completely inconsistent. By adjusting the levels of each piece to a uniform loudness, the overall sound of the podcast will be consistent and much more professional.

For instance, say you've added some music to your voice recording (see Figure 7-10), but the music has much higher levels than your voice track. In fact, the music track is almost clipping, yet the voice track maintains a level of between –12dB and –6dB, give or take. To even out the sound of the podcast, you'll need to normalize the tracks, so they have a more unified sound (see Figure 7-11).

We've used a multitrack application for this example, but you can easily normalize sections of a continuous recording without using separate tracks. Simply highlight the area you want to normalize and apply the process.

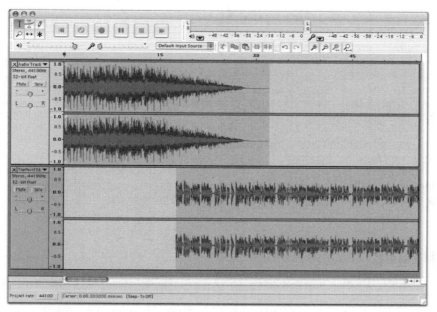

Figure 7-10. Example of normalization for a sample podcast where the music track (upper) is almost clipping, yet the voice track (lower) has nice, even levels

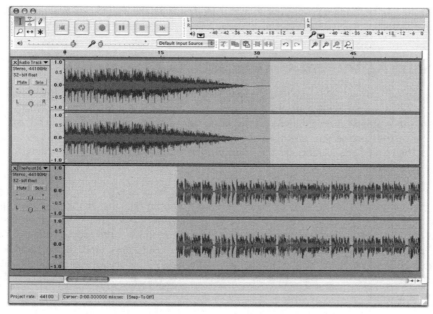

Figure 7-11. Example of normalization for a sample podcast after normalizing the music track to reduce its volume. The two tracks now mesh together beautifully. The change seems minor, but it makes a huge difference in sound quality.

Creating an audio mixdown

If you're using a multichannel workstation, you'll need to create a mixdown when your pieces are all in place. This is just a matter of taking your multilayered project and combining the layers into a single stereo or mono file. This file will be what you end up encoding into an MP3. How exactly you get your system to do a mixdown will depend on the editing software you're using. (In Audacity, this involves simply selecting File ➤ Export as WAV.)

Before you do your mixdown, triple-check that the volume of each of your individual tracks is exactly where you want it, and that the overall sound of the tracks, when played simultaneously, is what you want. You will not be able to make these kinds of adjustments to the resulting file, so do them now. Of course, if you're unhappy with the results, go back to your multitrack master, tweak your settings, and try again.

Adjusting the volume

Your podcast has come together nicely. There is just one last step in this final "mastering" process: you need to adjust the overall loudness. If the volume of your podcast is too low, it will be difficult if not impossible to listen to under anything but the most ideal circumstances. Since podcasts are meant to be listened to in just about any situation, it is critical that you ensure your show is loud enough (without being obnoxious).

The following sections discuss how to successfully adjust the volume of your recordings for the better.

Normalizing the entire podcast

Normalizing is also used to adjust the overall loudness of a file to a specific volume as the final stage of mastering. Something to keep in mind when doing this is that normalization doesn't have an effect on the dynamics of your recording in any way. It simply adjusts the volume of the section you are normalizing. So, if it makes the loud parts louder, it also makes the quiet parts louder and the noise louder. That is why a quality recording free of noise is so important.

Most compact discs these days are produced to be as loud as physically possible and are therefore mastered to as close to 0dB as possible. People feel that if the space is there, they might as well fill it. With this same thinking, many podcasters will master their shows to as close to 0dB as possible, so the file is as loud as possible. There are no solid rules for this, and no set of podcasting standards, yet serious podcasters tend to try to stick to audio standards set forth by the broadcast community. With the increasing opportunities for podcasters to have their material broadcast, it never hurts to put your best foot forward.

If you have mastered your audio correctly to this point, you can use peak normalization or a gain increase (same thing) to set your finished audio to –0.2dB. We, and many other podcasters, have been using this standard with great success. Remember, this guideline is based on our assumption that you have followed our instructions to this point. For most podcasters, this setting will result in superior audio that will stand head and shoulders above the rest. Count yourself fortunate to have stellar audio from the get-go; not all podcasters can make this claim. (But then, that's part of the reason you bought this book.)

What—still around? Not satisfied yet? You say stellar audio is not enough—you want the best? Well, so do we. What we're about to cover is for the über podcaster. It is by no means required, but since we do it, we thought we'd share it with you. It's the kind of thing you don't tell your podcast pals because you'll get blank stares in return—they'll have no idea what you're talking about. Meanwhile, everyone will keep complimenting you on your audio. Ready?

Calculating root-mean-square

To really, really get the perceived sound levels right, you need to understand **RMS**. RMS stands for **root-mean-square** (look out, math majors, here we come!), and it's a way to measure the magnitude of a set of numbers or, in our case, the overall magnitude (loudness) of a sound recording over time. To calculate RMS, you take all of your peak sound level readings, square each one, find the average of all of those squared numbers, and then take the square root of that number. Confused? So were we.

Here's the bottom line. Peak normalization measures the difference between the current peak level in the audio and the desired final peak level, and then increases the overall magnitude by that amount. As an example, in Figure 7-9 the peak level of the middle section of audio is –6.58dB. Peak normalization of the audio to a final peak level of –0.2dB simply increases all the levels by 6.38dB. The rightmost section of Figure 7-9 shows the results.

RMS normalization does something different. True RMS normalization looks at the average loudness of the audio and allows you to adjust that value. There are effectively three steps involved in RMS normalization:

1. Scan the audio to determine the current RMS loudness value.

2. Increase (or decrease) all samples so that the *average* RMS value achieves the new target.

3. As part of this process, compress or limit peaks that would otherwise exceed the selected threshold.

These steps result in gains that often can be seen as fattening up the lower and middle levels. While peak levels are easy to see visually, the average "loudness" (RMS level) is what your ear will hear. Thus, for the podcaster who wants to go the extra mile, having a set standard for RMS levels will result in consistent audio for all the shows that person produces.

Want to know what our suggested RMS settings are? Simple: −12dB RMS with a peak setting of −0.2dB.

Be aware that there is a downside to RMS, though. Not all audio-editing applications will do true RMS normalization. Usually, this kind of processing is reserved for professional-level audio-editing applications. Sound Forge, Adobe Audition, and some plug-ins such as Ozone 3 from iZotope (see Figure 7-12) can assist with RMS normalization.

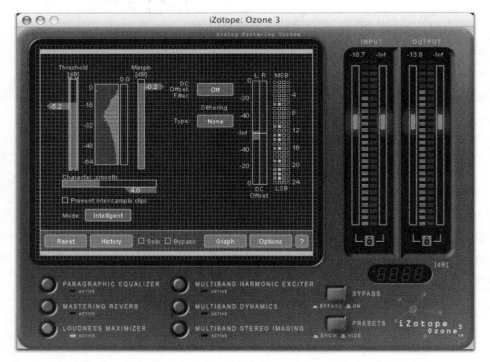

Figure 7-12. Adjusting the loudness based on RMS in iZotope's Ozone 3 using the Loudness Maximizer function

As we mentioned, RMS normalization is not available in all applications, but if your audio-editing software can do it, by all means take advantage of the functionality. You will be awash in compliments on the great quality of your recordings from your podcast listeners.

Summary

We can't emphasize enough the potential to make your podcast really great in the post-production and mastering stages. This is your chance to take out anything you don't like, tighten up anything you think is too loose, and add the connective tissue you'll need to make your podcast flow. These processes can make or break a podcast, turning a decent studio take into a piece of podcasting gold or an overproduced mess.

We'll end this chapter with a quick example of what finished audio should look like. The audio represented in Figure 7-13 was produced by our good friend Doug Kaye, who is responsible for "IT Conversations" (www.itconversations.com). When we first started podcasting, we used Doug's audio as an example of what to shoot for.

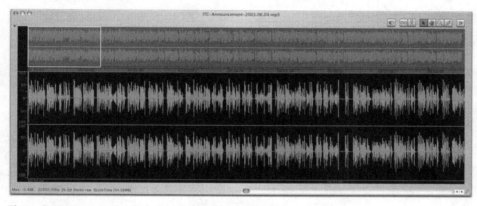

Figure 7-13. An example of what audio should look like

The production process is now officially over. You've done all to this episode you're ever going to do. You've buffed and polished your little baby until it shines like a diamond. (Well, shines like your first podcast, maybe.) Now it's time to encode your podcast to MP3 format. You don't really expect people to download your 250MB beauty, do you? In the next chapter, we'll take a look at the encoding process and how to use ID3 tags as embedded marketing tools.

8 PREPARING YOUR FILE

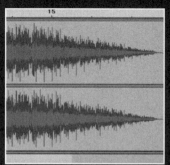

The last few steps before you upload your podcast for the world to listen to involve converting your sound file to the MP3 format and **tagging** it, so people know where the file came from, who was involved, and how to find more. Luckily, the hardest parts of preparing your podcast are over. Now you just have a little bit of processing to do and you're ready to send your podcast off into the wild cyber yonder.

In this chapter, we'll cover the following topics:

- Encoding and compressing to MP3
- Using podcast encoding standards
- Encoding with iTunes, Audacity, and LAME
- Adding ID3 tags and "album art"
- Following podcast naming conventions

Encoding and compressing to MP3

Your raw sound file is just too darned big to expect people to download it. Frankly, it would take too long for you to upload it. Maybe someday it will be no big deal to upload and download a 250MB file, but not today.

Because of today's file size limitations, podcasts are compressed using the MPEG-1 Audio Layer-3 (MP3) format. MP3 is the audio compression component (Layer 3) of MPEG-1. All that really means to us is that by encoding a sound file using the MP3 **codec** (**compression/decompression standard**), we can reduce the size of our sound files significantly. This compression is achieved by literally throwing out bits of information in the sound file. The codec is designed to balance file size with sound quality. It does this by trying to distinguish between those things that are important to maintain audio fidelity and intelligibility and those that are not.

Any way you slice it, compression deteriorates sound quality; however, a surprisingly good balance can be struck so that the audio is pleasing to the ear and the file is small enough for easy download. MP3 codecs do this by using **perceptual coding**, a process that uses algorithms designed to encode and compress the audio signal using psychoacoustic principles. In plain English, MP3 codecs try to compress the bits while maintaining fidelity for the human ear. Some do a better job than others, but with a little care, your sound files can come out sounding perfect for podcast purposes.

Podcast encoding standards

Nobody is likely to get an angry mob with pitchforks and torches together and come after you if you don't encode your podcast to what many are using as their "podcast standards," but why risk it? You never know!

The sample rate and bit rate at which you encode is completely up to you, but most podcasters stick to two relatively standard encoding settings, as shown in Table 8-1.

Table 8-1. General podcast sample and bit rates

Podcast Format	Sample Rate	Bit Rate	Compressed File Size
Talk	22.050kHz	64 kbps	≈ .5MB/minute
Music	44.100kHz	128 kbps	≈ 1MB/minute

Why these settings? First of all, they offer a great sound-to-compression ratio, providing wonderful sound reproduction considering their reasonable file sizes. Also, these bit rates and sample rates play well in the most players. Compatibility is key. New podcasters frequently wonder why their podcasts sound funny on some of the podcast players that the podcast directories have set up for sampling new shows. The reason is simple: they are using sampling rates other than those we have suggested. Nothing turns off a potential listener more than when she samples your show and finds that you sound like a chipmunk. We're all about getting heard, and if encoding at a different setting is going to keep even a few potential listeners away, we're not interested.

For maximum player compatibility, always encode in stereo. Even if the source recording is mono, encode in stereo. Some players can't handle mono MP3s. Don't worry, MP3s aren't like WAV files: a stereo MP3 isn't twice as big as one that's mono.

Now, all this being said, higher bit rates (and therefore fewer artifacts) would actually make more sense logically for *talk* podcasts, rather than music podcasts, since music is so full of sounds that artifacts are easily masked. In voice files—especially those with no background music—artifacts of the encoding process are much more noticeable (and potentially much more annoying). It is because of this that we have some very specific encoding advice (coming later in this chapter) that will all but eliminate artifacts, even at 64 kbps. So, let's get to encoding . . .

Encoding software

Many software packages available today will do a great job of encoding. You may even be able to export your file as an MP3 straight from your recording software. If not, a good place to start is with Apple's iTunes (www.apple.com/itunes) or Audacity using the LAME encoder. Both are free, easy to use, and available for both Windows and Mac OS X. Frankly, you may end up using both applications: Audacity to record, one or the other to encode, and then iTunes to manage the information stored within the MP3 as ID3 tags.

For the sake of demonstration, let's first encode your new podcast using iTunes, and then we'll show you how to incorporate LAME MP3 encoding into the iTunes system. After that, we'll go through the same process using Audacity with LAME. These steps differ from the steps you'd take in other applications, but the general concepts and settings are the same. If you know you'll be using Audacity, go ahead and skip down to that section now.

8

Encoding in iTunes

To encode in iTunes, follow these steps:

1. Launch iTunes.

2. Select iTunes ➤ Preferences to access the iTunes Preferences window.

3. Click the Importing button at the top of the Preferences window. The Importing panel will appear, as shown in Figure 8-1.

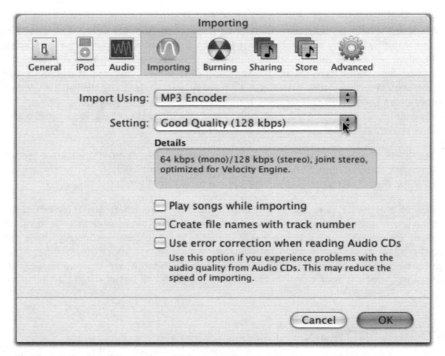

Figure 8-1. Settings for a podcast in the Importing panel in iTunes Preferences

4. Set the Import Using option to MP3 Encoder.

5. In the Setting drop-down list, choose either Good Quality (128 kbps) for a music podcast or Custom for a talk show.

6. If you chose Custom, the MP3 Encoder window will open (see Figure 8-2). Set the Stereo Bit Rate to 64 kbps and the Sample Rate to either 22.050 kHz or Auto. Set the Channels to Stereo and set Stereo Mode to Joint Stereo. Click OK.

7. Check that the information in the Details area (see Figure 8-1) in the Importing window reflects the settings you were aiming for:

- **Talk**: 64 kbps, 22.050 kHz
- **Music**: 128 kbps, 44.100 kHz

8. If everything looks good, click OK.

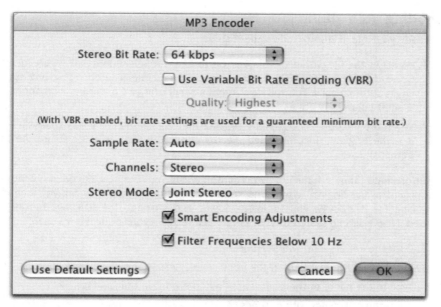

Figure 8-2. Setting your bit rate and sample rate for a talk-style podcast in the iTunes MP3 Encoder

iTunes will use the settings you just established every time you encode a file to MP3 (until you change them).

Importing into iTunes

Now you need to import the sound file into iTunes. There are several ways of doing this, but the way we recommend here will sidestep some of the idiosyncrasies of iTunes. When a sound file is imported into iTunes, it is automatically moved into the iTunes folder on your hard drive and renamed based on the ID3 tags (we'll get to those soon). At this point, it's likely that the file you used to be able to easily find is now buried deep inside the iTunes labyrinth on your hard drive. Instead of falling into a mini wild goose chase, simply follow these steps:

1. Create a new directory within iTunes (File ➤ New Playlist) and give it a unique name such as Encode or Convert. This playlist will be for sorting and encoding your podcasts.

2. Find your edited sound file and drag it to the playlist window in iTunes. The file will then be imported, renamed, and so forth, but it will be easy to access through the playlist.

3. Change the name of your WAV/AIFF file to something easily recognizable, such as My First Podcast. Doing so will actually adjust the title in the ID3 tags for the file. We'll explain this in greater detail in a moment, but for now just know that you'll want to change the name of your podcast within the tags so it is easier to find within iTunes.

Encoding your file in iTunes

To encode your file in iTunes, follow these steps:

1. Highlight the file within the playlist. Go to Convert Selection to MP3 (Advanced ➤ Convert Selection to MP3) to start encoding your file. The encoding process will begin automatically. You will notice that a small orange Converting icon appears in the left column of iTunes.

2. When the encoding is complete, rename the original in such a way that you know it is the original, uncompressed file (by adding original, wav, or aiff to the title, perhaps).

The unfortunate thing is that iTunes won't automatically put the new, encoded file into the same playlist as the original. Why? Who knows. That would be too easy. So, you'll need to go looking for it. Luckily, you took our advice and changed the ID3 tags before you encoded. Now a simple search of your library will retrieve your podcast in a snap:

1. Click the Library icon within iTunes.

2. Click within the text field in the upper right, next to the magnifying glass.

3. Type in the name of the podcast as you entered it in the ID3 tags.

4. All of the other files within iTunes will fall away, leaving only your new podcast MP3 (see Figure 8-3). Drag that MP3 into the folder you created before encoding.

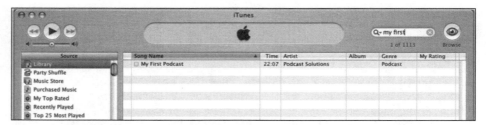

Figure 8-3. Searching the iTunes Library for your new podcast

You've just successfully created an MP3 version of your podcast in iTunes. Now you're ready to get all the tags, the artwork, and the information for the Comments tag in order (you'll see this shortly). If you're interested in a slightly different way of encoding to MP3 using iTunes that will yield potentially superior audio after compression, read on. If you're happy with the results you've achieved in iTunes (you most likely are), skip to the section titled "Updating ID3 tags and artwork."

LAME

LAME (which originally stood for **LAME Ain't an MP3 Encoder**) is an open source MP3 encoder that offers, in our opinion, superior compression. (A lot of MP3 encoder enthusiasts agree with us on this point. Entire discussion forums are devoted to how to squeeze every last drop of quality out of a file using LAME.) It is highly configurable, letting you manipulate how the file will be encoded. Because most standard MP3 encoders are built with simplicity in mind, they make some compromises in how they encode the file. They are usually optimized for music rather than speech, a preference that might be out of line with most podcasts. LAME allows you to select very specific settings for how you want it to go about its job. It is not a freestanding application, but it can be built in to, or used in conjunction with, other applications. For geeks, it can also be accessed from the command line. (If that last sentence doesn't excite you or you don't know what it's referring to, just forget we mentioned it.)

In the steps in this section, we'll use iTunes-LAME to do a better job encoding than we just did with iTunes alone.

Throw away unnecessary audio. Is this necessary? No, but it will give you the best-sounding MP3 processing money can buy. Use an 80Hz hi-pass and a 13Khz low-pass filter. Even at 128 kbps, MP3s don't do a great job with audio in the highest octave of human hearing. Likewise at the very bottom. If you eliminate this information (data) yourself before encoding, you help the encoder's psychoacoustic model understand what's really important and what's not. More bits will be dedicated to what you really care about: the sound you can and want to hear. You can do this in the audio editing software prior to encoding if you are using iTunes or a similar application. Alternatively, if you are using LAME as detailed next, you can do it with encoding options.

iTunes-LAME

Follow these steps to use iTunes-LAME:

1. Install iTunes-LAME. (Available at http://blacktree.com/apps/iTunes-LAME/.)
2. Launch iTunes-LAME.
3. In the playlist that you created earlier in iTunes, make sure the radio button next to the name of the WAV/AIFF version of the podcast is selected.
4. In the text field within iTunes-LAME, type in your settings. To start, try -h-b 128 for high-quality, 128 kbps constant bit rate (music; see Figure 8-4), and -h-b 64 –resample 22.05 for high-quality, 64 kbps constant bit rate (talk). To change these settings, refer to the iTunes-LAME Encoding Options help by clicking the question mark button.

As we mentioned, you can control a lot in LAME. Here is a setting one of us has been using for a high-quality talk-format show: --preset cbr 64 -a --lowpass 15 --lowpass-width 1 --highpass 0.054 --highpass-width 0.04 --cwlimit 7 --resample 22.05 --noshort. As you can see, there is a lot of power built into LAME. The settings just presented are a jumping-off point. Frankly, if you dove into this section on LAME, then you'll probably want to experiment to find the best settings for your particular situation.

8

Figure 8-4. Using iTunes-LAME for superior encoding

5. Click the Import button. The encoding will begin, with progress being shown in a drop-down window within iTunes-LAME.

The good news is that when you encode this way, LAME puts the new, encoded version of the file into the same spot as the original. So now both versions are in the same playlist, and you won't need to do any hunting. Phew!

Encoding using Audacity with LAME

LAME is not built into Audacity—you must download it and tell Audacity where it is. Then you can export your sound files as MP3s directly from your Audacity project window.

1. Download LAME.Lib (see http://audacity.sourceforge.net/help/faq?s=install &item=lame-MP3 for complete download information).

2. Unstuff or unzip the file and copy it to your hard drive.

3. Open the file you'd like to convert to MP3. When it is open, go to File ➤ Export As MP3.

4. Audacity will ask you where you'd like to save your file. Choose the appropriate directory/folder and click Save.

5. The first time you select Export As MP3 in Audacity, you are asked to locate the Lame.Lib file (you are asked to do this only the first time). Once you've found the file for Audacity, a window will appear for the ID3 tag information (we know, we know—we can't put off getting into it much longer!): Name, Artist, Album, and so on. Don't worry about those fields much right now. When you get to the next section, you'll really sink your teeth into using those fields to your advantage. For now, just enter your name and the name of the podcast.

6. Click the OK button. The encoding begins!

Here's how to change the bit rate and sample rate of your encoding:

- **Windows**: Go to Audacity Preferences (*CTRL*+P) and click the File Format tab. In the lower-left side of the tab, you can select a new sample rate from the Bit Rate drop-down (see Figure 8-5).

- **Mac**: Go to Audacity ➤ Preferences, and then click the File Formats tab. At the bottom of the Formats window, you'll see the MP3 Export Setup area. Within the drop-down menu, you will find several sample rates to choose from. Choose the sample rate at which you want to encode and click OK.

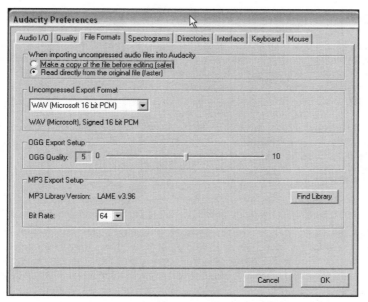

Figure 8-5. The File Formats tab within the Preferences window enables you to change the sample rate of your LAME encoder.

The encoding is finished. Now your rather large master sound file is a shadow of its former size. You have just a couple more small steps to perform before you upload: putting in the ID3 information and changing the filename.

Updating ID3 tags and artwork

You can store plenty of information in your MP3 file. Since your podcast will be uploaded, downloaded, and potentially passed around the Internet, you want to make sure that when it ends up in someone's media player, it's easy to discover where the file came from, who was involved in creating it, and how to find out more information about the file.

This information is stored in the form of **ID3 tags**, which are chunks of data that media players can read, making information about each MP3 file easily available. Since these tags were originally designed for handling music files, they are very music-centric: Name, Artist, Album, and so on. Still, as podcasters we use these tags to make sure people know the name of our podcast and podcaster, our URL, our listener voice mail phone number, our e-mail address, and any other information, including artwork, that we don't want separated from the file.

Creating ID3 tags

In this section, you're going to change the ID3 tags of your new podcast in iTunes. While many podcasters have come to rely on iTunes to manage their ID3 tags (remember, iTunes has a free Windows version), a number of good ID3 tagging applications have been built for all computer platforms, so just use whatever you are comfortable with. (Tag & Rename is a powerful ID3 editor for Windows only, for example.)

First, you must find your file within iTunes. If it is not readily available in a playlist but is in the Library, find it using the steps outlined in the "Encoding your file in iTunes" section (see Figure 8-3). Once you've tracked down your MP3, follow these steps:

1. Click the track to highlight it.

2. Go to File ➤ Get Info (⌘+*I* in Mac OS; *CTRL+I* in Windows). A window will open with several tabs to choose from: Summary, Info, Options, and Artwork.

3. Click the Summary tab. You'll want to double-check that you have the right file. If your original is still in iTunes, at this point it will have the same name as the MP3 version. The summary information appears, giving you the file's size, sample rate, bit rate, format, and so on. Make sure the format says MPEG-1, Layer 3, and that the sample and bit rates are what you expect from your encoding settings. If everything looks acceptable, click Info.

4. In the Info area, you'll see several text fields (Name, Artist, Album, etc.). These fields represent different metadata for the file. Obviously, you're free to put anything you want into these fields, but you'll likely find that conforming to the following guidelines makes your podcast more accessible (see Figure 8-6):

   - **Name**: The name of that edition of your podcast.

   - **Artist**: Your name/your group's name.

   - **Album**: The name of the podcast (series).

   > *Please note that because MP3 devices such as the iPod and the Zen have small screens, you may want to truncate or abbreviate some words in your podcast's name to make the information easier to read on these players.*

   - **Track Number**: The number of that edition of your podcast (e.g., if it is the fourth show, insert 4).

   - **Comments**: Your URL, e-mail address, listener voice mail phone number, "Thanks for listening" message, or whatever.

   - **Genre**: Insert Podcast, which is universally recognized as the appropriate genre tag for ease of sorting.

5. Click OK to save your changes.

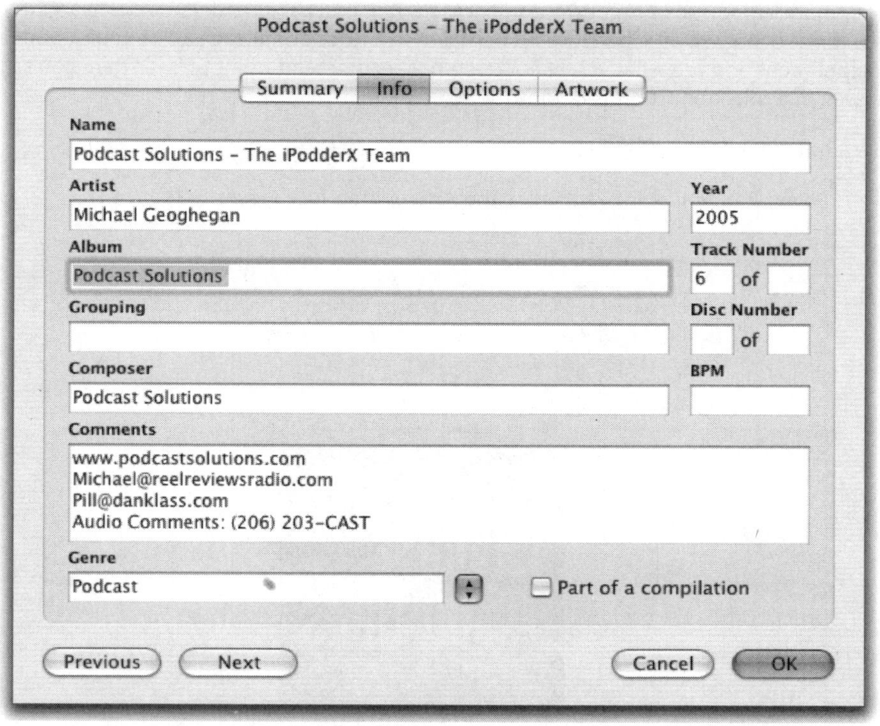

Figure 8-6. Completing ID3 tags in iTunes

The Comments field is capable of holding quite a bit of information, so include in that field any and all information you want to. However, the problem with inserting a lot of information into this field is that you can't add a line break from within iTunes. If you press the *ENTER/RETURN* key, you will activate the OK button instead of putting in a carriage return. Oops. Since you will most likely be putting the same information in the Comments field for each show, we recommend typing up your show information in a text editing application, and then cutting and pasting the information into the Comments field each time you do your tagging. Voilà!

Adding "album art"

You can add a piece of "album art" to your podcast MP3 file. This is a great way to include a visual representation of your show right in the file. For people who don't visit podcast websites, this may be their only exposure to any visual representation of your show. Make it good! The artwork pops up currently in iTunes and in iPodderX, and it may appear who knows where else in the future, so use this feature to its fullest advantage.

Your album artwork can be up to a full screen, but it usually renders more clearly if you keep it reasonably small. There are no hard and fast rules about the size of your album art, so experiment and see what you like. We do not recommend using GIFs, as they don't render well if reduced in size for viewing.

Here's how to add album art:

1. Select File ➤ Get Info and click the Artwork tab (see Figure 8-7).

Figure 8-7. Inserting art into MP3 ID3 tags

2. Click the Add button.

3. Find the image you want to use on your hard drive and double-click to select it. The artwork will be imported into iTunes and added to your ID3 tags.

4. Click OK to save your changes.

Naming your MP3 file

Apparently, some podcast listeners are picky. Not only are they picky about how the information is stored in the ID3 tags, but they want to have the podcasts named in a certain way, too. The name of your podcast has absolutely no bearing on whether or not it gets downloaded, but following podcast naming conventions makes podcasts easier to sort through on cluttered hard drives and keeps picky podcast listeners nice and calm.

Note that naming your MP3 file is different from assigning a name in the ID3 tags. One is the name "on the file," and the other is the name "within the file," respectively. As an example, in Figure 8-6 we named the podcast "Podcast Solutions – The iPodderX Team." When the file is downloaded and played in an MP3 application, that is the name that appears. However, the downloaded MP3 file itself is named PS-2005-05-12.mp3. As you can see, these names are quite different: one is designed for easy organization on the Internet, and the other is designed for easy organization once a listener has downloaded the file.

Following naming conventions

You'll need to set up for yourself a naming convention for your podcast that includes the name of the podcast (or an abbreviation of the name) and the number of that edition or the date of its creation/publication. How you handle the naming is up to you, but most podcast listeners will at the very least demand that you are consistent.

One of the most common styles of filenaming is the classic *Podcast initials-edition number* method. So if your podcast is called "Podcast Solutions" and this is the sixth episode, you would name the file PS-6. This is a nice and clear way to name your show. The problem with this sample name is that once you get to the tenth show, the shows will be listed out of order on most people's hard drives. So, to compensate, change the name to PS-06. There, now the problem is fixed . . . as long as you have no intention of doing more than 99 shows. So, you may add another zero or two. Eventually, you realize that this is getting silly and if you're doing that many shows, how will people remember which is which? If someone wants to refer back to a previous show, how can they easily remember which show to look for?

This leads us to another common naming convention: the old tried-and-true *Podcast initials with date* method. So, with this in mind, the sample podcast becomes PS-2005-05-12, meaning it was published on April 12, 2005. Naming a file in this way seems to require that you begin with the year, then the month, and finally the date (although Europeans may do it year-date-month). This makes the podcasts easy to sort through on crowded hard drives and makes it easier for listeners to find an old show, as long as they can guess when they first heard it. You'll notice a lot of variation in filenaming among podcasters, but the vast majority includes the publication date in their filenames.

To make things easy on yourself, here's a tip if you're using iTunes to do your encoding and/or tagging. Instead of hunting through your hard drive for the finished MP3, simply drag it from a playlist onto your desktop. That way, it's at your fingertips. Rename the file there, and it will be easy to find for uploading.

8

A word about foresight and files

We may have said this already, but either way it bears repeating: *Save the master of your edited file.* You never know what the future brings, and you may want to repurpose that podcast later. Whether you want to syndicate the file's content to radio, press it onto audio CDs, or simply make it available at a higher bit rate, you'll be glad you have the original file.

Summary

Well, that's it! You've made a podcast. From start to finish, from planning to encoding, you've done it all. Congratulations! (Is all this back patting getting sickening?) You've prepped your file by compressing it down to a manageable size and tagging it with all the information about your podcast that anyone might need. Now it's time to get that baby out into the world and globetrotting from media player to media player. You've raised it right—now it's got to leave the nest and fly. Let's get the podcast onto the Internet in its own space, and then let's get it downloaded and into your listener's headphones.

9 **SERVING IT UP**

  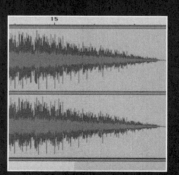

It's time to get your podcast on the Internet and establish its web presence. The process is really pretty straightforward. First, you'll find a place on the Internet to host your files. Next, you'll upload your files and set up a website or blog to tell everyone what your show is about. Finally, you'll create the feed to let subscribers know that there is a new podcast available for download.

There are many ways to handle setting up a website for your show, and we'll offer several suggestions on how you can get set up without having to take a night class in web design. It is important to note that the decisions you make at this point will have an impact on how your feed is created and maintained as well as where your files will reside. While that might not sound like too much of a big deal, some of these decisions are akin to deciding to move to a new house. Once you get settled, deciding to move again can be a big hassle, so you need to plan carefully. We'll take things step-by-step so we don't get too far ahead of ourselves.

Here's what the chapter covers in a nutshell:

- Registering and securing your domain
- Hosting and uploading your MP3s
- Creating your website
- Setting up an RSS feed

Registering your own domain

You don't need to have your own domain to do a podcast. As long as your MP3s are on the web and people know how to find them, your podcast will be heard. Many podcasters have a **URL** (**Uniform Resource Locator**; the address you type in your browser) completely unrelated to their podcast. However, in our opinion, the best move will always be to secure your own personalized domain name, rather than choosing some less-than-ideal free hosting solution. For example, the location of your podcast will be much more memorable if it's located at www.myfarmingpodcast.com, rather than www.freeuserhosting. org/~user125448_ntvvvgh06/webfeed/default.html.

A **domain name** is your "dot-com" (or dot-org, or dot-net, etc.). It's your personal address on the Internet that you control and maintain. You should be careful to choose and register a domain *before* you name your podcast. As hinted at earlier, we recommend coming up with as intuitive a name as possible. As another example, take one of our podcasts, "Grape Radio." Want to guess what its web address is? We made it easy: www.graperadio. com. As you might imagine, if someone were to hear the name of the podcast, it would be easy for that person to also remember its web address.

However, this late in the "Internet land grab," finding a suitable domain name is a bit of a crapshoot. You will be surprised at how many domains have long since been snatched up. If you wait until you have a few shows under your belt, you may find that the domain you want is taken. Instead, first think of several names for your podcast and see which domains are available. This is the reality of doing business on the Internet—to a certain extent, the availability of a domain name will dictate the name of your podcast.

Unlike most of the early podcasters, I never had a blog or website before I started pod-casting. Since most podcasters were using a blog as their launch pad, I went ahead and set up my site. `www.mwgblog.com` (easy enough to remember, right?). Things went swim-mingly as I started doing my podcast "Reel Reviews – Films Worth Watching."

As my show got more popular, I began to realize that it would be much easier if the name of my site were closer to the name of my show. Truth be told, I did not really even consider myself a blogger—I considered myself a podcaster. The only reason I had a blog was so I could podcast. I also had a few interesting reactions from movie studios when I called about getting advance copies of DVDs. Everything would go great until I gave them the name of my site, MWGblog.com. More than once I got the response, "Oh, it's just a blog." I knew that, right or wrong, my credibility had taken a hit.

For a few months I toyed with new names for my site. The person who owned `www.reelreviews.com` would not return my phone calls, so I settled on `www.reelreviewsradio.com`. The problem was that I had thousands of people who had sub-scribed to my feed at `www.mwgblog.com`, as well as countless links and references in the press all pointing to the old site. To ensure that all the old links would forward correctly to the new site and, more important, that my subscribers would continue to receive the show, I had to have someone come in and help with all kinds of custom coding. It was a huge hassle.

Learn from my mistake. Plan for success with your podcast and take your time when naming your show, website, and domain.

—Michael Geoghegan

To secure and use a domain name of your own, you need to register it and then have the domain hosted. Registering a domain name is easy and inexpensive. It wasn't long ago that Network Solutions handled all domain name registrations. The company continues to do a terrific job, but as you can imagine, when Network Solutions was the only one doing it, registration fees were rather high. Nowadays, dozens of companies handle domain regis-tration, including Network Solutions, Register.com, Yahoo!, and GoDaddy.com (the service we both use).

Securing your domain

Once you've decided on several possible domain names, it's time to see what's available, choose an available domain, and register that domain in your name. It's a very simple process that is fairly uniform from site to site:

1. Go to a registration website (see the previous section for a selection of registration sites).

2. Search for your first choice of URL. Simply enter your prospective domain name into the Search field and press ENTER/RETURN.

3. The search will give you its results, showing the status of the domain you entered and offering up several similar options that you may also want to register. If the domain you want is available, select it and proceed to the next step in the process.

   If the domain you want is not available, check over the list of proposed alternatives to see if anything strikes your fancy. These options will most likely be less appealing versions of the domain you searched, with terms like "online" or "site" tacked onto the end. Also, you may want to consider searching for the .net and .org versions of your domain name of choice, in case that would work better for you than the other names on your list. If not, proceed to the next domain name idea on your list and repeat the search process. Continue until you find an available domain name that you like and that fits your podcast.

4. You may be asked if you want to also register the .net, .org, .biz, and so on versions of your domain, to protect the name. Doing so is entirely up to you—it mostly depends on whether you feel not doing so would weaken your "brand."

5. If you are an individual (as opposed to a business), we recommend opting to have your domain listed as "private" in the WHOIS database. The database lists complete information on the registrar of every domain in cyberspace, including the registrar's address and phone number. Unless you want this information made available to everyone and anyone on the Internet, pay the extra couple of dollars for some peace of mind.

Once you own your domain, you can either have it point to an existing website or blog, or have it hosted by a hosting service. This will all make more sense when we talk about websites and blogs in a moment.

Hosting your MP3s

You need to find somewhere for your podcasts to live. They need to be posted on the Internet and made available for download. How do you do that? Well, we're assuming that you don't have access to Internet storage through your job or school and that you will need to get some of your own. To tell the truth, you may already have Internet space available for your use and you don't even know it.

Hosting through your ISP

We're going to take a leap of faith and assume that you have Internet access at your home or office. You surf the Net, you check e-mail, and you pay a monthly bill or two. What you may not realize (because perhaps it was not a concern until now) is that many Internet service providers (ISPs) make hosting and storage space available as part of their service package. Many ISPs include in their service agreements a set amount of Internet space to be used for a personal website, file storage, and so forth. That space is just sitting there, ready for your podcasts.

However, you have to be careful. Most of these ISP hosting plans are set up with the expectation that the user will be hosting only tiny web pages or the occasional photo album. They are usually not priced to accommodate the demands of a successful podcast.

Read your ISP's service agreement carefully. There will undoubtedly be restrictions on the amount of traffic passing through the service (i.e., **bandwidth**) that is allowed per month. Surpassing that bandwidth allocation can be very expensive.

We do not recommend that you use this type of storage as the only hosting solution for your MP3s. It is too limited. But when you're just getting started, this might be an option, since it's there and already paid for.

Deciding on a web hosting provider

You will be much better served by finding yourself a bona fide web hosting company to provide file storage and hosting for your site. These companies offer domain hosting, e-mail forwarding (to you@yourdomain.com), storage, and a decent amount of allotted traffic per month. Depending on the service plan, you will be provided enough storage and bandwidth to keep your podcast humming along for months.

Or will you? As your podcast becomes more popular, bandwidth will become an issue. If you're doing a 30-minute podcast that is a 15MB MP3, and 1,000 people download it the first month, that is 15GB of traffic for that month. As you can see, it can add up quickly, especially if your plan provides only 30GB of bandwidth per month. Do the math and get a rough idea of how much storage and bandwidth you'll need per month before settling on a plan for your hosting. It is important that you do some very careful comparison-shopping here to find a plan that meets your needs and budget.

While we'd love to give you recommendations, there are just too many hosting companies to list here, and they change their plans all the time in order to remain competitive. One suggestion is to post questions to some of the podcast discussion boards we've mentioned in the book and find out what services others are using to host their files and would be willing to recommend. You might even find that some of the more popular podcasters are hosting their shows from multiple sites to spread the bandwidth load of their shows. These are still the relatively early days of podcasting, and new and improved podcast hosting solutions seem to be popping up every week.

If you don't carefully approach the bandwidth problem, you could easily get burned. Most plans charge subscribers exorbitantly high fees for going over their allotted bandwidth. It is crucial that you not only look at the storage and bandwidth offered by each plan (like anyone would, right?), but also *compare the cost for going over your bandwidth*. These costs can add up quickly, and you could suddenly be faced with a huge bill you didn't expect. It's like mobile phone overages—only worse.

One way to get around the bandwidth concern is to find a web hosting service provider that does not restrict your podcast traffic. Liberated Syndication (www.libsyn.com) is a web hosting company created especially to serve the needs of podcasters. They seemingly originated the "no bandwidth restrictions" model of service, which means that (unlike most other service providers) you will not be penalized with higher charges if and when your podcast becomes popular. Regardless of the number of people downloading your files, you pay only for the amount of *storage* you want to use, *not the download traffic*. This is ideal for the needs of the average podcaster. Many of the music podcasters we've spoken to use Liberated Syndication; it's perfect for them, since their files are larger than those of talk shows (more on that shortly).

9

Whatever web hosting service provider you choose, make sure to read all the fine print, and make certain that you understand everything you're signing up for. Most services involve no long-term commitment, but you don't want to end up with a surprisingly high bill that could have easily been avoided.

Uploading your MP3s

You may be able to upload your MP3s to your new hosting provider via the host's website. Most hosts have a way to easily choose files from your hard drive and upload them from your browser window. You will also have the opportunity to make new folders and subdirectories within your space. While this may seem like the easiest way to do it, it can actually be very frustrating, and it can be too big a burden for a browser to handle. Usually there is no way to monitor the progress of your uploads and no way to upload in the background while you take care of other business. Well, we're all about taking care of other business, so we recommend uploading through the browser only as a last resort. Instead, you should be using an FTP client.

A **File Transfer Protocol (FTP)** client is a software application that makes it easy to upload files to the web. There are many to choose from for every platform, all with the same basic functions. Check out Cyberduck (http://cyberduck.ch; open source and free to use) and Fetch (http://fetchsoftworks.com) for some reliable Mac FTP clients. If you're running Windows, you might want to look into SmartFTP (www.smartftp.com; free for personal use) and FileZilla (http://filezilla.sourceforge.net; open source and completely free).

The object of using a decent FTP client is to make uploading as effortless as possible. To get your FTP client running smoothly, you'll need the host name, the username/ID information, and the password your hosting service provided you (see Figure 9-1). This information will be stored in the FTP client, so that each time you go to connect to your server space, you'll be able connect easily. *If you have any trouble setting up the FTP client and getting it to connect successfully, contact your hosting provider.* They will give you all the information you need to get you connected properly.

Figure 9-1. The New Connection window in Fetch. All FTP clients will ask you for the same basic information: host, user ID/username, and password.

Once you are connected, you may see a series of directories and folders within the account window, many of which will have cryptic names. Check with your hosting provider about which folders to use for which files. Odds are excellent that if one of the folders is named public_html, that is the folder into which you should put all your files. (But check with your ISP to be sure!) Click the public_html folder to open it. Now you're ready to upload.

> *As a matter of organization, you may want to create a subfolder for your podcasts to keep them separate from any image files, web pages, and so forth that will undoubtedly end up in your server space. Whether you do this or not, you need to know exactly where you're putting your MP3s, so you'll know the address of each. This is essential for when you're linking to the podcasts from your website and for inclusion in your RSS feed.*

Assuming you've uploaded your podcast into a folder called MP3, your podcast MP3's address might be http://www.yourdomain.com/MP3/podcast1.mp3. This means that your file podcast1.mp3 is within the MP3 folder on your domain's "root" directory. If anyone were to go to that URL using his or her browser, your podcast would start to play.

Creating your podcast's website

Don't worry, you're not going to have to learn HTML, PHP, or anything else to get yourself set up with a website. You don't need an elaborate website, with pages and pages of information, links, shopping carts, and animated buttons. What you do need, however, is a place where your listeners (and potential listeners) can go to find out about you and your show. At the very least, you need a web page with the name of your podcast, links to the MP3 files, and information on how to subscribe to your show. You can accomplish this by setting up a blog or creating a standard HTML website.

A **weblog**, or **blog**, is a type of website (usually created using dynamic code linked to a database) where information can be posted to the web almost instantly. The person maintaining the blog (the **blogger**) can easily type in new text and, with little or no formatting, publish the text to the web. That text can then be read by web-based newsreaders, since most blogs are set up to output an RSS feed that these newsreaders can interpret and display. Converting a blog feed to a podcast feed is relatively simple; therefore, most podcasters maintain their podcast's web presence by using a blog.

Some podcasters prefer to use a traditional HTML website for their podcasts. (HTML is the standard computer language that website code is written in.) HTML websites are made up of static information, so to update them, you have to directly update the HTML pages, which can be more time consuming than blogging. However, HTML is also easier to understand from a code point of view.

The choice is up to you regarding which to use, so let's look at a few pros and cons of each, to give you an idea of which way you'd like to go. We'll also examine some of the tools you can use to get your site up and running.

9

Blog site vs. HTML site

In general, blogs are easy to update and usually require minimal knowledge of HTML. People with very little web development experience can set them up, because they usually feature a fairly intuitive creation procedure. They also usually have fairly robust support communities.

On the other hand, serious HTML website creation tools can be a bit intimidating to novices, although, once you get the hang of their basic functions, they are pretty straightforward. Also, with an HTML site your imagination is your only limit. You can do whatever you please, and you don't have to work within the framework of the blog service or software.

Table 9-1 shows a comparison of other considerations when choosing between a blog and a traditional HTML website for your podcast.

Table 9-1. Blog and HTML Website Comparison

Consideration	Blog	HTML Website
Uploading updated pages and images	Blogs upload pages with the click of a button. With some blogs, images can be uploaded from within the blog software; sometimes the images are uploaded separately.	Many web tools offer convenient, seamless uploading.
Layout and dating	Blogs will format your "postings" based on the format of the blog's template. Very little layout/design is required for each new post, and adding new postings, podcasts, and so on is nearly foolproof. This ease comes at a price, however, in that it is often difficult to customize individual postings and pages, and changing the template of the blog changes the look of the entire website. To some, this is quite an advantage; to others, it is a hindrance. It all depends on the amount of control the user is hoping to have over the site.	Web tools offer much greater flexibility in creating different page layouts. With that flexibility comes the ability, of course, to mess things up if you're in a hurry and not accustomed to web design conventions and standards. You have not only the luxury of designing each new posting, but also the burden of making sure each posting works properly. HTML is completely static, so it's much more difficult to make a mess of in general.
Feed creation	Most blogs will either create an RSS feed that can handle your podcast enclosure automatically or at least create a feed that can be converted to RSS.	If you create your site using HTML, the RSS feed must be created separately, either by hand or using a stand-alone application.

Consideration	Blog	HTML Website
Feedback	Most blogs are set up to accept "comments" from readers/listeners. With the click of a button, people give you feedback about your podcast, chime in on your latest topic, and tell you about themselves. This is a great way to maintain a dialogue between you and your audience, and it's a must-have for any podcast.	HTML sites are not set up to accept comments as easily as a blog. If you choose to go the HTML route, look into setting up a message board or forum, so listeners can "discuss" your shows online.
Price	Most blog software is free, although you may need to find someone to help you get it up and functioning properly.	A good, high-end web development application is expensive.

OK, from the comparison in Table 9-1, there doesn't seem to be much of a contest: an HTML site has its advantages, but a blog setup usually comes out on top. The use of blogs is so commonplace in podcasting that you really can't go wrong setting up shop that way. Ultimately, you may even choose to use both solutions: a blog for new podcast posting and feed creation and an HTML site for other areas of your website (links page, bio page, contact information, etc.). You won't regret it.

Building your HTML site

If you're serious about creating a website using traditional web development tools, we strongly suggest going with one of the two 800-pound gorillas in the web development game: Macromedia Dreamweaver or Adobe GoLive. Now, as we've said before, these packages can be intimidating at first. They are simple enough for a beginner to set up a basic page and robust enough to handle just about any requirement you'll ever have down the road. You do not need to know anything about programming to set up a professional-looking site. Adding pictures, creating hyperlinks, and embedding movies and Flash animations is all automated. As long as you know which button to click, you are set.

> *For a good example of an HTML-based podcast site, check out our friends Greg and Lisa from "Viva Podcast" (http://vivapodcast.com). In talking to Greg, he pointed out that one of the advantages of an HTML-based podcast site is that you are not constrained by a template, as you are with a blog. Using HTML, you are free to make each page look any way you please.*

9

Choosing your blog platform

While we wanted to be fair, it's probably clear that we are more in favor of using a blog as the launching pad for a podcast. You have many choices when it comes to picking your blog service or software. Like anything else, each has its pros and cons. In the sections that follow, we'll cover the three most common methods used by podcasters today:

- The fast and easy Blogger
- The just as fast and slightly more functional blog offered free to Liberated Syndication users
- The very complex but rewarding "serious blogging" tools WordPress and Moveable Type

Blogger + FeedBurner = easy and free

If you want to create a blog quickly and painlessly, and you already have a way of uploading and storing your MP3 files, then Blogger (www.blogger.com) may be for you. There's almost nothing to set up, there's nothing to learn but some simple HTML (to include pictures and links within your posts, as shown in Table 9-2), and the service is free.

The Blogger home page claims you can get a blog going in three steps, and it's true. All you need to do is create an account, name your blog, and choose a template for the look and color palette of your site. Blogger has dozens of templates to choose from, all created by professional graphic designers, so finding one that suits your needs is easy. Eventually, you may want to play around with the template of your blog to customize it a bit, but Blogger gives you enough choices up front to get you started.

You need to make sure your Blogger blog is creating a feed from your posts. The major drawback of using Blogger is that (as of this writing) Blogger can output only what is called an **Atom feed**. This is a type of news feed similar to RSS. However, since most of podcasting is built around RSS, you'll need to convert the Atom feed to a podcasting-friendly RSS 2.0. Luckily for us, FeedBurner (www.feedburner.com) offers a service that will take the Atom feed from Blogger and convert it to RSS for podcasting.

Setting up your blog at Blogger To set up a Blogger blog, simply go to www.blogger. com, sign up, decide on a name for your blog, create a URL for your blog (typically http://yourpodcast.blogspot.com), and choose a template. Voilà! Your blog has been created. Once that's done, you're immediately taken to a window where you can type in the text for your first post. Simply type whatever you want into the text field and press *RETURN/ENTER* to break lines. Inserting images and text formatting requires a bit of simple HTML; see the cheat sheet in Table 9-2.

Table 9-2. HTML Cheat Sheet for Blog Entries

Purpose	Tags	Example
Create bold text	`<strong></strong>`	Put it `<strong>under </strong>`the table . . .
Create italicized text	`<em></em>`	She was the `<em>only </em>`one who showed up . . .
Create links in text	`<a href="LINK URL"></a>`	For more information, go to `<a href="http://www. podcastsolutions.com">` Podcast Solutions`</a>`.
Open a link in a new window	Add `target="_blank"` to `<a href="LINK URL">` tags	Visit `<a href=http://www. podcastsolutions.com target="_blank">`Podcast Solutions`</a>`.
Add an image	`<img src="IMAGE URL">`	`<img src="http://www. podcastsolutions.com/ images/logo.gif">`
Use an image as a link	`<a href="LINK URL">` `<img src="IMAGE URL">` `</a>`	`<a href="http://www. podcastsolutions.com">` `<img src="http://www. podcastsolutions.com/ images/logo.gif"></a>`

9

The only downside at this point is that your blog isn't yet set up to help you podcast. To do so, follow these steps:

1. Click the Settings tab above the new post text field.

2. Click Formatting. (You will eventually want to go through all of these tab choices and set up your preferences, but right now you're focusing on getting podcast-ready.)

3. Scroll down to the next to last choice, Show Link Field, and select that radio button. Now when you go to create a new post, you will see a Link field just below the Title field in the new post window (see Figure 9-2). This field is where you need to put the URL of your uploaded MP3. This URL is information that will eventually end up in the `<enclosure>` tag of your RSS feed, making automatic downloads of your podcast possible.

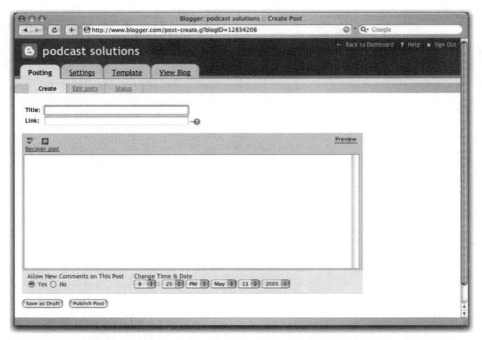

Figure 9-2. In the Blogger Posting Create window, make sure to include the URL of your podcast MP3 in the Link text field. That is what will eventually create the podcast enclosure.

4. Within the main text area of the post, type in whatever information you want to post about your podcast: the topic, the length, the rating, whatever.

5. Click Publish Post. Within a few moments, your first post will be formatted based on the template you chose and ready to view.

6. Go back to Settings ➤ Site Feed. You need to note the information listed beside the heading Site Feed URL. That is the information you will need to input into FeedBurner. It should look like this: http://yourpodcast.blogspot.com/atom.xml.

Setting up FeedBurner Now let's set up FeedBurner to take that Atom XML feed and convert it into not only a podcast-ready RSS feed, but ideally an iTunes-ready feed as well. Don't worry if you still don't understand what we're talking about here—just follow along and everything will be fine, we promise. (We'll discuss RSS feeds in *great* detail later.)

1. Go to www.feedburner.com.

2. The site will ask you for your blog or feed address. Type in the site feed URL you just got from Blogger.

3. Click Go. You'll be taken to a page listing the various things FeedBurner can do to your feed before it spits it out the other end. Frankly, you don't need to worry about any of these items save one. All the others will give you this bell or that whistle, but that's not what you're working toward—you're working toward a podcast.

4. Scroll down until you see the SmartCast area, and then click the radio button. The details of the SmartCast system will appear (see Figure 9-3). Make sure you select the Ping audio.weblogs.com choice.

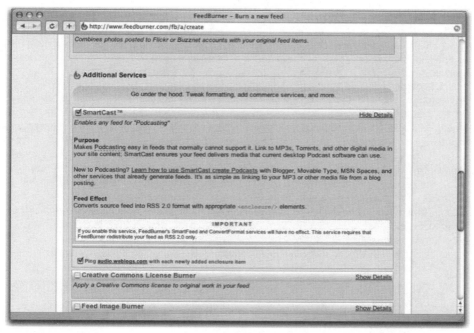

Figure 9-3. Selecting the SmartCast option FeedBurner will turn your Blogger feed into a podcast feed.

> `http://audio.weblogs.com` *is a site that tracks when new podcasts are posted. If you ever want to experiment with a few random podcasts, you can view the site, which lists the last 100 podcasts posted. By pinging the site, you may attract some listeners who are just watching for new and interesting podcasts.*

5. Scroll down until you reach the FeedBurner URI section. The feed URL that follows is your podcast feed. This is the URL that your listeners will need to put into their podcatchers to get your podcast automatically. (More information on that to come later in this chapter.)

And that's it—you're ready to go. When you've finished uploading a new podcast MP3, create a new posting, include the link to point to the MP3 as outlined previously, and publish the post through Blogger. Everything else will take care of itself. You will never need to worry about FeedBurner again—once it's set up, it continues to translate your blog feed to a podcast feed automatically each time you post.

Podcast hosting + blog = Liberated Syndication

To discuss Liberated Syndication is to jump around a little bit and talk about blogs, hosting your files, and the RSS feed all at once. Liberated Syndication is an ISP that was created especially to service the needs of podcasters. It has a rather inventive "no bandwidth restrictions" model of service, which means that (unlike with most other service providers) you will not be penalized with higher charges if and when your podcast becomes popular. As we mentioned earlier in the chapter, whether you have one person download your files or one million, you only pay for the amount of *storage* you want to use, but *not the download traffic*. Yes, that's right: it's the seemingly perfect ISP for future podstars.

But actually, it gets better. Not only does Liberated Syndication not charge for excessive traffic, but also it gives you a monthly allotment of storage space to use. So, instead of having 100MB of total space to use, you might have 100MB of *new* storage space each month to use. At the beginning of each billing cycle, you are automatically allotted fresh space. Your existing files are **archived** (i.e., moved from Liberated Syndication's fastest servers to their less speedy but storage-rich brothers) and remain online until you stop using the service. Yes, it seems too good to be true (or it will once you have 100MB of podcasts to juggle), but true it is. Even better, each account comes with a foolproof blog built in that will automatically create your RSS feed for you. Simply choose whether it's a podcast or text post, upload your file right from the page, attach the file to the post using a pull-down menu, type in your text, and publish (see Figure 9-4). You can even easily add graphics and ping http://audio.weblogs.com.

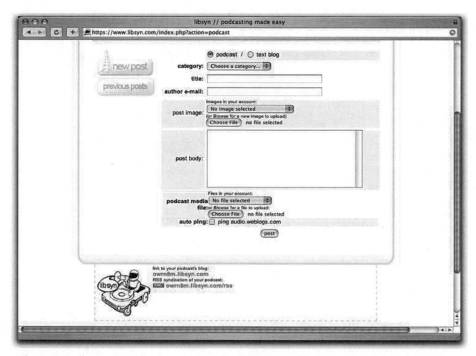

Figure 9-4. Liberated Syndication's blog tool, which is free with every account and perfect for podcasters

"Real" blogs: WordPress and Moveable Type

If you want to be a "power podcaster," you'll want to set up a power blog. The methods outlined in the previous sections are great, and they certainly get the job done, but to have real control over your blog, you'll want to use a top-of-the-line blog platform such as WordPress (www.wordpress.org) or Movable Type (www.movabletype.org). WordPress is free, and a limited version of Moveable Type is also available for free.

Setting up one of these two powerhouses is complicated enough to exceed the scope of this book. However, there are extremely detailed, easy-to-follow tutorials available on the web that will take you through the entire setup process. Don't be intimidated. If having total control over your podcast site is appealing to you, then you should check out these blog applications. Each is full of features and gives you the last word on the content and layout of the blog. Sure, using these applications involves more of a learning curve than the other two methods just described, but the difference in the results is night and day.

Want our recommendation? We prefer and recommend WordPress. WordPress (which as its creators so eloquently put is "both free and priceless") is highly customizable, and developers are constantly creating new and improved plug-ins to further extend its flexibility. If you decide to use WordPress, there is a very active support community (www.wordpress.org/support). Also, because so many people use WordPress, you can easily find everything from step-by-step setup instructions to complex plug-ins that will allow you to do almost anything you can imagine.

> *Want to see some WordPress setups? Check out* www.reelreviewsradio.com *and* www.podcastsolutions.com.

9

Your domain, revisited

Now that you've set up your blog or website, whether it's hosted by Blogger or on your own server, you now have a place on the Internet to call your own. It's time to set up your domain so that when people try to connect to it, they are taken to your site. All you'll need to do for this is go back to your registry service (GoDaddy.com, for instance) and make adjustments to your account there. Up until now the domain has just been "parked," sitting idly doing nothing. Now that you have someplace to point it, get it pointing.

If your site is being hosted by a hosting service provider (like Liberated Syndication), you will need to get that company's **Domain Name Service (DNS)** numbers. These are the magic numbers that tell browsers to go to the host's servers when looking for your web pages. Like we've said before, if you have any questions regarding setting up your domain to point to your host, contact your service provider for all the information.

If your site is a blog being hosted by a blog provider (like Blogger) or is uploaded to your ISP account, you may want to set up your URL to "forward" to that web address. Then when people type your URL into their browser, they will be forwarded to whatever URL you designate (your web page, your blog, etc.). That way, instead of telling people to go to www.pocastsolutions.blogspot.com, or to www.earthlink.net/~pocastsolutions/index.html, you just point them to www.pocastsolutions.com, and they are automatically taken to the correct page. Your registry service will have easy-to-follow instructions on how to set this up, which usually involve asking you for the URL you'd like your domain to forward to and whether or not you want the forwarding to be "hidden." Simple as can be.

The RSS feed

Gulp! You're finally going to have to learn to write code, right? Well, no. It's time to set up the RSS feed, but you still won't have to write any code. Yes, you may want to get to know the code a tiny bit, just to ensure that you have some idea of how it works. That way, if something ever goes wrong, you stand half a chance of figuring out why. For that reason we have included an uncommonly "geeky" (for this book), in-depth description of the RSS feed. It is here as a reference and is not required reading, but speaking from experience, we wish someone had laid it out for us like we have here so we could have avoided all the struggles we went through when we first started out. So here it comes.

Really Simple Syndication (RSS) is written in Extensible Markup Language (XML), as we discussed earlier. The "feed" is simply a page of raw code that is stored on the Internet to be read by podcatchers and other newsreaders. So, let's take a look at the XML and see what it includes. If you find all this code stuff too mind-boggling, just skip down to the section titled "Creating the feed"—you won't miss anything crucial.

OK, here's the XML code for a sample Podcast Solutions podcast, with one MP3 enclosure. This is a fairly straightforward version of a feed, created in Feeder (www.reinventedsoftware.com). We'll first give you the whole feed here, and then we'll talk about some of its key elements in the next section:

```
<?xml version="1.0" encoding="utf-8"?>
<rss version="2.0">
  <channel>
    <title>The Podcast Solutions Sample Podcast Series</title>
    <link>http://www.pocastsolutions.com</link>
    <description>
      A series of sample podcasts, intended to make the RSS feed
      more easily understood.
    </description>
    <generator>
      Feeder 1.0.4 http://reinventedsoftware.com/feeder/
    </generator>
    <docs>http://blogs.law.harvard.edu/tech/rss</docs>
    <language>en-us</language>
    <copyright>
      Copyright 2005, Michael Geoghegan and Dan Klass
    </copyright>
    <managingEditor>
      Michael@podcastsolutions.com (Michael Geoghegan)
```

```
    </managingEditor>
    <webMaster>Dan@podcastsolutions.com (Dan Klass)</webMaster>
    <pubDate>Tue, 03 May 2005 18:22:02 -0700</pubDate>
    <lastBuildDate>Tue, 03 May 2005 18:22:02 -0700</lastBuildDate>
    <image>
      <url>http://www.podcastsolutions.com/logo.jpg </url>
      <title>the Podcast Solutions Sample Podcast Series</title>
      <link> http://www.podcastsolutions.com </link>
      <description>Podcast Solutions logo</description>
    </image>
    <item>
      <title>#1: Trying to Understand the RSS Feed</title>
      <description>
      <![CDATA[
        <img src="http://www.podcastsolutions.com/podcast_icon.jpg">
        The first in our series of sample podcasts.  This one shows
        how the RSS feed looks when you look under the hood at the
        raw XML code.  It's not actually as baffling as you thought
        it would be, right?
      </description>
      <author> Dan@podcastsolutions.com (Dan Klass)</author>
      <pubDate>Tue, 03 May 2005 13:51:57 -0700</pubDate>
      <enclosure url=http://www.podcastsolutions.com/sample1.mp3
                        length="19908738"
                        type="audio/mpeg"/>
    </item>
  </channel>
</rss>
```

Before we get into how to effortlessly create your feed (like we did a bit when talking about FeedBurner), let's take a look at a few elements of the RSS code next, so you understand how each element is important to not only getting the feed to work, but promoting your podcast as well.

Examining the naked XML

Wow, that code listing in the previous section is a mess, right? Well, not really. Actually, it makes a lot of sense, and once we go through it and explain what's what, you'll realize that if push came to shove, you'd be able to update your code by hand without a hitch. Let's take a look, piece by piece. We'll first present the code, and then we'll explain it.

```
<?xml version="1.0" encoding="utf-8"?>
<rss version="2.0">
```

These elements are simply an indicator that the particular version of XML/RSS the following code is written in is XML, version 1.0, and RSS, version 2.0. Don't worry about the deeper ramifications. You'll never need to worry about this part.

```
<channel>
```

Everything in the feed must be between the opening channel tag, `<channel>`, and the closing channel tag, `</channel>`. In XML, like HTML, all tags that open (the opening tag is between angle brackets, `< >`) must close (the closing tag looks the same as the opening tag except it has a backslash before its name, `</ >`). This being the case, there is a closing `<channel>` tag at the end of the code, right before the tag that closes the RSS.

```
<title>The Podcast Solutions Sample Podcast Series</title>
    <link>http://www.pocastsolutions.com</link>
    <description>
      A series of sample podcasts, intended to make the RSS feed
      more easily understood.
    </description>
```

These tags establish the name (in `<title>` tags) of your series of podcasts, the main web address for the podcast (in `<link>` tags), and a description of the podcast series (in `<description>` tags). This description is more important than it seems: it shows up in pod-catchers, directory listings, and online podcast players, so make sure it is a thorough, well-thought-out, and well-written description of your podcast. It will end up being one of your most valuable marketing tools.

```
<generator>
    Feeder 1.0.4 http://reinventedsoftware.com/feeder/
</generator>
```

The application used to create the feed is indicated within `<generator>` tags.

```
<docs>http://blogs.law.harvard.edu/tech/rss</docs>
```

This is a link to a Harvard Law School website, which includes in-depth information on RSS, including a very nice description of everything we're discussing right now! Why does it seen to end up in most RSS code? Who knows. Someone's just trying to be complete, we suppose.

```
<language>en-us</language>
```

This `<language>` tag tells the world that the feed is written in American English. If you are in another country and/or wish to podcast in a different language, refer to the RSS specification found at http://blogs.law.harvard.edu/tech/rss to find the right language tag to use here.

```
<managingEditor>
    Michael@podcastsolutions.com (Michael Geoghegan)
</managingEditor>
```

This line gives the e-mail address of the person to contact with questions or concerns about the content of the feed.

```
<webMaster>Dan@podcastsolutions.com (Dan Klass)</webMaster>
```

This line gives the e-mail address of the person to contact with questions or concerns about the feed itself.

```
<pubDate>Tue, 03 May 2005 18:22:02 -0700</pubDate>
```

This line gives the date and time when the material in the feed was published. Typically, this will be the same as the "last build date."

```
<lastBuildDate>Tue, 03 May 2005 18:22:02 -0700</lastBuildDate>
```

This is the date and time when the feed was last updated. For the podcatchers to know to download your latest MP3, it is crucial that this date is correct. If this dates ends up out of whack, your podcasts may not be downloaded by your subscribers.

```
<image>
      <url>http://www.podcastsolutions.com/logo.jpg </url>
      <title>the Podcast Solutions Sample Podcast Series</title>
      <link> http://www.podcastsolutions.com </link>
      <description>Podcast Solutions logo</description>
</image>
```

Everything within the <image> tag is optional. This tag embeds an image (typically the logo of the podcast series) within the podcast that will accompany the feed when read by some readers/podcatchers. This series of subtags includes the URL of the image itself, the name of the image, a link that clicking the image would direct a browser to, and a description of the image.

```
<item>
```

Now, we are shifting from tags containing descriptions of the podcast series as a whole to tags containing descriptions of a single edition of that series. So, everything within the <item> tag only pertains to one particular podcast (in this case, sample podcast #1).

```
<title>#1: Trying to Understand the RSS Feed</title>
      <description>
        <![CDATA[
        <img src="http://www.podcastsolutions.com/podcast_icon.jpg">
        The first in our series of sample podcasts.  This one shows
        how the RSS feed looks when you look under the hood at the
        raw XML code.  It's not actually as baffling as you thought
        it would be, right?
      </description>
```

So, this time the <title> and <description> are for our sample podcast, "#1: Trying to Understand the RSS Feed." Again, this description is important, as it will not only sell your podcast, but also the text within it will end up in newsreaders and other sites that aggregate these feeds, turning the description into text that search engines crawl through. Descriptive words you use here will get picked up in searches, and that could mean new listeners. Don't skimp on the descriptions!

9

```
<author> Dan@podcastsolutions.com (Dan Klass)</author>
    <pubDate>Tue, 03 May 2005 13:51:57 -0700</pubDate>
```

This part is fairly self-explanatory, given what we're covered thus far.

```
<enclosure url=http://www.podcastsolutions.com/sample1.mp3
            length="19908738"
            type="audio/mpeg"/>
```

Finally we come to the <enclosure> tag—the magic bullet that turns simple news feeds into podcast heaven. This is the tag that the podcatchers need, because it is the code that points to the location of your podcast MP3 file. Without it, the feed is fairly useless, consisting of titles and descriptions, but no podcast.

The <enclosure> tag includes three elements: the location of the podcast MP3 (in the form of a URL), the length of the podcast in bytes, and the type of file the enclosure is. In the case of your typical podcast, it is an MP3 file. Truth be told, this exact code would work with image files and movie files. The images and movies would be downloaded by the podcatcher, and sorted automatically (presumably, depending on your system).

```
</item>
</channel>
</rss>
```

These tags close the item, the channel, and the RSS.

Now, if we were coding by hand and wanted to add another episode to this series, we would reconstruct all the information within the <item> tag, updating the information to reflect the new podcast. Cutting and pasting come in very handy in these cases. Dan did his RSS for "The Bitterest Pill" by hand for almost 6 months, with very few glitches (and he's no computer programmer!). The main thing to remember when doing the code by hand is to *never use an ampersand*! Ampersands (&) are code killers. If you *have* to use an ampersand within your description, use the code-friendly version (&)—but don't worry, odds are you won't be handling the code in its raw state anyway. There are better ways to build a feed, as we discuss next.

> *The iTunes Music Store uses additional tags to get the host's name, artwork, and other information to appear correctly within their podcasting section. We thought about including the tags in this chapter, but they appear to be in flux currently. To take a look at the raw iTunes tags, see the PDF document at* http://phobos.apple.com/static/podcast_specifications.pdf.

Creating the feed

A podcaster needn't write his RSS from scratch. Why waste the time? After prepping, recording, editing, and processing, who wants to sit and write code anyway? In the sections that follow, we describe a few different ways to get an RSS feed built effortlessly: using an automatic RSS creator, using a stand-alone application, and having your blog build the feed.

Using an automatic RSS creator

There are websites and bits of Java code floating around that will automatically generate RSS based on the information stored in your MP3's ID3 tags. Simply make sure that all the information you want to end up in the feed is included within the appropriate tags (depending on the configuration set up by the particular creator), and run the MP3 through the website/code.

This may be an attractive solution for podcasters looking to shave some time off their production schedule, but it is so limiting it is hardly recommended for serious podcasters. "Real" RSS has the ability to include text links, images, and a lot more information than can be stored within the ID3 tags. By using this method, you are limiting yourself unnecessarily. You will find that including links and images within the RSS feed will enhance your presence within directories and podcatchers. This is where you'll attract listeners, so you must put your best face forward.

Using a stand-alone application

Several stand-alone applications are available that will create beautiful, robust RSS for you, without your having to use a blog to post your code. Feeder for the Mac OS is what Dan switched to after giving up on hand coding, and he hasn't regretted it. Feeder works in much that same way as any blog platform, except that it doesn't publish blog posts—only RSS and RSS for podcasts (including iTunes tags). Still, the formatting and functionality is much the same, and Feeder, or another application like it, is an ideal choice for podcasters who choose to use a traditional nonblog website (or make the mistake of hand coding at the beginning like Dan did. We live, we learn). The only real downside of going this route is that you are potentially duplicating work: you are updating your website and your RSS separately.

Having your blog build it

Yes, your blog will build the feed for you, automatically. Any blog platform worth its bandwidth (WordPress) will be able to take your posts and add an enclosure fairly simply. The blog post becomes the contents of the `<description>` tag, and the title of the post becomes the `<title>` tag (see, aren't you glad we talked about this already?). You will be asked to designate a file to be attached as an enclosure, and that is automatically built into the feed code as well. When you publish your new blog post, it will create and post an update to your XML file. Simple. Just make sure that your blog is exporting an RSS feed and not an Atom feed.

> DON'T FORGET: Put a link in each blog posting to the corresponding MP3 file, so visitors can just click and listen.

9

Displaying your feed

No matter how you create your RSS code, the one thing that every podcaster has to do is display the feed address. Until all podcatchers have seamless "one-click" subscribing, some podcast listeners will need to know your feed's URL. You don't want to alienate any potential listeners just because they are using one catcher rather than another. In fact, you may want to take this idea a step further and create a place on your blog or website that explains exactly how to subscribe to your podcast (see Figure 9-5). It can't hurt.

Figure 9-5. To make it easy for people to subscribe manually, Michael displays his feed URL prominently on his site.

The future of podcasting services

We must admit, this is an interesting time in podcasting. As we are writing this book, a number of services are on the horizon that promise to make podcasting even easier. Most seem to focus around a unified recording and posting interface that removes the need to deal with setting up a site, much less worry about a RSS feed. Both PodShow and Odeo (see Figure 9-6) hope to accomplish this. The problem is that none of these services has gone into public release as of yet. In addition to offering solutions for recording and posting content, they also propose to assist podcasters in monetizing their content. We have seen advance glimpses of both these services. It looks like they will offer yet another attractive choice for people wishing to get started in podcasting.

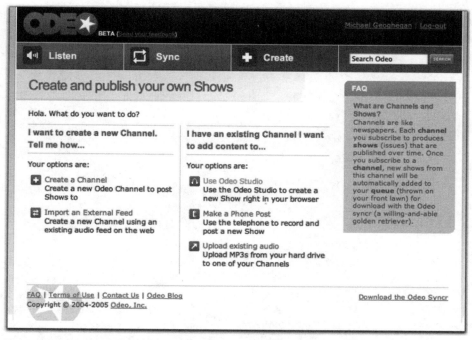

Figure 9-6. Odeo's content creation screen has lots of choices!

Summary

There is this tremendous temptation to congratulate you at the end of each chapter, and it's getting a bit old. But let's be honest, you've come a long way. And now you're done. You have a podcast. Start to finish. Everything else we cover in this book from here until the end is gravy: promoting your podcast, getting listed in directories, making money at podcasting. All of that can be done or not, and it doesn't change the simple fact that you've been through the process and you've put a podcast into the world. If you've followed along and followed through on each step, you could put your RSS feed into an iPodder, click Check Subscriptions, and lo and behold, your podcast would download. Yes, you can deny it no longer: you are a podcaster! (Now all you need to learn is the secret handshake . . .)

Honestly, the thrill only lasts so long. Being a podcaster just isn't enough. You want to be a podcaster with an audience, right? Thought so. So, let's get the word out that there's a new 'cast in town. Let's get you known and generate a little buzz!

9

10 GETTING HEARD

  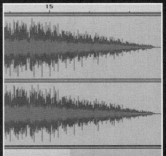

After all the hard work you've put into creating your show, it's difficult and possibly upsetting to imagine your podcast MP3 just sitting there on the server, being downloaded only by the two or three family members you can get to actually understand podcasting. Let's be very clear about something right here and now: just because you think you're "podcasting" and there are thousands of podcast listeners out there doesn't mean that your podcast is going to instantly have an audience. People can't listen to a podcast that they don't know about or can't find. You need to get your podcast out to the podcast community and out to the world.

As the number of podcasts continues to skyrocket (especially the number of big-budget corporate podcasts), it's becoming harder and harder to carve out a slice of the audience pie. However, there are still ways you can generate attention and encourage people to check out your podcast. The key to building an audience is to *get heard* (perhaps this seems too obvious, but bear with us). Sure, not everyone who hears your show is going to love it, but *nobody* can love it if they don't hear it first.

So, without further ado, let's look at how you can get your podcast the exposure it deserves. In this chapter, we'll cover the following topics:

- Listing your podcast in the major podcast directories
- Networking with other podcasters
- Getting your podcast reviewed
- Sparking interest in your podcast from the mass media

Getting listed in the major podcast directories

First and foremost, you need to get your show listed in the major **podcast directories**. Podcast directories are an essential part of any podcaster's promotional arsenal. Listeners go to podcast directories to find new shows, rate their favorite shows, and even to listen to shows. A well-put-together directory has the potential to be the virtual "town square" for thousands of podcast listeners and producers worldwide.

Podcast directories represent a growing and extremely competitive area in the podcasting universe. The creators and caretakers of these podcast databases know that podcast listeners (and the media) go to podcast directories when they want to search for new favorites. New listeners means more traffic, and more traffic means potential increased revenue to the directories in the form of ad sales.

Most directories are on a tireless quest to better service their visitors and the podcasts they list, hoping to be *the podcast directory*. Podcast directories need podcasters as much as podcasters need directories, so the directories are constantly improving and streamlining their sites, inside and out, to make the experience of getting listed and getting listened to as easy and as powerful as possible.

In this section, we'll cover how to create your podcast directory listing, get your show information posted in the most popular and influential podcast directories, and ping pod-catchers to let them know your show is out there.

Crafting your listing

Before you submit your listing to a single podcast directory, you'll want to do a little think-ing up front about how you'd like to "position" your show. Not only will potential listeners see the name of your show, but also they'll be able to view a description of your show and the category your show is listed in.

Just as with the description of your podcast within your RSS feed, the description you sub-mit to a podcast directory should be concise and descriptive enough to entice people to listen to your show. (In the case of some directories, the description of your show that gets displayed *is* the description from your RSS feed.) This is one of those golden opportunities to sell your show to potential listeners. Make sure that you tell them exactly what your podcast is about and who might like it, and give a feel for the overall tone of the show. Consider this your sales pitch in paragraph form. Make it count.

> *Here's an example of the description from Dan's show, "The Bitterest Pill":*
>
> *The Dan Klass Show: Comedy, commentary, and music from a stay-at-home dad/shut-in.*

You will often be asked to list your podcast in a particular category. The category structure of the directories is an incredible benefit for both the podcaster and the podcast listeners. By breaking down the podcast listings by category, the directories make it that much easier for potential listeners to find the types of podcasts they're looking for. By the same token, if you choose to list your show in the wrong category, it could mean that your podcast is overlooked by your target audience, which can only be a bad thing. Choose the categories you wish to be listed in carefully. Most directories use a wide enough array of categories that you're bound to find one that suits you. If not, drop the directory in question an e-mail and suggest a new category.

10

> *We aren't kidding about suggesting a new category to a directory—we've each been the first in a category on a directory. For example, "Reel Reviews" was the first movie-oriented podcast at the time I created it, so I asked Adam Curry to create a "Movie" category (node) in iPodder.org since I thought that category title was a better fit than "Entertainment."*
>
> *If the category makes sense to you, then it will probably make sense to the kinds of people you are trying to reach.*
>
> *—Michael Geoghegan*

Submitting your listing to the main directories

We talked a bit about specific directories in Chapter 2. As we examine directories in this chapter, it's from the point of view of a podcaster, as opposed to a podcast listener. In the sections that follow, we'll look specifically at iPodder.org (www.ipodder.org), iTunes Music Store (www.apple.com/itunes/store/podcasts.html), and Podcast Alley (www.podcastalley.com). We want to make sure you get your show listed in at least these three directories, and they're the biggest on the scene currently. If you aren't listed in these directories, you aren't really listed at all. We'll also cover other available directories that are definitely worth investigating.

iPodder.org

iPodder.org (see Figure 10-1) is home to the oldest (and still the most useful, in our view) podcast directory. The directory is broken down into an exhaustive list of categories and subcategories, with each **node** maintained by its own editor. Each node's editor makes updates to the directory manually, so depending on who is managing a particular category, your new listing could take moments or days to be included.

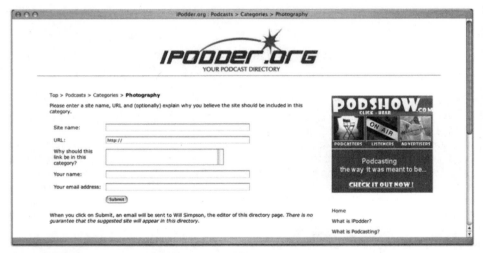

Figure 10-1. An iPodder.org podcast submission form

The iPodder.org directory also feeds the directories built into iPodder and iPodderX, so getting listed here is extremely important. People new to podcasting tend to automatically search for shows from within their newly downloaded podcatchers, as opposed to seeking out directory websites. To be found in most podcatchers, you need to be listed on iPodder.org.

To get listed, go to www.ipodder.org and follow these steps:

1. Click Podcast Directory, and then click Categories.

2. Select the directory category that best suits your podcast.

3. On each category's page, you will see a list of all the podcasts currently accessible through iPodder.org in that category. At the bottom of the list will be the name of the list editor, the date of the last update to the list, the number of podcasts listed in that category, and a Suggest a link link. When you click the Suggest a link link, you're taken to a short form to fill out, where you submit the name of your podcast, the URL of your website or blog, your name and e-mail address, and a brief explanation of why your podcast should be in that particular category.

4. Click Submit to send the information directly to the node's editor, and you're all set.

Keep in mind that iPodder.org will list your podcast in multiple categories. Use it, don't abuse it. Get yourself listed in every category that legitimately reflects the content of your podcast, but don't go overboard. If people surfing around iPodder.org start seeing your podcast listed in too many categories, they will begin to think you don't have anything specific to say, and they'll turn a blind eye and a deaf ear to your podcast.

Apple iTunes

Apple iTunes may not have the most comprehensive directory, but let's face it, it's the 800-pound gorilla of podcasting. iTunes is responsible for bringing untold numbers of new listeners to podcasting every week, and its importance to podcast producers is immeasurable. Since so many people already use iTunes, there is no need for them to download new software or search the web for podcasts. If users are already familiar with the iTunes Music Store, they are halfway to your podcast.

You need to be listed in the iTunes podcast directory without question, and to get listed, you'll need to play by the iTunes rules. You need to use an iTunes-compatible feed, using iTunes RSS tags (see Chapter 9). Unfortunately, there is no clear-cut way of verifying that your feed is truly iTunes compatible without simply beginning the submission process and seeing how iTunes interprets your code. Luckily, submitting is the easy part:

1. Go to the Podcasting section of the iTunes Music Store (www.apple.com/itunes/store/podcasts.html).

2. Look for the Publish a Podcast area, and click the link there.

3. You are now at the Publish Podcasts to the Music Store page. Type or paste the feed URL of the podcast you are submitting into the text field at the bottom of the page (see Figure 10-2) and click Continue.

10

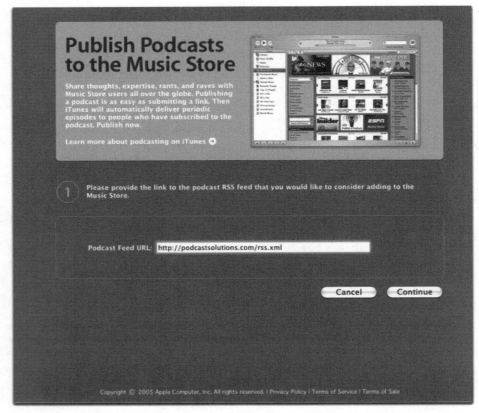

Figure 10-2. Type or paste your iTunes-compatible feed information here.

4. On the Review Podcast page, you can see how iTunes will interpret your feed. As it says on the page (see Figure 10-3), you cannot make changes from this page. This page only reads your code; it cannot help you change your code. For that, you need to go back into your feed and make the appropriate modifications, either to clean up the code itself or to add missing information.

5. If/when the information displayed looks right to you, click Publish.

6. Then wait. As of this writing, iTunes is very slow to add podcasts, very slow to update changes in podcast information, and very slow to update podcast episode listings for each show. When iTunes looks for new episodes of podcasts a user has subscribed to, it seems to read the current version of the feed. But when it displays the podcast "page" within iTunes, it relies on a cached version for some time.

Figure 10-3. iTunes reads the feed and shows you how the information will be displayed within the iTunes Music Store.

Here's a great iTunes-related trick: you can easily create a link on your blog or website that will take listeners directly to your "page" within iTunes. Simply go to your podcast page and right-click (Windows) or CTRL-click (Mac) on your podcast's artwork. A pull-down menu will appear with the choices iTunes Help *and* Copy iTunes Music Store URL. *Choose the latter option to send the URL of your show's iTunes page to your clipboard. Go to your website and create a link to that URL. Now whenever someone wants to find your show in the iTunes Music Store, it's just a click away!*

Podcast Alley

The other main directory you'll want your show to be listed in is Podcast Alley. This site (see Figure 10-4) has become an incredibly popular place for podcast listeners to go looking for new shows. As such, it is an essential submission for all podcasters. Podcast Alley has also become a town square of sorts for the entire podcasting community, with listeners and producers stopping by daily to see who's hot, who's not, what the discussion topics are for that day, and much more. The power of Podcast Alley and its "Top Ten" list is quite impressive, as exposure on the Top Ten has led directly to national and international press coverage for many podcasters.

> See our interview with Podcast Alley's Chris McIntyre at www.podcastsolutions.com.

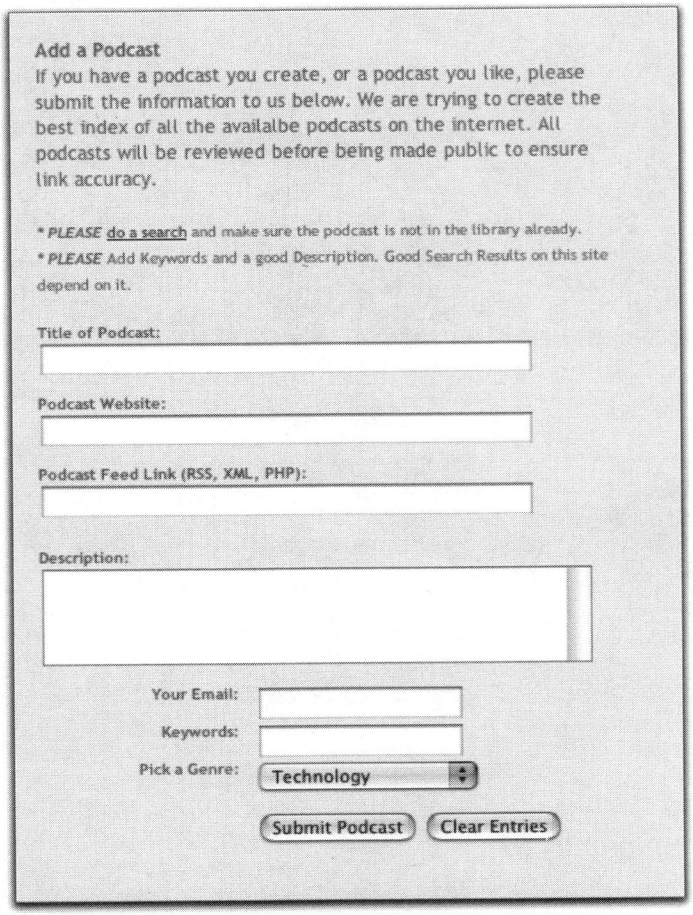

Figure 10-4. Podcast Alley podcast submission panel

To get listed on this important site, follow these steps:

1. From the Podcast Alley homepage (www.podcastalley.com), click the Add a Podcast link.

2. On the submission form that appears, insert your podcast title, website, feed (RSS), and e-mail address. You'll also be asked for a description of the podcast and some "keywords" to further describe your show. Podcast Alley warns, "Add keywords and a good description. Good search results on this site depend on it," and we couldn't agree more.

Other directories

There are perhaps dozens of other podcast directories, all vying to be an alternative to iPodder.org, iTunes Music Store, and Podcast Alley. Time will tell which ones make it in the long run and which don't. Still, it never hurts to get listed in as many directories as possible. The other directories we recommend checking out are as follows:

- PodcastPickle.com (www.podcastpickle.com)
- Podcast Central (www.podcastcentral.com)
- Podfeed.net (www.podfeed.net)
- PodNova (www.podnova.com)
- Podcast Bunker (www.podcastbunker.com)

We'll all have to watch how the relationships between the directories and the podcatchers change over time, especially now that Apple's iTunes has podcast features built in, and as some directories are inevitably swallowed up by corporate concerns.

It seems that almost every day we receive notice of a new directory that claims it will soon be the best. When you start submitting your show information to directories, do yourself a favor and search around a bit. The situation is fluid enough at the moment that by the time you have digested the contents of this book and are ready to publish your podcast, there might be some new, "must-list" directories available.

Pinging podcast trackers

A great way to let the world know that you have just posted a new episode of your podcast is to **ping** podcast trackers (i.e., make them aware of you) such as http://audio.weblogs.com, a service run by one of the original podcasters, Dave Winer. This service keeps a running list of the "freshest podcasts in the known universe." When you visit the homepage, you will see a list of the 100 most recently posted podcast episodes on the Internet, along with their RSS feed links (represented by the white-on-orange XML buttons).

Most blog software allows for pinging of tracking services such as this. If you are not sure how to do it with your blog software, you can manually let http://audio.weblogs.com know you have a new podcast up by visiting http://audio.weblogs.com/pingform.html. Enter the name of your podcast and the address of your RSS feed. The service will then

10

respond by letting you know whether or not it sees your podcast as new. If not, it probably just means the service has already logged it. How did it do that? Magic.

The list moves pretty quickly these days, as new podcasts are posted now at an alarming rate (we remember when it took a day or two to cycle off and be dropped from the 100 most recent list!). Even so, this service is used by many to see what is new in the podcasting world. In addition, the site features a great tool, a podcast feed debugger, which you can access through a link in the checklist of common problems at www.podcatch.com/howToPing.

Networking with other podcasters

A great way to generate new listeners is through networking. Nobody understands what it's like to try to connect with an audience quite like your fellow podcasters. They have been there and done that. Other podcasters can be a resource for attracting new listeners, or they can at least give you advice on how best to build some awareness. In the next few sections, we look at how to network effectively.

Sending show promos to other podcasters

Back when we discussed how to find podcasts in Chapter 2, we talked a bit about listening to the podcast promos being played on your favorite shows. Well, now you're on the other side of that listener/podcaster fence, and it's time to listen again, but from a new angle. Now when you hear a promo for a podcast being played on another show, take special note: what is it about this promo that works or doesn't work? Does it make you want to listen to that show, or does it make you want to write a nasty e-mail to the podcaster who played the promo?

You should definitely consider developing your own podcast promos to send to other podcasters. When you're putting together your own promos, keep in mind that you're targeting two very distinct audiences: the other podcaster's audience and the other podcaster. Get to know the other podcaster's audience and understand what they've come to expect from that podcaster's show. You can't send an adult-themed promo to a family-friendly show and expect it to get played. Hopefully you're sending your promo to a podcaster whose audience is similar to your own, so that sort of consideration is moot. Still, consider every angle. More important, consider the other podcaster. Does he ever play promos? If so, what are they like? Are they long or short? Funny or serious? Is the other podcaster more likely to play the promo if it's written in iambic pentameter? If so, break out your quill, Shakespeare!

When you send a promo, send an MP3 file and be sure to maintain your usual "post–*Podcast Solutions*" sound quality. Keep in mind that your promo MP3 will be played, recorded, and then re-encoded for the other podcast. That is a lot of encoding and decoding for one file. To maintain your promo's sound quality and the sound quality of the podcast you hope will play your promo, encode your promo at *twice the bit rate* of the receiving podcast. For instance, if the receiving show is usually encoded at 64 kbps, encode your promo at 128 kbps. Your promo should be relatively short, so file size isn't a concern (compared to the lousy sound of sending something at a lower bit rate); in fact, you could even send a WAV file. The other podcaster will appreciate your forward thinking, technically speaking.

The art of promoting without promoting

If you send a popular podcaster a three-minute promo extolling the virtues of your new show, she may not play it. Why not? A better question is, Why should she? That podcaster's time is precious, and she is probably not in the promo-playing business. You need to approach promoting your podcast through other podcasters with some stealth. Everyone knows everyone else is doing it; it just needs to be done with tact.

> *I don't play promos where the people go on and on about how great they are. I play promos where the people go on and on about how great I am.*
>
> —*Dan Klass*

Promote yourself by promoting the other podcaster. Now, this should really be done only if you truly enjoy the work of the podcaster for whom you've recorded the promo. A simple minute-long recording of how much you enjoy said podcaster's show sprinkled liberally with your own podcast's URL is a perfect way to kill two birds with one promo.

Start by sending a promo to Adam Curry for his "Daily Source Code" show. Adam plays several podcast promos each day, and exposure on his show is a guaranteed ratings boost for you.

> *You always have the option to create a stand-alone promo and include it in OpenPodcast.org, the automatically generated, anyone-can-contribute podcast. With over 1,500 subscribers, it is an easy gateway to the ears of many potential listeners. Simply e-mail a promo that's less than five minutes long to* submit@openpodcast.org. *The promo is dynamically included in the feed. That's it. Of course, your promo will be in a feed with dozens (hundreds?) of others at any given time, but if yours stands out, you can catch 1,500 fresh ears.*

10

Keep it short and simple

Great things can come in small packages, especially when it comes to podcast promos. You're asking another podcaster to give up time on his show to promote your podcast. Exactly how much time are you willing to ask for? Five minutes? No way. Three? Too much. Remember, those seemingly endless commercials you used to listen to on the radio were only 60 seconds long. (Apparently, 60 seconds can seem like forever if you go about getting people's attention the wrong way.) Shoot for a minute, give or take. If you can't say what you need to in 60 seconds, you're trying to say too much. This is another benefit of your having come up with a short, snappy description for your podcast. Let's take a look at a standard, no frills (and easily acceptable to other podcasters) promo you might send (or phone in) to a show:

> *"Hi, this is (your name) from (your podcast), (one-line description of your podcast). I really loved your show about (a topic you sincerely liked). (Your take on that same topic, or more congratulations to the host for being such a genius). Keep up the great work! Bye."*

You're mentioning your name and the name of your podcast, and you're even telling a little bit about it. But, most important to the other podcaster, you're adding to the content of his show in a constructive way. Rest assured,

> *"Hi, this is (your name) from (your podcast), (one-line description of your podcast)."*

will start to roll off your tongue in no time. That is who you are now, so you need to introduce yourself that way.

The podcast badge exchange program

OK, there is no such program, but there might as well be. Those mini badges (see Figure 2-2 in Chapter 2) are a mainstay of most podcast websites, and they reflect a podcaster's tastes and allegiances. If you become friendly with a podcaster and have established a rapport with him, consider asking him to put one of your podcast badges on his site in exchange for putting one of his on yours. Or, if the direct approach doesn't work for you, put badges from all your favorite (and the hottest) podcasts on your site. Those podcasters may feel guilty and, in the spirit of community, reciprocate.

Bulletin boards and user groups

If you're going to be a podcaster, you might as well become involved in the podcast community. Checking the new forum topics at Podcast Alley alone will keep you up to date on what's at the top of many podcasters' minds. Sure, the bulletin boards can sometimes turn into gripe-a-thons, but they can also be an invaluable source of podcasting dirt. Also, several podcasts have thriving online communities of their own, built on blog comments and bulletin boards. If the podcasts you enjoy have bulletin boards, don't hesitate to get involved.

By contributing to a bulletin board thread, whether it's asking a question, helping answer someone else's question, or just chiming in on a topic, you're getting your name (and the name of your podcast) out into the world. (But be careful not to make a nuisance of yourself.) Legitimate discourse and interaction within a bulletin board community will help spread the world that there is another legit podcast out there worthy of a listen.

The same holds true for user groups and mailing lists. We both belong to the Yahoo! Podcasters User Group (http://groups.yahoo.com/group/podcasters) and receive list mail all day long on topics ranging from how to market a podcast, to what equipment to use, to decency and censorship issues. Contributing to these mailing lists, as well as bulletin boards, will get your name out there. If you seem to be an expert on a particular subject, or you're just especially insightful or humorous, people will be moved to check out your podcast, without your even suggesting it. Joining various mailing lists can also be a big help in putting you in touch with other podcasters to share promos with.

In addition, bulletin boards and user groups are great sources of information, news, interaction, and advice about all things podcasting. The community as a whole is very helpful, particularly to newbies, and there are no "bad" questions when it comes to getting involved. Yes, there are threads on boards where people can get snotty with each other and have month-long disagreements and flame wars, but these are the exceptions rather than the rule. The podcasting community is by and large a positive, hospitable group to be part of. Welcome.

Getting your podcast reviewed

There are surprisingly few podcast review sites, especially when you consider just how many podcasts there are to weed through these days and how many new listeners are doing the weeding. The oldest (and still the best, if not the most active) of the few is called "The New, New Podcast Review" (www.podcastreviews.net). Cori Schlegel (aka kinrowan) reviews podcasts with fairness and insight, and rates each one based on content, presentation, audio production, and usefulness of ID3 tags. He is, if nothing else, thorough.

If your reviews are glowing, don't hesitate to pull a couple of quotes and feature them front and center on your website. This is a great way to quickly add credibility to your podcast for new site visitors (and it will do wonders for your ego). The truth is, people sometimes need the affirmation of others, whether it's a trusted friend or a known critic, before they're willing to try something new. If you have the opportunity to give them a gentle push, why not do so? Be as proud of your reviews as you are of your podcast.

Even if the reviews are lukewarm, you can often do a little creative cosmetic surgery on the text in the form of copyediting to make the review seem more glowing, and your podcast will appear to be the greatest thing since Thomas Edison. Don't feel guilty; Hollywood does it all the time (and worse) in movie marketing, so why not learn from the experts of promotion? Now, we're not suggesting that if a review reads "It's a shame this podcast isn't the least bit funny!" you should edit it down to say ". . . funny!"—you can't make an outwardly bad review great—but we are suggesting that it's not unheard of to cut and paste a little. This is promotion, after all. Promote!

Why let those great comments on Podcast Alley go to waste? If people are leaving comments about your show on the directory sites, in bulletin boards, or wherever, why not pull from these quotes for other great promo quotes? True, your website might start to look a bit cheesy and self-aggrandizing if you have hundreds of glowing quotes on the front page. So, create a separate "What People Are Saying" page and stow them there. People love to be involved with something successful.

10

Getting your story to the mass media

If we've learned one thing about the media, it's that they need a good story. Every day, in every city in the country—no, strike that: every city in the *world*—news directors, magazine editors, and book publishers are looking for the next hot topic, the next great story. What's the up-and-coming technology? Who's an up-and-coming celebrity? Who's cashing in? Who's crapping out?

> When I learned about podcasting, I knew that it was going to be huge and that friends of ED needed to do a book on it. That's when I shot Michael Geoghegan an e-mail about it, and our great journey started, culminating in the amazing book you hold in your hands.
>
> Now, where's my coffee? I need some sleep . . .
>
> —Chris Mills, keyboard slave and editor of Podcast Solutions

Podcasting was still in its infancy when the media outlets arrived, smelling a story. And the stories are there. They've covered the technological side of podcasting. They've covered the business side of podcasting. They've covered the celebrity side of podcasting. The mass media will continue to cover podcasting as long as there is something *newsworthy* to say about podcasting. At the rate podcasting is growing and evolving, it will be an awfully long time before they run out of things to report.

Press coverage translates directly to an increase in listenership. It's that simple. If you're on television, talked about in a newspaper, or mentioned in a magazine, that's guaranteed to drive potential listeners to your show.

You may be lucky enough to have the media come to you. Whether your podcast is on the Podcast Alley Top Ten list or your show happens to have a particularly catchy title, you may suddenly get a call or an e-mail from someone in the media. Or, if you want some coverage and are sick of sitting by the phone, there are things you can do to stack the deck and help usher the press in your direction, as we'll discuss in the following sections.

Hand them a story

What better way to get someone's attention than to make that person's job a whole lot easier? For your show to get noticed, there has to be something to notice—some reason that you get the call over another podcaster. What is it about your podcast, or you as a podcaster, that might make a good story? What sets you and your show apart and makes you "newsworthy"? Depending on your show, it might be quite simple: you may be the youngest podcaster or the oldest. You may podcast every day from your car on the way to work (it's been done). You might podcast from your bathtub (ditto). News writers and their editors are always looking for an angle—a bend in the story that actually makes it a *story*.

You'll hear a lot of people say, "Hey, you should write a press release about your podcast and send it around," but they never follow that up with advice about how to actually *write a press release*. A good press release is your gift to a news editor. We said "hand them a story"—well, this is it. Your press release needs to tell who you are, what your podcast is about and, most important, why you are newsworthy. You do this by skipping over the news writer and writing the story yourself. Hand them the story, written, typed, proofed, and ready to roll. Will they print it as is? No, but that's not the goal. The goal is to help them see that an interesting, engaging news story can easily be written about you and your podcast.

News stories are written with a very particular flow. First, you put the most important and specific information up front. This is not a "story" story; this is a news story. You are not trying to build suspense or slowly develop a character. You are hooking the reader with a strong lead, for example:

> "From a small apartment over a dry cleaner on Crest Ave., with only his PC and a microphone, Poddy Caster does a new kind of radio show that is heard in 17 different time zones around the world . . ."

Holy cow, really? Over the dry cleaner? Seventeen different time zones around the world? OK, now you've got my attention. What is this story about? How can I hear this show? How did this guy even know he could do something like this?

Your story's lead must be specific; it should probably the single most specific and narrow sentence in the entire piece. After the lead, keep the story as specific as possible while slowly introducing more and more general information. Think of the structure of your news story as being like a pyramid, with the lead being at the tip, and the story getting broader and broader as you continue along. Think about the reader and the questions she may have as she reads, much like in the example just shown. Have all the answers flow from the questions that logically follow your lead. Continually ask yourself, "What is interesting about my podcast, podcasting, and everything else relevant to this story?"

10

> When I was in college, I had a very hard-nosed journalism professor who would always berate his students with the same two words: "Who cares?" He would read our stories aloud, stopping after every sentence to ask, with great disgust, "Who cares?" These are the last two words in the English language you want to hear after someone's just read your story, but their brutality is revealing.
>
> Ask yourself the following two questions when you write your story to keep you grounded: "Will someone care about this, or is it extraneous information that does nothing for the news I'm trying to relate?" and "Am I leaving out something that people would care about?"
>
> —Dan Klass

Think globally, start locally

One of the easiest ways to get a little coverage is to start at home. Podcasters are spread out all over the world, and since we're not producing shows from huge corporate studios (we're likely creating our shows in spare bedrooms and empty conference rooms), nobody knows where we are. There could be podcasters right there in your hometown and nobody would know it. Hey, you're a podcaster in your hometown! Nobody even knows! Tell them.

> *I took this "start locally" approach early on. I had been featured in a number of articles on podcasting, but none that had run locally. I contacted a reporter from my local newspaper and explained that I was involved in something that was getting national media attention and thought the paper might be interested in covering the local angle. Sure enough, that initial contact led to local coverage and a large photo "above the fold" on the front page of the paper's business section.*
>
> *—Michael Geoghegan*

Make it easy to contact you

A reporter from the *New York Times* isn't going to leave a comment on your blog. That's not how this sort of thing works. That reporter wants to get someone on the phone. Right now. If he can't get the first person he tries to reach on the phone, he'll try the second. There is no shortage of podcasters to interview, but there is almost always a shortage of time the reporter has to put a story together. Make sure that you have some sort of contact information prominently displayed on your blog or website. This is another great reason to set yourself up with a voice mail account. With a voice mail account, people can contact you by phone, without the hassle of having your home phone number posted on the Internet.

Be yourself

The truth is, if you do get contacted by someone in the media, you may not know why. You never know what the angle of the piece the reporter or producer is working on is until you see it on the air or in the paper. She may be looking for someone who is taking podcasting to the limit with thousands of dollars worth of equipment and a determination to make millions, or she may be looking for a lonely guy in his basement who uses a tube sock as a pop filter. You never know. All you do know is, like on your podcast, you have to be yourself.

Summary

Always keep your eyes and ears open for new ways to promote your show to new listeners. Make sure your podcast information is in the signature of all your e-mails. When you post on a bulletin board, don't forget to say what podcast you're from. Mention your podcast at every turn. Yes, you may call your doctor's office to make an appointment and accidentally address yourself by your URL, but, hey, your doctor could be a podcast listener, right?

Once you feel like you have a good-sized audience, and you see it's steadily growing, you may decide it's time to try to turn some of those listeners into income. Yes, it may sound a bit crass to the more artistic, but is there anything wrong with trying to lessen the financial burden of bandwidth and new mic cables? No. So, unless you're doing this solely for self-expression, read on, and we'll discuss how to make money through podcasting.

10

11 MAKING MONEY WITH PODCASTING

Before too long, your podcast will be up and running. You'll have your production process down to a science, your content will be focused and inspired, and your audience will be growing at a nice, steady pace. There's nothing like the days of your podcast's youth, watching what was recently a mere concept bloom into a full-fledged ongoing concern. You're busy now with your new offspring, checking download stats, answering e-mails, and worrying over your ranking on your favorite podcast directory.

When your show has matured a bit and you've gained some experience as a podcaster, you'll start to wonder, "What's next?" The show is going well and you're getting great responses from your listeners, but in what ways can you grow the show and mobilize your newfound audience in new and exciting ways? Like many before you, your mind may turn to—dare we say it—*money*.

Plenty of podcast purists strongly believe that podcasting is an art form, and that a person should do a podcast for its own sake. Bravo to someone so selfless, because podcasting is hard work. The prep is hard work; the recording, editing, and mastering is hard work; and the encoding and updating blog entries is hard work. OK, maybe it's not *hard* work, but it's a lot of work nonetheless. Since podcasting is work, why not get paid for it?

There's been a lot of talk about "monetizing" podcasting. Apparently, **monetizing** is a business term for "turning it into a business." Fair enough. People have been fretting over how to monetize this new medium since moments after its inception. So, why all the fretting? Podcasters can easily borrow from the tried-and-true business models that have served radio, TV, and independent artists for decades. Now, if you have an advertising sales staff in your basement, you're probably fairly clear on how you could sell some time on your podcast. But for everyone else, we'll start slowly with a few simple ways to earn, well, perhaps not millions, but at least enough money to cover your expenses.

In this chapter, we'll look at a few ways you can take podcasting to another level. We'll discuss the following topics:

- Making media money
- Learning about your audience
- Implementing donations/memberships and paid subscriptions
- Selling your own merchandise
- Selling other people's merchandise
- Understanding advertising and sponsorships
- Finding advertisers and sponsors
- Becoming a podcast producer for hire
- Moving beyond podcasting

Making media money

Before we get into the specifics of how to monetize your podcast, let's be very clear about how making money in the media works (since that's what we're actually doing here). Not to be too blunt about it, but for you to make money, you need to get someone to give you his or her money. Simple, right? Well, just how do you do that? You leverage your audience.

Your audience is your greatest asset, bar none. Without your audience, it's just you and a mic and some audio equipment. Your audience is that ten or that ten thousand people who listen to your show on a regular basis. They actively participate in your podcast, whether by e-mailing in comments, phoning you, or simply just downloading and listening your show.

So, how do you leverage your audience to make money?

- Offer your listeners something they would pay money for.
- Offer your listeners as a target market to someone who is dying to reach them.
- Offer your audience to businesses as proof that you know how to actually reach and build an audience, and hire yourself out as a podcast producer.

We'll discuss these points throughout this chapter. We'll start off by covering ways you can learn about your audience, which is the basis for any marketing and advertising steps you take next.

Learning about your audience

Who is your audience? This is an important question to be able to answer, because from this answer comes all of your marketing, all of your merchandising, and every sales pitch you will make regarding your show, whether it's to your audience or to the head of a media company. As you sit back and enjoy your daily barrage of fan mail, take note of where it's coming from, who's sending it, and what they're attracted to about your program. Are they mostly male or female, or is it an even mix? Are they married, single, American, European, Asian, tech-savvy, tech newbies? If your show has a narrowly defined focus, you'll be able, with little work, to define your audience. If, for instance, your podcast is a movie review show (like Michael's "Reel Reviews"), it's safe to assume that your audience is made up of movie lovers, right? Here again is the advantage of the narrowly defined concept we talked about in Chapter 4. For the podcasters who do shows about religion, movies, sports, beer, sex, Windows, Mac, Linux, sci-fi, and so on, it's easy to make certain assumptions about their core audience. For others, you have to ask.

Survey says . . .

Don't be afraid to ask your listeners to fill out a survey. It doesn't need to be a 13-page opus or anything fancy; you just need to gather enough information from your listeners to get a sense of how you can market them and market *to* them. Ask for your listeners' gender, age range, and annual income range (we know, that sounds a bit personal, but you haven't asked for their names!), and ask any other questions specific to your podcast that might yield helpful answers. A slower, less aggressive approach is to just hang loose and get to know your listeners naturally. In due time, you will get a sense of who's who and what your show means to them.

11

Keep in mind, though, that if you take the time to do a "formal" survey, potential advertisers will know you're serious. They'll be able to glean the demographics of your show, which they need to make a decision about whether to advertise with you. Remember, you are now competing against print, radio, and TV for ad dollars. Potential advertisers will appreciate that you are taking it seriously. Surveys also help you to ensure you are aligning with advertisers/sponsors who will provide a real benefit for your listeners.

Determining what your listeners are willing to pay for

Pinpointing exactly what your audience is willing to pay for may be tough. Luckily for us, it doesn't take much effort to figure it out. Setting up donation links or offering an array of merchandise may have once required a considerable up-front investment in time and money. These days, thanks largely to the Internet, we can set up online transactions in no time.

Ask yourself what sorts of "stuff" your audience would want, given who you believe they are. Can you think of something to offer, at a reasonable price, that they would really like and enjoy, and that is a natural extension of your podcast? Or is offering the podcast itself enough?

Implementing donations/memberships and paid subscriptions

Going straight to your listeners for donations or membership fees is something that you may have mixed feelings about. Asking for money is something that some people just aren't comfortable with. The flip side of the situation is, however, that your listeners may be more than happy to help subsidize the show. Whether it is to feel more connected to the show, show their appreciation, or just help to avoid your having to look for sponsors, your audience may be willing to share a bit of your new financial burden. Let's take a look at some of the ways you can seek support directly from your listeners, whether through donations, memberships, or paid subscriptions.

Donations and memberships

In mid-June 2005, Jason Evangelho from "Insomnia Radio" (www.insomniaradio.net) sent a dollar to Dan's PayPal account out of the blue. Why, you might ask? According to Jason, "I'm sending a dollar each month to all the podcasts I listen to. Maybe it will catch on." Now, yes, this is a testament to Jason's good nature, but it's also a shrewd and forward-thinking move. What does it cost Jason each month to send $1 to each of the podcasts he subscribes to? Five dollars? Ten? Twenty? Most of us are paying well over $20 a month for the cable TV we barely watch (not including premium channels and Pay Per View), $15 a month for Netflix, and more than all that put together to go to the movies (especially if you have kids). Yet we're paying nothing for the hours and hours of podcast entertainment we download each month. Not a cent. For the form of entertainment that for some of us has taken up all the time many other kinds of entertainment once dominated, *we pay nothing*.

Now, Jason isn't the first podcaster to have this type of idea. Many podcasters have had a PayPal (see the next section) "tip jar" on their podcast sites for ages. The striking thing about Jason's gesture is that it is a small but regular contribution to his favorite podcasters (Dan is honored to be among them). And because of Jason's (and other podcasters') kind gesture, eventually some money will start coming back to him. If all of Jason's listeners did what he has vowed to do, he would no longer have to cover his storage and bandwidth costs out of his own pocket. Actually, if we can guess at Jason's listener base, he could devote *a lot more time* to working on his fantastic podcast and a lot less time to, well, working.

For a podcaster, that $1 a month per listener could mean the difference between needing a second job or not. It's a movement worth pushing forward. In the meantime, asking for donations is not unheard of. You're offering your listeners a wonderful program and asking for very little in return.

Instead of asking for donations, you could consider taking a cue from the folks at National Public Radio (NPR) or the Public Broadcasting Service (PBS). These organizations rely heavily on donations to continue to produce and broadcast some of the most interesting news and entertainment programs available (sounds like podcasting, right?). One way that they have maintained a certain level of donations flowing in is through offering memberships and conducting membership drives. Listeners/viewers pay a certain amount of money to become a member, and in return they get discounts on merchandise and are eligible to win sweepstakes and prizes. Also, for joining, members get a little free swag (e.g., a magazine subscription, a logo mug, etc.) and a good feeling from knowing they've contributed to a worthy cause.

As we talk more later about creating and selling your own merchandise, keep the idea of member gifts in the back of your mind. It's a great way to build community and offer an incentive to give.

PayPal

PayPal (www.paypal.com) is an online service whereby you can send money over the Internet. The money is withdrawn from your checking or credit card account and "sent" to another PayPal user. PayPal is a great way for smaller websites to accept payments or for individuals to pay for goods and services. PayPal is owned by eBay (www.ebay.com), and it's a secure and well-protected service. You might use PayPal if you're accepting donations, selling merchandise that you stock at your home or office, buying equipment through the eBay auction site, or doing any other transaction that doesn't involve a major online retailer.

PayPal makes it very easy to set up a donation button for your website (see Figure 11-1). People can simply click that button and send any size of donation they choose.

11

Figure 11-1. A donation button in action in the top-right corner of the "IT Conversations" homepage

Paid subscriptions

You always have the option, of course, to directly charge listeners to receive your podcast. At the time of this writing, there is no clear-cut way to easily set up a paid subscription feed without having some serious technical savvy. That being said, now that PodShow and Odeo are opening up shop, and Apple has included podcasting functions in its iTunes music player, the day may be close at hand when a podcaster can easily set up a subscription channel that requires a per-download payment. (In fact, we're positive this functionality is coming—it's just not yet available.) How much will listeners be willing to pay for a podcast? That remains to be seen. People all over the world are paying the equivalent of $.99 for a single three- to four-minute song from iTunes. What might they pay for a 30-minute podcast?

While there are not any current subscription-only services for podcasting in widespread use, some podcasts do offer a "subscription" model where the subscription fee is more akin to a membership than a gateway to the content. The most successful of these services at the time of this writing is "This Week In Tech" (www.thisweekintech.com), a show hosted by Leo Laporte and a number of other former TechTV hosts. They have a recurring $2-per-month donation choice, as well as an annual $20 donation option. Of course, listeners are free to donate any amount they are comfortable with and, as we mentioned, donations are not required to listen to the content. Because this show is produced by people who make their professional living talking about technology, it is an interesting experiment to see if they can use a pseudo subscription model to keep traditional advertising out of the show and still succeed in reaching their revenue goals.

The best use of a paid subscription in the long run may be to charge for a "premium" feed that is an alternative/addition to a standard, free feed. The free feed is there to hook new listeners and to maintain the listener base that will not pay for the show. The premium feed is for the hard-core fans and offers more content than the free feed ("best of" segments from shows no longer on the server, outtakes, special editions, etc.), at a much higher sound quality.

Selling your own merchandise

We assume you don't have a bunch of stuff sitting around your house that you'd like to unload on your unsuspecting listeners, which is good. When we talk about selling to your listeners, we aren't talking about selling anything and everything you can get a digital photo of. We're talking about offering something to your audience they might want— something connected to the show. Whether it's a t-shirt with your podcast name on it or a bumper sticker that reads "Kill Your Radio: Podcasts Are Better," you'll want to offer your listeners something they connect with (sound familiar?).

Products on demand

For those of us with a do-it-yourself mentality, this has got to be the best time in history to put together our own swag. Gone are the days of having to pay to silk-screen hundreds of t-shirts in varying sizes or getting stuck with boxes and boxes of unsold *How to Care for Your Pet Rock* paperbacks. Now there is the Internet, and with the Internet and the advances (and advantages) of the digital world, we now live in the age of **products on demand**. You could be selling t-shirts, buttons, coffee mugs, hats, books, and bumper stickers in a half hour with no cash outlay at all, thanks to the relatively new on-demand services available on the Internet.

In the sections that follow, we'll discuss a couple of options for offering your merchandise to your listeners.

CafePress.com

If you don't know about CafePress.com, you need to. CafePress.com (www.cafepress.com) is the premiere on-demand product service, and through the CafePress.com site, you can set up your own online store selling shirts, hats, sweatshirts, CDs—you name it—in no time, free of charge.

You pick which products you'd like to sell, upload graphics according to the site's specifications, and determine the amount of profit you'd like to make. CafePress.com handles order taking, printing, packaging, receiving payments, and shipping. You pay nothing. CafePress.com's payment comes from shipping and handling costs and the base price of each item, upon which you add your profit.

There is no inventory for you to pay for and maintain. When someone orders one of your products, CafePress.com produces the item on demand. Because there is no inventory, there is no initial investment on your part.

Setting up a basic CafePress.com store (see Figure 11-2) is free, but you are restricted to selling only one version or design of each item at a time (e.g., only one design for the basic t-shirt, only one design on the trucker hat, etc.). The site also offers upgraded "premium" stores for a monthly fee, where you can sell as many variations of each product as you desire. The choice of products is extensive, and new seasonal products are added regularly to keep things fresh.

11

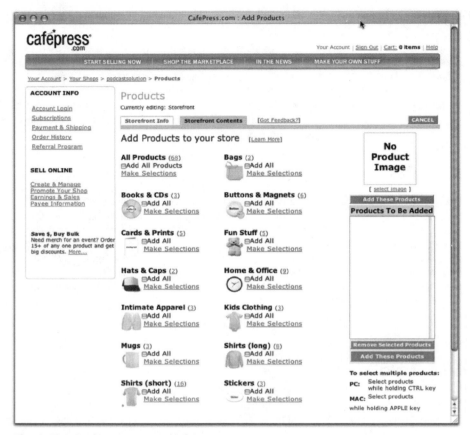

Figure 11-2. Setting up a store at CafePress.com

The print quality of CafePress.com products is good, though not perfect, but for what you're getting for no up-front cost, CafePress.com is a perfect solution for the podcaster who wants to offer some merchandise.

Lulu

Lulu (www.lulu.com) is very similar in concept to CafePress.com, except it specializes in on-demand books and comics. You upload your manuscript in the form of a PDF, and you upload graphics for the front and back covers. Lulu sets up a sales page for your book on its site, and prints and binds each copy as it's purchased. Lulu also can make your book available through Amazon.com and Barnes & Noble.com, to give your book a "professionally published" appearance.

Lulu's print quality and binding is top-notch, and the prices are quite reasonable. The site charges a standard setup fee based on the dimensions and binding of the book, a per-page charge (a few cents per page), and the equivalent of 25 percent of your profit (if your profit is set at $4, Lulu charges an additional $1). Not a bad deal to have an entire book published.

Now, yes, we understand that not many podcasters have books cluttering their hard drives. We also realize that anything a podcaster might write, she could just as easily publish on a blog and have people read it for free. But, from the point of view of the listener, a blog entry doesn't make a very good birthday gift; it's not a tangible keepsake of a podcast listened to regularly. Publishing something for your listeners to enjoy and treasure is not such a crazy idea. Stow it away in the back of your brain, because someday you may have just the thing to get printed up.

> *Dave Slusher of the "Evil Genius Chronicles" (*www.evilgeniuschronicles.org/wordpress*) has put together a real win-win way of providing revenue for his podcast. Dave offers listeners a chance to support his podcast and the band, Gentle Readers, that graciously allow Dave to use their music as his theme song and music bed, through the purchase of a "stuff package." The package includes an "Evil Genius Chronicles" shirt and a Gentle Readers CD (*www.evilgeniuschronicles.org/stuff*). Everyone wins: the listeners, the band, and Dave. Now that is a great way to monetize. Best of all, Dave continues to keep up the interest among audience members by posting on his site pictures of listeners wearing their "Evil Genius Chronicles" shirts.*

Selling other people's merchandise

You can also capitalize on your podcast through **affiliate programs**, which are arrangements with major online retailers for you to sell their products through your website. Here's how it works, generally speaking: you post an ad for a specific company or product on your site. If someone clicks through that ad link and makes a purchase, you get a cut of the action. Sound simple enough? It is.

In the sections that follow, we discuss a few of the major affiliate programs you can participate in.

Amazon.com Associates program

You use Amazon.com. We use Amazon.com. Presumably everyone who shops online at one time or another purchases something from Amazon.com. The site carries not only books and compact discs, but also things like professional audio equipment, clothing, and kitchen appliances. You name it, Amazon.com sells it. The benefit of having such a wide array of products for sale is that it makes it very easy to find things on Amazon.com that you own, use, and recommend. If you talk about a new CD or DVD that you particularly enjoy on your podcast, why not include an affiliate link to Amazon.com's listing of that CD or DVD on your site? If you've recommended the item that highly, and the listener is moved to purchase it due to your recommendation, why shouldn't Amazon.com give you a piece of the pie?

Signing up and being approved as an Amazon.com Associate is relatively easy (https://associates.amazon.com/gp/flex/associates/apply-login.html). In practically no time, you are given an affiliate code that is embedded into the URL of the items you want to promote. When someone clicks an affiliate link on your site, he is taken to that product on the Amazon.com site just as he normally would. What the user doesn't see is that his every move is being tracked with the help of your affiliate code. After he enters the Amazon.com site from your affiliate link, a percentage of *anything* he purchases, whether it is the linked item or not, is put toward your affiliate earnings.

Podcast Solutions

Michael Geoghegan

Best Price $16.49
or Buy New $16.49

Buy from amazon.com

Privacy Information

Amazon.com makes it very easy to set up links with your embedded code, and you can choose from general-category ads (e.g., "All import CDs 10% off!") to item specific displays (see Figure 11-3). With Amazon.com's performance fee structure, associates stand to earn as much as 4 to 6.5 percent on the sales of electronics, audio and video, and camera and photo items. This is above and beyond the standard 1 percent for "Easy Link" items (general category banner ads) and 2.5 percent for "Direct Link" purchases.

Figure 11-3.
An Amazon Associates link to *Podcast Solutions*.
(Hey, where's Dan's name?)

Family shows can have links to kid-friendly movie recommendations. Political shows can link to biographies and tell-all books. A great example of the use of the Amazon.com Associates program is the common practice of podcasters posting links to the audio equipment they use. Any podcaster doing a decent show will get e-mails asking what hardware and software she uses to record her podcasts. What a great way to display the equipment, maybe help a newbie out with some information and insight, and help pay for the show.

CD Baby

When it comes to music in podcasts, it's all indie. Since most podcasters doing music shows are almost exclusively playing independent artists on independent labels, they can't promote the music they play through affiliate links to Amazon.com's exhaustive catalogue of major label discs.

The good news is that many independent artists sell their CDs through CD Baby (www.cdbaby.com), who offers a wonderful affiliate program through which podcasters can promote and sell the music they play. Whenever Dan is putting together a new edition of

"Old Wave Radio," he checks to see if any of that week's artists have CDs listed with CD Baby (see Figure 11-4). If so, he makes sure their album is prominently displayed on that podcast's blog entry, complete with affiliate links. Why not? Everybody wins.

Figure 11-4. A posting from "Old Wave Radio" featuring several affiliate links to artists on CD Baby

CD Baby also offers rudimentary shopping cart functions and several ways to set up and style affiliate displays. Be aware that the site is not as professional-looking as Amazon.com; it's indie and it looks it.

LinkShare

Easily the mother of all online affiliate marketing companies, LinkShare (www.linkshare.com) manages affiliate programs with some of the biggest retailers in the country: Target, Netflix, KB Toys, Disney Direct, Apple, Delta Air, TimeLife.com, and Champion, just to name a few. LinkShare clearly offers something for everyone. Determining which participants are currently involved can be a bit confusing, and each participant requires separate registration and approval. LinkShare is not one-stop-shopping to sign up for affiliates, but it's a great resource for finding major companies who offer affiliate programs that you never knew existed.

Understanding advertising and sponsorships

Clearly, one way you can capitalize on your podcast is the way most media does: through advertising and sponsorships. Since you are a podcaster with a podcast and a website, both of which get a lot of traffic, you are in the enviable position of having two potential revenue streams: selling time and selling space.

Before you can really get started acquiring advertisers, though, you need to know a bit about how advertising works money-wise and how ad rates are calculated. Then you'll need to find advertisers looking to market to your audience. To do this, either you can use a service that will bring the ads to you, or you can find your own.

How ad rates are set

Selling time is fairly straightforward: you determine how much your show is worth, based on how many listeners you have (or realistically expect to have) and how targeted your audience is in marketing terms.

Ads rates on web pages are slightly more complicated. Payment and charges for web ads are usually based on either **click-throughs** or **impressions**. A click-through is exactly what it sounds like: someone sees a linked ad on your side, clicks it, and you get paid. Payment for impressions is based on how many times the page with the ad is loaded in a given period of time. Think of it as a very accurate Neilson rating. The advertiser pays for exactly how many people see the ad.

Cost per click

In a **cost per click** (**CPC**) arrangement, the person hosting the ad (in this case, you) is paid only when someone clicks that link. Our theory is that CPC ads are most beneficial to the person placing the ad, not the person hosting the ad. The ad sits on the page and is exposed to every viewer of that page. Visitor after visitor sees the name of that product, service, company, or whatever. It's free advertising every time that page is loaded, except on those occasions when someone clicks the ad.

In what other ad medium is the advertiser charged only if the media people can prove that the ad actually grabbed viewers' attention and moved them to action? Radio stations get paid for their airtime whether or not the ads they air get listened to. The same is true for magazines, TV shows, you name it.

As you might imagine, CPC is an invention of the Internet age, dating back to the early days of online ad placement. Since so few people believed that advertising on the web would be worth paying for, the CPC structure was devised to prove to advertisers and their agencies that there was value in advertising on the Internet. But those days are over. We've long since proven that Internet advertising works.

CPC ads only really work for you if the ads are so targeted (e.g., a link to an affiliate program where you are literally choosing the products being sold) that they are almost guaranteed to be clicked. While CPC may not be ideal for a primary revenue source for your podcast, it is certainly something to consider on your site. Many people use Google AdSense, which is a CPC-based system that features targeted ads (see the "Having the ads come to you: Google AdSense" section).

The flip side of the CPC coin is that if and when *you* decide that you'd like to start advertising your podcast on other websites, the right CPC setup might be the perfect way to get a lot of exposure for your podcast at very little cost to you. Remember, you are not paying every time someone sees the name of your podcast or the URL; you are paying only if someone clicks that link.

Cost per thousand impressions

Having links on your site, particularly large graphic links, exposes visitors to your page to the message those links convey. That should be enough, and you should be compensated for it. In this way, you are being paid using a structure similar to that of any media outlet: you are compensated based on the size of the potential audience for the advertiser's message. Now, this is not to say that every **cost per thousand** (**CPM**; the "M" stands for the Roman numeral for "thousand") impressions arrangement is fair, but it looks inherently fairer than a CPC agreement.

CPM is how all ad rates are determined in the real world for print and electronic media. You will eventually (if you decide to go looking for sponsors and advertisers) need to determine your *podcast's* CPM and use that to calculate what you would charge for an advertisement on your podcast or to sponsor your podcast.

As traffic to your website increases, and the number of people downloading your shows rises, more and more advertisers and sponsors will be willing to pay to get their message in front of your audience. That much almost goes without saying. The challenge is finding those advertisers and sponsors.

Having the ads come to you: Google AdSense

When you're looking for something on the Internet, if you're anything like us, you probably go straight to Google (www.google.com). Through Google, you often can find everything you need on the web in little to no time at all. And, yes, Google can even find advertisers for you. Not only is Google the search engine of choice for many, but also they offer an easy-to-set-up and fairly unobtrusive system of including ads on your website. You choose between text and graphic ads, the ads' dimensions, and their placement on your site. Google gives you a code to cut and paste into the appropriate section of your site and uses that code to push fresh ads to your page whenever it is viewed. The ads displayed are chosen by Google's system, which scans the text of each page for keywords and then uses that information to determine which ads might work best for your site. For instance, if you mention Johnny Depp, The Ramones, and Australia in a blog post, the Google ads on that page might be for movie posters, MP3 downloads, and travel packages.

Google AdSense (www.google.com/adsense) income is based on CPC. Each time a page with Google AdSense ads is loaded, an invisible auction takes place behind the scenes to determine which ads will be the most profitable to display on that particular page. For this reason, Google does not pay publishers a fixed amount per click or impression. Revenue varies based on the actual CPC or CPM impression paid by the specific advertiser for each ad that ends up appearing on your site. Some ads have higher CPCs or CPMs than others; therefore, it is not possible to say precisely how much someone might earn for a given number of clicks or impressions.

Finding your own advertisers and sponsors

By now, you've figured it out: to be a successful podcaster, you need to be a radio host, an audio engineer, a blogger, and an advertising sales rep. Hey, nobody said this was going to be easy. To be clear, attracting and keeping potential advertisers and sponsors is *work*. You need to make sure that the revenue you are expecting to produce is in line with the amount of work you are going to put in. Interestingly, it takes as much time to attract a $500 sponsor as it does a $5,000 sponsor. Don't undersell your podcast's value. Luckily for all of us, when we go looking for sponsors and advertisers, we're at least selling a product we believe in: our podcast.

Advertisers vs. sponsors

It may seem like a fine line between someone being an advertiser on your podcast and a sponsor of your podcast. To split the hair, an **advertiser** is someone who gives you money to promote his or her products, goods, services, or what have you. In exchange for money (well, hopefully money), you spend a certain amount of time on your podcast or set aside a certain amount of space on your website to promote the advertiser's wares. A **sponsor** is a person, group, or organization that supports your podcast and/or website financially, in part or as a whole. In exchange, you are expected to tell everyone who is sponsoring you.

So, what's the big difference? Well, the difference definitely seems semantic at best. Typically, nonprofit ventures and public media outlets (e.g., PBS and NPR) have sponsors, whereas corporate endeavors like major TV networks and radio stations have advertisers (and lots of them). Since podcasting is still so young, and still adjusting to life with advertisers and sponsors, it is commonly expected that if you are accepting money from someone for "promotional consideration," it is in the form of sponsorship. Still, we are not naïve enough to think that podcasting will continue to grow and thrive forever without an influx of ad dollars. Therefore, we will continue talking about advertisers and sponsors and, for the sake of our convenience, not worry about which word we use.

Selling the category

At the time of this writing, one of the major stumbling blocks to selling a podcast show to potential sponsors is the fact that too many people still don't know anything about podcasting. It is astounding that so few people are aware of this movement, though this is also changing at a pace that is astonishing to all. Before anyone is going to buy your podcast, they have to understand what podcasting is. That is why it is so important for all podcasters to get out of the podcast community every once in a while and into the greater community to start spreading the news. Until more people know what podcasting is and how it can be used for marketing, we will only be selling the category, not the individual shows.

The great thing about podcasting, and the thing that puts it head and shoulders above most other media out there today in terms of reaching an audience, is that the audience pays attention to the *entire program*. Most podcast listeners will tell you that they start a podcast, they listen to a podcast, and then they listen to another podcast. Since there is no expectation of long, horrible ads, and no expectation that some part of the program won't suit their tastes, they listen intently to each podcast in its entirety. This is the great advantage of the audience getting exactly what they want, when they want it.

You could go to an advertiser right now and say, "Listen, I can get your new sales message into the ears of three thousand people by Tuesday," and actually do it.

Understanding your audience

Go back to the survey of your audience, and your endless checking and rechecking of your download statistics. You know how big your audience is, give or take. You know who your listeners are—perhaps not as individuals, but as a group. That is a group to market to. Recognize that and offer it up to those who are dying to reach that particular market.

From that bit of market information, ask yourself, "Who is most likely to benefit from reaching my audience?" Computer sales websites? Sport drink manufacturers? DVD rental companies? In the case of today's on-demand culture, and by virtue of the nature of podcasting, the more narrowly defined your audience is, the easier it will be to attract advertisers desperate to reach that audience.

Creating a sales kit

You'll need to put together a **sales kit**, which is a collection of information that tells about you, your show, your audience, and why it would be a great opportunity for advertisers to get involved in your podcast. Tim Bourquin of the "Podcast Brothers" put together a superb sales/media kit for his "Endurance Radio" podcast. He made sure it looked great, sounded professional, and included Arbitron information (Arbitron is the company that handles quantifying the ratings of radio stations), listener stats, and contact information. He was selling not only airtime on his podcast, but also the banner at the top of every page of the Endurance Radio website. He prepared mock-ups of the site for prospective clients, showing them what it would look like if their ads appeared on his site.

11

Tim was gracious enough to make his sales kit available to download for reference and inspiration at www.enduranceradio.com/EnduranceRadioMediaKit.pdf.

Then Tim started pounding the pavement with his sales kit. Much to his surprise, he wasn't getting any offers. His media kit looked great, he had the sales pitch down, and his ad rates were affordable, but still no one was interested. Eventually he realized his ad rates were too low, and they were working against him. According to Tim, "Big companies just don't write checks that small, especially for advertising buys." So he adjusted his rates and approach. Rather than selling multiple ads at $250 apiece to various advertisers to appear on the shows, he bundled the whole package and sought a sole advertiser/sponsor for monthlong periods (see Figure 11-5). He set the rate at $4,000 per month and landed Gatorade as the sole sponsor of "Endurance Radio" for several months.

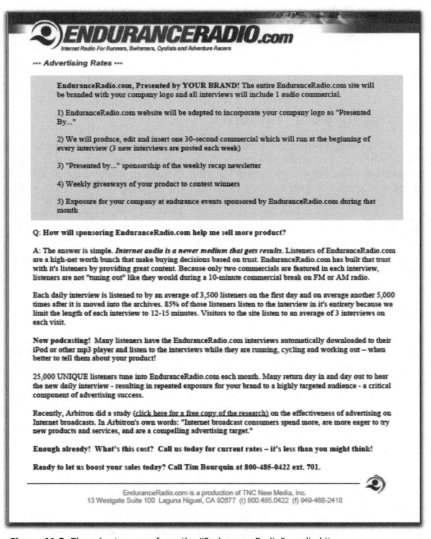

Figure 11-5. The ad rates page from the "Endurance Radio" media kit

Joining a podcasting association

For smaller advertisers, spending a couple hundred dollars to sponsor a podcast may be a big deal, but the real money is going to be found with big companies—companies so big, in fact, that they may simply dismiss your podcast because you couldn't possibly offer them the audience size they'd need to make it worth their while.

This is why several groups and associations have sprung up where podcasters band together to provide a larger audience to advertisers and potential sponsors. There's power in numbers. Dan's own Jacket Media (www.jacketmedia.com) is such an association. Starting with a handful of top-rated shows, and hoping to expand to literally thousands of participating podcasts, Dan is approaching advertising executives and media buyers in major markets around the United States, offering podcasting as the ultimate "alternative media" (apparently that is a big buzzword with ad people these days). The promise of podcasting is clear: tell us who you want to reach, and how many of those people, and we can get your message directly to them in a matter of days. Well, even hours. Whether the advertisers need 10,000 sci-fi geeks or 20,000 music lovers, podcasting associations can deliver them almost instantly.

Developing advertising and promotion policies

A podcaster's most important currency is the trust of her audience. Once you start accepting money for advertising or sponsorship, you need to deal with the reality that some listeners may view your credibility with a little more suspicion. Are you talking about how much you love that computer program you are using because you genuinely like it, or is it because the maker happens to sponsor your show? Of course, you are an honest person who would never sell out—never! As such, it is a good idea to develop a policy regarding these issues. One approach is to segregate paid announcements and disclose them as such, both in your podcast audio and on your website. How you choose to develop your advertising and promotion policies is entirely up to you, but you should address these issues well in advance of signing on advertisers and sponsors.

11

A good example of an advertising and promotion policy is the one we developed for "Grape Radio" (www.graperadio.com). At "Grape Radio," we often get wine producers and vendors who offer to send us samples of their wine. While we're happy to accept these samples, we decided it was important to develop a written policy that disclosed our "sample wine policy." When vendors offer to send samples, we forward the following disclosure to them:

"Sample Wine Policy

Grape Radio does not solicit samples of wine-related products. Should a vendor decide to send samples, Grape Radio's acceptance of such samples does not imply an evaluation will be conducted. In addition, should Grape Radio decide to evaluate a sample, vendors are advised that Grape Radio does not warrant such reviews will be made public, nor that such reviews will be positive."

We post this policy in the "About Grape Radio" section, so that anyone—including our listeners—can read it. As a point of interest, we have had some vendors who ended up not sending us a sample after receiving our notice.

— Michael Geoghegan

Becoming a podcast producer for hire

Unlike you, not everyone is willing to plow through a 200+-page book about RSS, RMS, and XML to get the word out. They may want to put a podcast together but lack the time, skill, patience, and/or wherewithal to do so. That is where you come in. Once you've established your own show, you may be presented with the opportunity to produce other people's podcasts, your show being the ultimate proof of your podcasting savvy. This may be a great way for you to earn some money without the sweat and heartache involved in looking for sponsors and designing t-shirts.

If you have the knowledge and expertise to put a podcast together for yourself, you surely could be doing it for others as well. At the time of this writing, the most prominent (and possibly the most lucrative) podcaster-for-hire experience was had by our own Michael Geoghegan. Michael was hired by Disneyland in Anaheim, California, to podcast its entire 50th Anniversary celebration, complete with behind-the-scenes "sound-seeing tours" and celebrity red-carpet interviews.

You should approach projects such as this with your eyes wide open. Large companies are not used to dealing with small operations; as a result, if you are interested in pursuing corporate podcast hosting and production, we suggest aligning with a public relations (PR) agency or company. That way, the PR company can offer your services to their current clients. They will also be able to better deal with the complications of negotiating with and getting paid by larger companies.

The Disneyland podcasts Michael produced turned out to be a podcaster's dream (see Figure 11-6). The vice president in charge of the event certainly understood where podcasting fit into the coverage of Disneyland's 50th Anniversary celebration and gave Michael exclusive access to interviews with celebrities, Disney executives, park guests, and others who help to make Disneyland such a special place. This experience was a highlight of Michael's podcasting career so far. You can find the Disneyland podcasts at www. disneyland.com/podcast.

Figure 11-6. Michael getting ready to do celebrity interviews on the "gold carpet" for Disneyland's 50th Anniversary celebration. Over his shoulder is Greg Cangialosi, who was helping out with the podcast.

11

Not all corporate podcast hosting experiences may be as positive as Michael's was with Disneyland, however. Some companies may be interested in just getting in on the "newest" or "hottest" thing. We know of other podcasts where the client companies would not post the podcast prior to a review of a transcript and in some cases demanded postproduction edits. This is big-league stuff. No one is fooling around at this level. When money and corporate reputations are involved, the sensibilities of the podcaster are not the primary concern. Make sure you are clear well ahead of time on exactly what is expected regarding content, timeline, review process (if any), and music rights issues.

If you can balance producing an exciting and entertaining podcast with fulfilling the needs of your client company, you've got yourself a business. Think about how valuable this type of production is to the company hiring you. To have countless customers and potential customers listening to 20, 30, or even 45 minutes or more of content specific to the company or its products and services is an advertiser's or publicity person's dream.

Let's do some math. What do you think it would be worth to Ford Motor Company to have a podcast available of a recent Mustang promotion event where celebrities and professional racecar drivers were invited to drive the newest Mustang GT on a racetrack? Let's say that in addition to inviting traditional media outlets, Ford also hires a podcaster to produce a podcast based on the event. Just imagine the audio the podcaster could get. In-car audio of the cars going around the track and the sounds of screeching tires as cars accelerate away. Interviews with celebrities the listeners would identify with describing how much they enjoyed driving the cars, all the while speaking with the excitement of someone who just experienced something that got his adrenaline flowing. Professional racecar drivers talking about the handling characteristics of the car on the track and how that would carry over to street performance. Perhaps interviews with a person who helped design the car describing the design decisions made and an engineer discussing some of the innovative technology behind the performance increases. Anyone from Ford listening? We think we may be onto something here.

Now here is the kicker: unlike with TV or radio, there is no requirement to get all this information conveyed as quick sound bites to fit before the next segment. The podcast could be 45 minutes long if there were enough material and quality content (though this often has more to do with the skill, planning, and execution of the podcaster than anything else). Most important, unlike a two-minute spot on the evening news seen by everyone, including people who could care less about performance cars, who do you think is going to subscribe to and download this podcast? Obviously, the people Ford would be most interested in: Mustang fans and potential customers who can listen to it over and over if they like.

Now back to the math. What is it worth to a car manufacturer such as Ford to have 50,000 potential customers who by choice listen to 45 minutes of podcast audio like this? We leave that question to you, as we're sure you get the point.

Using the Ford Motor Company example, you'd think every company would be getting involved in podcasting and producing great audio content. The reality is, though, that most of the corporate-backed podcasts available today are, for lack of a better term, terrible. Why? Because they are produced by ad agencies and PR people who try to turn the podcast into a 45-minute ad that the company will like rather than something listeners will enjoy and share with their friends. Listeners can hear the inauthenticity from a mile away and instantly get turned off by it. This might change over time, but most companies have the wrong people helping them try to attract a podcasting audience—they just don't get it yet (but you always hear that, don't you?). A perfect example is some of the earliest corporate attempts at podcasting, which were podcasts of audio from "visual" events. We remember one of the first that got some hype, where in the first few minutes of the podcast, a new product was unveiled. The hosts kept referring to how beautiful the item was and asking the audience to "gaze upon it" while an executive read from a prepared speech—not very compelling listening.

Clearly, there are some great opportunities for aggressive, yet professional podcasters who can plan, produce, and execute compelling content that listeners will enjoy and corporate clients will appreciate. Approached correctly, corporate podcasting may prove to be a profitable addition to your podcast production abilities.

Moving beyond podcasting

We're just beginning to see some of the more entrepreneurial people involved in podcasting put together companies based on products and services inspired by or at least related to podcasting. For example, some new companies are trying to syndicate audio advertisements in podcasts or are attempting to create podcasting associates (e.g., Dan's Jacket Media). Podcast networks are forming, and people are trying to figure out ways to make the sale of podsafe music more efficient for the bands involved. Then there are more specialized uses of the underlying technology, such as Michael's newest venture, PrivaCast (www.privacast.com), which is an enterprise-level solution for secure corporate and educational communications among organizations and their employees or constituents.

The bottom line is that new businesses as well as a new media segment are emerging. It's an exciting time to be involved in podcasting. If you get bitten by the podcasting bug, you'll find a way to make your passion your business.

Summary

If you are interested in monetizing your podcast, the key is to consider it all: t-shirts, magnets, trucker hats, advertisers, sponsors, click-throughs, and affiliate programs. But again, we have to stress that you start with your podcast and your audience, and let them dictate how you approach making money with your podcast. Keep trying and revamping your strategy until you find the combination of advertising and merchandising that's right for you and your show. It could be that you're better off just asking for a monthly donation and leaving well enough alone. Or you may end up with a huge online superstore. You never know.

11

CONCLUSION

  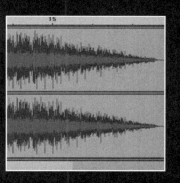

And, that's that. Podcasting in a nutshell. Sure, a 7.5" × 9" nutshell, but you get the idea.

We've given you everything we believe you need to know to get yourself not only up and running with your own shows, but also fully immersed in the world of podcasting. Little did you know that a book with a title as seemingly single-minded as *Podcast Solutions* would actually cover audio production, voice-over techniques, advertising and marketing, media relations, and news writing—well, such is the world of the serious podcaster.

Podcasting is growing and evolving every day. Although this book was written with that constant change in mind, you may still need to keep up through the various online resources we've listed in Appendix B. These are the resources we use to keep our fingers on the pulse of podcasting, and they will serve you well in the months and years to come.

We hope you are as excited about the endless possibilities of podcasting as we are. Podcasters as a community are only just beginning to scratch the surface of the true potential of podcasting. We will continue to explore new ways to put this new medium to work, whether it is to deliver college lectures (as Duke University will soon be doing with our help), to enhance internal corporate communications, or to distribute new forms of television and film. We hope this book has sparked an interest in you to explore the medium, too. Podcasting has changed the way content is delivered. Let's keep pushing forward to see exactly what that can mean for everyone.

Our best,

Michael and Dan

www.podcastsolutions.com

A **GLOSSARY**

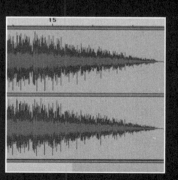

The following is a list of terms you will have encountered earlier in the book. For each term, we have provided a definition and, optionally, some links to follow for further reading about the subject.

AAC

Abbreviation for *Advanced Audio Coding*. AAC is a new breed of codec for encoding audio that provides more efficient compression than older formats such as MP3. It is used by many modern Internet, wireless, and digital broadcast systems. Apple heavily supports AAC in iTunes. For more information, see www.vialicensing.com/products/mpeg4aac/standard.html and www.apple.com/mpeg4/aac.

See also: *codec*.

aggregator

A piece of software or a website (service) that collects disparate content and presents it in one place, making it much easier for users to keep up with important news stories, websites of interest, or the latest edition of a favorite podcast. Podcatchers such as iPodder Lemon and iPodderX (which you'll find on this book's companion CD) are aggregators focused on retrieving podcasts. An aggregator is also often referred to as a *feed reader* or *feed aggregator*.

AIFF

Abbreviation for *Audio Interchange File Format*. A file format (similar to WAV) that is popular on the Mac platform for storing digital audio waveforms. It is widely used in professional audio production programs such as BIAS Peak, Sound Forge, and DSP Quattro. Like WAV, it is a lossless format. For more information, see www.borg.com/~jglatt/tech/aiff.htm.

AMP

Acronym for *Association of Music Podcasting*. An association of podcasters and independent record labels that seeks to promote new music through podcasting. The group operates with agreements stipulating that the music is to be licensed to allow it to be legally played on podcasts. For more information, see www.musicpodcasting.org.

ASCAP

Acronym for *American Society of Composers, Authors, and Publishers*. A for-profit performing rights society. ASCAP licenses public performing rights for musical compositions, so if you want to perform someone else's song on a record or television show, for example, and the original composer/artist's song is licensed under ASCAP, you have to pay a fee to ASCAP for legal permission to do so. For more information, see www.ascap.com.

Atom

An XML format and HTTP-based protocol for syndicating web content. An Atom feed describes web content (such as a podcast) and allows it to be collected by an aggregator. Proponents suggest that it is supposed to solve some of the problems with RSS (by offering improved security and interoperability), although some critics have argued that it just creates more confusion. For more information, see http://en.wikipedia.org/wiki/Atom_(standard) and http://ietf.org/html.charters/atompub-charter.html.

See also: *XML; aggregator; RSS.*

bit rate

The speed at which digital information is transmitted or stored, measured in bits per second (bps).

BMI

Abbreviation for *Broadcast Music, Inc.* A for-profit performing rights society. BMI licenses public performing rights for musical compositions, so if you want to perform someone else's song on a record or television show, for example, and the original composer/artist's song is licensed under BMI, you have to pay a fee to BMI for legal permission to do so. For more information, see www.bmi.com.

clipping

An effect that happens in a recording when the recording level of an audio signal (be it musical or vocal) is too high and exceeds the ability of the digital system to represent the waveform (you just run out of numbers!), causing a loss of audio signal information in the recording and a horrible distortion of the sound. You need to avoid clipping at all costs when recording a podcast.

codec

Acronym for *compressor/decompressor*. An encoding algorithm run on a piece of hardware or as software that compresses audio or video files into a format suitable for transportation over the web or for storage. The codec is also used to then decompress the file again at the end.

CPC

Abbreviation for *cost per click*. The method of determining how much an Internet ad costs, based on how many times people click the ad link.

A

CPM

Abbreviation for *cost per thousand exposures* (note that the "m" in the abbreviation represents the Roman numeral for "thousand"). The method of determining the cost of advertising based on the number of people potentially exposed to the ad.

Creative Commons

A nonprofit organization dedicated to allowing creative types to share their work through the use of free licenses known as *Creative Commons licenses*. These licenses offer a flexible range of protections and freedoms for authors and artists alike. For more information, see www.creativecommons.org and www.creativecommons.org/licenses/by-nc-sa/1.0.

dB

Abbreviation for *decibels*. The logarithmic units used to describe sound amplitude or intensity.

domain name

The unique identifying name of a server or site on the Internet that allows web browsers to find it. For example, the domain name of the website found at http://www.podcastsolutions.com is podcastsolutions.com.

DSP

Abbreviation for *digital signal processing*. Audio processing (usually to improve clarity, or for a specific sound effect) carried out through the use of hardware or software such as can be found on this book's companion CD.

EQ

Abbreviation for *equalization*. The process of modifying audio by amplifying or attenuating different frequencies (e.g., high-pass filtering to eliminate low-frequency sounds).

FCC

Abbreviation for *Federal Communications Commission*. The U.S. government agency responsible for regulating electronic communication (e.g., radio and television broadcasts). The FCC currently has no jurisdiction over podcasts transmitted via the Internet. For more information, see www.fcc.gov.

FTP client

Abbreviation for *File Transfer Protocol client*. A piece of software that allows you to open a connection with an FTP site, and transfer data to and from it. This is an important means by which you can get your podcasts uploaded to the web for others to access.

HTML

Abbreviation for *Hypertext Markup Language*. A markup language used to structure the vast majority of the content on the Internet. For more information, see `www.w3.org/MarkUp` and `www.w3schools.com/html`.

ID3 tag

A tag used to attach metadata to an MP3 file containing information such as album name, artist name, track name, track number, and so on. This information can be edited using an ID3 tag editor (such as the one provided by iTunes), and it can be very useful when searching for tracks.

ISP

Abbreviation for *Internet service provider*. A company or service that provides Internet access via services such as dialup, cable, and DSL. Examples of ISPs include AOL, CompuServe, and NTL.

LAME

Acronym for *Lame Ain't an MP3 Encoder*. An open source MP3 encoder that is ideal for turning your podcast WAV or AIFF files into MP3s. For more information, see `http://lame.sourceforge.net` and `www.apple.com/downloads/macosx/ipod_itunes/ituneslameencoder.html`.

latency

The time it takes for audio signals to travel around your system. In audio terms, latency comes into play when a delay is caused in the audio due to processing or transmission. As an example, if you are recording on your computer and using a number of audio effects, the audio being monitored in the headphones may have a delay between when you speak and when you hear your voice in the headphones. Latency is also a big issue when using Skype and other Internet telephony programs.

A

mastering

The process of preparing audio into a final form (in terms of tone and levels of the different elements contained in the audio) on a wide range of audio playback devices, using software and hardware tools such as equalizers and compressors.

MP3

An audio file encoded using the MPEG-1 Audio Layer-3 (MP3) format.

PHP

Abbreviation for *PHP: Hypertext Preprocessor*. A dynamic web scripting language that allows you to write web pages that will display different information depending on variables such as user input, time of day, and so on. The pages are processed, and the results are then turned into HTML for display in a web browser. PHP is an ideal language to create blogs in. For more information, see www.php.net and www.w3schools.com/php/default.asp.

See also: *HTML*.

plosive

A consonant pronounced by completely closing the lips or air passage and then releasing air suddenly (e.g., "p," "b," etc.).

podcast

An audio program available for download from the Internet via subscription by way of an RSS feed with MP3 audio enclosures.

podcast badge

A graphic (typically 80×15 pixels in size) used to promote a podcast.

podcatcher

Slang for *podcast aggregator*. Software used to manage podcast subscriptions and automatically download new episodes.

podroll

A list of favorite podcasts. Listeners typically share their podrolls with others by posting them on their blogs or websites.

pop filter

A windscreen or foam filter that helps reduce the popping noises created by breath or speech when a person says a plosive such as "p" or "b."

See also: *plosive*.

RIAA

Abbreviation for *Recording Industry Association of America*. A trade consortium that supports and represents the U.S. recording industry and strives toward a business and legal climate that protects its members' creativity and financial viability. For example, RIAA works to protect record companies' intellectual property rights, and it certifies gold, platinum, multiplatinum, and diamond sales awards. Over 900 companies are part of the RIAA, including BMG, EMI, and Sony Music. For more information, see `www.riaa.com`.

RMS

Abbreviation for *root-mean-square*. A way to accurately measure the overall magnitude (loudness) of a sound recording over time. To improve the mix of your audio, you should set the levels of the different tones that make up the audio in accordance with a recommended RMS value (we recommend −12dB RMS with a peak setting of 0.2dB). Various audio-editing applications have RMS normalization functions to help you do this (e.g., Ozone 3, which you can find on this book's companion CD).

RSS

Abbreviation for *Really Simple Syndication* (or *Rich Site Summary*). An XML format for syndicating web content. An RSS feed describes content (such as a podcast) and allows it to be collected by an aggregator. RSS is said to be a precursor to Atom, but it is still far and away the most common protocol for podcasts.

See also: *XML; aggregator; Atom*.

A

sample rate

The frequency at which analog data (in the case of podcasts, sound) is recorded or "sampled" and converted to digital information (e.g., 44,100kHz or 44,100 samples per second).

SESAC

Acronym for *Society of European Stage Authors and Composers*. A for-profit performing rights society. SESAC licenses public performing rights for musical compositions, so if you want to perform someone else's song on a record or television show, for example, and the original composer/artist's song is licensed under SESAC, you have to pay a fee to SESAC for legal permission to do so. For more information, see www.sesac.com.

URI

Abbreviation for *Uniform Resource Identifier*. A term for a classification of identifiers of resources on the Internet. For example, a URL is a type of URI. Other types include Uniform Resource Classification (URC), relative URL, and Uniform Resource Name (URN).

See also: *URL*.

URL

Abbreviation for *Uniform Resource Locator*. Also known as an Internet address, or link, a URL provides the location of a directory or file on the web (e.g., http://www.friendsofed.com or http://www.podcastsolutions.com).

VST

Abbreviation for *Virtual Studio Technology*. A format for audio plug-ins used with audio processing software.

WAV

The de facto standard file format (especially on Windows, where it originated) for storing raw, uncompressed sound. You'll deal with WAV files often as you record your podcast. A WAV file recorded at 44.1kHz and 16-bit samples offers quality equivalent to that of a CD, but its large file size means it isn't practical for delivering audio over the web. This is why podcasts are always turned into MP3s before they are published.

waveform

A graphic representation of a sound recording.

WMA

Abbreviation for *Windows Media Audio*. A proprietary Microsoft audio format similar to MP3. For more information, see www.microsoft.com/windows/windowsmedia/9series/codecs/audio.aspx.

XML

Abbreviation for *Extensible Markup Language*. A markup language that can be extended, allowing you to create your own custom vocabularies for describing data. RSS and Atom are two examples of XML vocabularies. For more information, see www.w3.org/XML, www.w3schools.com/xml/default.asp, and www.xml.com.

See also: *RSS; Atom.*

A

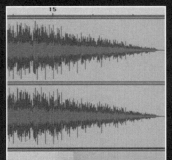

This appendix presents a short list of websites to check out and podcasts to listen to, to get your feet wet. Please note that this is not even an attempt at a complete list of anything—it's just the tip of the iceberg.

Podcasts: Entertainment

Reel Reviews – Films Worth Watching (www.reelreviewsradio.com)

The Bitterest Pill (www.thebitterestpill.com)

Grape Radio (www.graperadio.com)

Coverville (www.coverville.com)

The Daily Source Code (www.dailysourcecode.com)

The Dawn and Drew Show! (www.dawnanddrew.com; adult content)

Evil Genius Chronicles (www.evilgeniuschronicles.org)

Illinoise! (www.illinoise.net)

The Rock and Roll Geek Show (http://rockandrollgeek.podshow.com)

Verge of the Fringe (www.vergeofthefringe.com)

Viva Podcast (www.vivapodcast.com)

Podcasts: Music

Old Wave Radio: New 80s Music (www.new80smusic.com)

Accident Hash (www.accidenthash.podshow.com)

Coverville (www.coverville.com)

IndieFeed (www.indiefeed.com)

Insomnia Radio (www.insomniaradio.net)

Podcasts: Podcasting

Podcast Solutions (www.podcastsolutions.com)

Behind the Scenes (www.godcast.org/categories/behindTheScenes)

Podcast Brothers (www.podcastbrothers.com)

Directories

iPodder.org (www.ipodder.org)

Podcast Alley (www.podcastalley.com)

Podcast Central (www.podcastcentral.com)

PodcastPickle.com (www.podcastpickle.com)

Feed validators

Feed Validator (http://feedvalidator.org)

Podcast FeedCheck for iTunes compatibility (www.nobodylikesonions.com/feedcheck)

Podcatchers

Apple iTunes (www.apple.com/itunes)

Doppler (www.dopplerradio.net)

iPodder Lemon (http://ipodder.sourceforge.net)

iPodderX (www.ipodderx.com)

Podcasting resources

iLounge (www.ipodlounge.com)

Podcast Alley (www.podcastalley.com)

The Podcast Rigs Forum (www.podcastrigs.com/forum)

PodcastExpert.com (www.podcastexpert.com)

B

Podsafe music resources

15 Megs of Fame (www.15megsoffame.com)

Internet Archive: Live Music Archive (www.archive.org/audio)

GarageBand.com (www.garageband.com)

Magnatune (www.magnatune.com)

Podsafe Music Network (music.podshow.com)

Associations and networks

The Association of Music Podcasting (www.musicpodcasting.org)

The Godcast Network (www.godcast.org)

L.A. Podcasters (www.lapodcasters.com)

Podcast Media Group (www.podcastmediagroup.com)

The Podcastoutlaws Network (www.podcastoutlaws.com)

TechPodcasts.com (www.techpodcasts.com)

Mailing list

Yahoo! Podcasters Group (http://groups.yahoo.com/group/podcasters)

Our production companies

Michael: Willnick Productions (www.willnick.com)

Dan: Jacket Media (www.jacketmedia.com)

INDEX

friendsof

DESIGNER TO DESIGNER™

an Apress® company

Apress License Agreement (Single-User Products)

THIS IS A LEGAL AGREEMENT BETWEEN YOU, THE END USER, AND APRESS. BY OPENING THE SEALED CD PACKAGE, YOU ARE AGREEING TO BE BOUND BY THE TERMS OF THIS AGREEMENT. IF YOU DO NOT AGREE TO THE TERMS OF THIS AGREEMENT, PROMPTLY RETURN THE UNOPENED DISK PACKAGE AND THE ACCOMPANYING ITEMS (INCLUDING WRITTEN MATERIALS AND BINDERS AND OTHER CONTAINERS) TO THE PLACE YOU OBTAINED THEM FOR A FULL REFUND.

APRESS SOFTWARE LICENSE

1. GRANT OF LICENSE. Apress grants you the right to use one copy of the enclosed Apress software program collectively (the "SOFTWARE") on a single terminal connected to a single computer (e.g., with a single CPU). You may not network the SOFTWARE or otherwise use it on more than one computer or computer terminal at the same time.

2. COPYRIGHT. The SOFTWARE copyright is owned by Apress, with portions owned by Madison Media Software, Inc. iZotope, Inc., Reinvented Software, i3 S.r.L., MixMeister Technology, LLS, Berkeley Integrated Audio Software Adobe Systems Incorporated, Thunderstone Media, LLC, Rogue Amoeba Software LLC, Toysoft Development, Inc. The iSpider Team, and CombiTech, and is protected by United States copyright laws and international treaty provisions. The SOFTWARE contains licensed software programs, the use of which are governed by English language end user license agreements inside the licensed software programs. Therefore, you must treat each of the SOFTWARE programs like any other copyrighted material (e.g., a book or musical recording) except that you may either (a) make one copy of the SOFTWARE solely for backup or archival purposes, or (b) transfer the SOFTWARE to a single hard disk, provided you keep the original solely for backup or archival purposes. You may not copy the written material accompanying the SOFTWARE.

3. OTHER RESTRICTIONS. You may not rent or lease the SOFTWARE, but you may transfer the SOFTWARE and accompanying written materials on a permanent basis provided you retain no copies and the recipient agrees to the terms of this Agreement. You may not reverse engineer, decompile, or disassemble the SOFTWARE. If SOFTWARE is an update, any transfer must include the update and all prior versions. Distributors, dealers, and other resellers are prohibited from altering or opening the licensed SOFTWARE package.

4. By breaking the seal on the disc package, you agree to the terms and conditions printed in the Apress License Agreement. If you do not agree with the terms, simply return this book with the still-sealed CD package to the place of purchase for a refund.

DISCLAIMER OF WARRANTY

NO WARRANTIES. Apress disclaims all warranties, either express or implied, including, but not limited to, implied warranties of merchantability and fitness for a particular purpose, with respect to the SOFTWARE and the accompanying written materials. The software and any related documentation is provided "as is." You may have other rights, which vary from state to state.

NO LIABILITIES FOR CONSEQUENTIAL DAMAGES. In no event shall Apress be liable for any damages whatsoever (including, without limitation, damages from loss of business profits, business interruption, loss of business information or other pecuniary loss) arising out of the use or inability to use this product, even if Apress has been advised of the possibility of such damages. Because some states do not allow the exclusion or limitation of liability for consequential or incidental damages, the above limitation may not apply to you.

U.S. GOVERNMENT RESTRICTED RIGHTS

The SOFTWARE and documentation are provided with RESTRICTED RIGHTS. Use, duplication, or disclosure by the Government is subject to restriction as set forth in subparagraph (c) (1) (ii) of The Rights in Technical Data and Computer Software clause at 52.227-7013. Contractor/manufacturer is Apress, 2560 Ninth Street, Suite 219, Berkeley, California 94710.

This Agreement is governed by the laws of the State of California.

Should you have any questions concerning this Agreement, or if you wish to contact Apress for any reason, please write